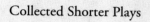

Collected Shorter Plays

# Collected Shorter Plays

## Eugene O'Neill

*Introduction by*
Robert Brustein

*Yale University Press   New Haven and London*

First published by Yale University Press in 2007.

*Hughie* © as an unpublished work 1959 by Carlotta Monterey O'Neill; © 1959
by Carlotta Monterey O'Neill.
Introduction © 2007 by Robert Brustein.
Copyright © 2007 by Yale University.

Set in Garamond type by Tseng Information Systems, Inc.
Printed in the United States of America.

Library of Congress Control Number: 2006928358
ISBN 978-0-300-10779-1 (pbk.)

A catalogue record for this book is available from the British Library.

10  9  8  7  6  5  4  3  2  1

CAUTION: Professionals and amateurs are hereby informed that all inquiries
regarding production rights to these plays should be addressed to William
Morris Agency, Inc., 1325 Avenue of the Americas, New York, NY 10019, Attn.
Samuel Liff. All other inquiries should be addressed to Yale University, Office
of the General Counsel, P.O. Box 208255, New Haven, CT 06520-8255.

THE EUGENE O'NEILL COLLECTION was founded at the Yale University
Library in 1931 by Carlotta Monterey O'Neill. It includes notes, photographs,
and the manuscripts of plays, among them *Hughie*.

# Contents

# Introduction

## ROBERT BRUSTEIN

O'Neill's best-known one-act sea plays—*Bound East for Cardiff, In the Zone, The Long Voyage Home,* and *The Moon of the Caribbees*—were all written between 1913 and 1916 and published together under the generic title *S.S. Glencairn.* They represent only four of twenty-four such playlets that O'Neill was composing around this time, and when they were produced at the Wharf Theatre in Provincetown (and later at the Provincetown Playhouse in New York), they made the playwright famous overnight.

O'Neill was not the first American to turn to one-act plays. Susan Glaspell and others were also writing them for the Provincetown Players. But there is no doubt that, largely under the influence of Strindberg, he perfected the form, just as Hemingway, a few years later, was to perfect the genre of the American short story. Encouraged by his father, the famous actor James O'Neill, to study playwriting with George Pierce Baker at Harvard, O'Neill at first found considerable inspiration in the short, terse, suggestive one-act play. His father, whom O'Neill depicted as the penny-pinching "Old Gaspard" in *Long Day's Journey into Night,* also financed his son's first collection of these works, *Thirst and Other One Act Plays* in 1914.

Like Hemingway, who compared the short story to an iceberg whose mass was mostly hidden beneath the water, O'Neill admired the short play more for what it implied than for what it said. At this point in his career, at least, he is interested more in anecdotes than in plots, engaged less with big philosophical statements than with a kind of terse, allusive pointillism. The man with epic ambitions who would later turn out dramatic marathons keeping audiences in their seats for four to eight hours is here content with making his theatrical points in twenty minutes or less.

The seven early sea plays included in this volume sometimes feature a number of the same characters. The American Yank, for example, appears to have died in *Bound East for Cardiff*, only to be resurrected in *The Moon of the Caribbees*, and again later as the considerably more primitive stoker in *The Hairy Ape* (though it is Paddy in *The Moon of the Caribbees* who is first called "a 'airy ape"). Similarly, the melancholy self-hating Smitty, who drinks to forget his blighted past, appears as a supporting character in *The Moon of the Caribbees* and then as the central tragic figure of *In the Zone*. In short, the international crew of Cockney, Swedish, Irish, Scottish, and Norwegian sailors form a kind of seagoing repertory company, partly based on some of the polyglot nationals with whom O'Neill sailed during his days in the merchant marine. Some of them speak an almost cartoon dialect (Cocky's "Gawd Blimey," Big Frank's "py chiminy Christmas," Scotty's "na doot"), while the Cockney whores in *The Long Voyage Home* seem to be verbal blood relations of Eliza Doolittle in Shaw's *Pygmalion*.

But dialogue was never O'Neill's strong point. What distinguishes these early sea plays is not their language but a sense of mood, of atmosphere, of local color. Each of the plays is set on a different body of water, ranging from the Atlantic to the Caribbean to the Arctic Sea, and in a different geographical location, from London to New York to the West Indies before World War I. Each exposes a different aspect of shipboard life as well. *Bound East for Cardiff* shows us the tragedy of sickness and death in the forecastle; *Fog*, a social protest play set on a lifeboat and the first example of O'Neill's enduring conflict between the artist and the businessman, is about the powerlessness of the poor; *Thirst*, also set on a life raft, characterizes a sea undulating with threat, loss, and accident; *The Long Voyage Home* is about the shanghaiing of the gentle Olson, who will never see home again; *Ile* brings us the first of O'Neill's obsessed characters, an almost Shakespearean whaling captain who sacrifices his wife to his overweening pride; *The Moon of the Caribbees* is a genre piece about bun boat whores selling whiskey and sex; and *In the Zone* is a drama of panic and paranoia during wartime. Whatever their subject, almost all of them are drenched in that spiritual fog that Edmund Tyrone so beautifully describes when telling his father about his seagoing life in *Long Day's Journey into Night.*

*The Hairy Ape* is a bit of an anomaly in this collection. Written at least five years after the earlier works, it is not really a one-act play at all, considering its length (more than an hour) and structure (eight scenes). And subtitled *A Comedy of Ancient and Modern Life,* it obviously has much more ambitious things on its mind than local color.

O'Neill's Yank is an early version of Tennessee Williams's Stanley Kowalski—an inarticulate hero inclined to substitute instinctive violence for coherent debate. O'Neill describes him as "Neanderthal Man" with a hirsute chest and long arms. And although the clumsy diction O'Neill invented for him ("Nix on dat old sailing ship stuff. All dat bull's dead, see?") is about as artful as the stiff upper-class speech he provides for Mildred ("How naïve age makes one"), it is at least an effort to demonstrate Yank's estrangement from the modern world.

Like so many of O'Neill's works, *The Hairy Ape* is a play about human alienation, and just as Edmund Tyrone, half in love with death, feels a sense of belonging only while on watch on the bridge merging with the Infinite at night, so the hairy stoker Yank ultimately can find his identity not in political action nor in human exchange nor even in the clasp of a murderous gorilla, but only in the embrace of death. Edmund says he "would have been more successful as a seagull or a fish." Yank is not even successful in the role of a primate.

*Hughie,* though set in 1928, was written in 1942 and belongs to the period when O'Neill was writing his last great plays, a sick man in a shuttered room, tortured by the sun, unable to hold a pencil in his hand. One critic has called it "a footnote to *The Iceman Cometh,*" and there is no doubt that just as the fog-ridden sea plays forecast the voyage into darkness and fog of *Long Day's Journey,* so Erie Smith's soliloquies in *Hughie* often sound a lot like Hickey's monologues in *Iceman.* *Hughie* is the only O'Neill one-acter not set on or near the sea, but like *The Iceman Cometh* it is clearly an underwater play.

More than twenty years after his earliest work, O'Neill's control of working-class dialect has not really improved ("Nix on that Mr. Smith stuff," says Erie in a typically tone-deaf passage), but his sense of character has grown infinitely more sophisticated. In a few deft strokes, O'Neill draws a portrait of a tinhorn gambler and Broadway sport, full of bluff and bluster, yet deeply lonely and near desperation, looking for any human contact to counter the loss of Hughie the desk clerk, the only friend he had. Although the piece ends positively, with Charlie replacing Hughie as Erie's good-luck charm, it is permeated with O'Neill's patented pessimism, now a deeply felt despair, that compelling urge to get "out of the racket," which is life itself.

Taken together, then, these short works reflect O'Neill's abiding weaknesses, yes, but also a lot of his strengths. They represent indispensable chapters in that spiritual autobiography that is his artistic testament. They show us O'Neill's earliest efforts to imagine those "fog people" that populate his last great plays. They show him attempting to forge an American drama out of the smithy of his early experience and his reading of European plays. They show us someone in process of becoming one of the world's most powerful modern dramatists.

*Bound East for Cardiff*
A Play in One Act

# Characters

YANK

DRISCOLL

COCKY

DAVIS

SCOTTY

OLSON

PAUL

SMITTY

IVAN

THE CAPTAIN

THE SECOND MATE

# Bound East for Cardiff

SCENE

*The seamen's forecastle of the British tramp steamer* Glencairn *on a foggy night midway on the voyage between New York and Cardiff. An irregular shaped compartment, the sides of which almost meet at the far end to form a triangle. Sleeping bunks about six feet long, ranged three deep with a space of three feet separating the upper from the lower, are built against the sides. On the right above the bunks three or four port holes can be seen. In front of the bunks, rough wooden benches. Over the bunks on the left, a lamp in a bracket. In the left foreground, a doorway. On the floor near it, a pail with a tin dipper. Oilskins are hanging from a hook near the doorway.*

*The far side of the forecastle is so narrow that it contains only one series of bunks.*

*In under the bunks a glimpse can be had of seachests, suit cases, seaboots, etc., jammed in indiscriminately.*

*At regular intervals of a minute or so the blast of the steamer's whistle can be heard above all the other sounds.*

*Five men are sitting on the benches talking. They are dressed in dirty patched suits of dungaree, flannel shirts, and all are in their stocking feet. Four of the men are pulling on pipes and the air is heavy with rancid tobacco smoke. Sitting on the top bunk in the left foreground, a Norwegian, Paul, is softly playing some folk song on a battered accordion. He stops from time to time to listen to the conversation.*

*In the lower bunk in the rear a dark-haired, hard-featured man is lying apparently asleep. One of his arms is stretched limply over the side of the bunk. His face is very pale, and drops of clammy perspiration glisten on his forehead.*

*It is nearing the end of the dog watch—about ten minutes to eight in the evening.*

COCKY
*A weazened runt of a man. He is telling a story. The others are listening with amused, incredulous faces, interrupting him at the end of each sentence with loud derisive guffaws.*
Makin' love to me, she was! It's Gawd's truth! A bloomin' nigger! Greased all over with cocoanut oil, she was. Gawd blimey, I couldn't stand 'er. Bloody old cow, I says; and with that I fetched 'er a biff on the ear wot knocked 'er silly, an'—
*He is interrupted by a roar of laughter from the others.*

DAVIS
*A middle-aged man with black hair and mustache.*
You're a liar, Cocky.

SCOTTY
*A dark young fellow.*
Ho-ho! Ye werr neverr in New Guinea in yourr life, I'm thinkin'.

OLSON
*A Swede with a drooping blond mustache—with ponderous sarcasm.*
Yust tink of it! You say she wass a cannibal, Cocky?

DRISCOLL
*A brawny Irishman with the battered features of a prizefighter.*
How cud ye doubt ut, Ollie? A quane av the naygurs she musta been surely. Who else wud think herself aqual to fallin' in love wid a beautiful, divil-may-care rake av a man the loike av Cocky?
*A burst of laughter from the crowd.*

COCKY
*Indignantly.*

Gawd strike me dead if it ain't true, every bleedin' word of it. 'Appened ten year ago come Christmas.

SCOTTY
'Twas a Christmas dinner she had her eyes on.

DAVIS
He'd a been a tough old bird.

DRISCOLL
'Tis lucky for both av ye ye escaped; for the quane av the cannibal isles wad 'a died av the belly ache the day afther Christmas, divil a doubt av ut.
*The laughter at this is long and loud.*

COCKY
*Sullenly.*
Blarsted fat 'eads!
*The sick man in the lower bunk in the rear groans and moves restlessly. There is a hushed silence. All the men turn and stare at him.*

DRISCOLL
Ssshh!
*In a hushed whisper.*
We'd best not be talkin' so loud and him tryin' to have a bit av a sleep.
*He tiptoes softly to the side of the bunk.*
Yank! You'd be wantin' a drink av wather, maybe?
YANK *does not reply.* DRISCOLL *bends over and looks at him.*
It's asleep he is, sure enough. His breath is chokin' in his throat loike wather gurglin' in a poipe.
*He comes back quietly and sits down. All are silent, avoiding each other's eyes.*

COCKY
*After a pause.*
Pore devil! It's over the side for 'im, Gawd 'elp 'im.

DRISCOLL

Stop your croakin'! He's not dead yet and, praise God, he'll have many a long day yet before him.

SCOTTY
*Shaking his head doubtfully.*
He's bod, mon, he's verry bod.

DAVIS

Lucky he's alive. Many a man's light woulda gone out after a fall like that.

OLSON

You saw him fall?

DAVIS

Right next to him. He and me was goin' down in number two hold to do some chippin'. He puts his leg over careless-like and misses the ladder and plumps straight down to the bottom. I was scared to look over for a minute, and then I heard him groan and I scuttled down after him. He was hurt bad inside for the blood was drippin' from the side of his mouth. He was groanin' hard, but he never let a word out of him.

COCKY

An' you blokes remember when we 'auled 'im in 'ere? Oh, 'ell, 'e says, oh, 'ell—like that, and nothink else.

OLSON

Did the captain know where he iss hurted?

COCKY

That silly ol' josser! Wot the 'ell would 'e know abaht anythink?

SCOTTY
*Scornfully.*
He fiddles in his mouth wi' a bit of glass.

DRISCOLL
*Angrily.*
The divil's own life ut is to be out on the lonely sea wid nothin'

betune you and a grave in the ocean but a spindle-shanked, gray-whiskered auld fool the loike av him. 'Twas enough to make a saint shwear to see him wid his gold watch in his hand, tryin' to look as wise as an owl on a tree, and all the toime he not knowin' whether 'twas cholery or the barber's itch was the matther wid Yank.

SCOTTY
*Sardonically.*
He gave him a dose of salts, na doot?

DRISCOLL
Divil a thing he gave him at all, but looked in the book he had wid him, and shook his head, and walked out widout sayin' a word, the second mate afther him no wiser than himself, God's curse on the two av thim!

COCKY
*After a pause.*
Yank was a good shipmate, pore beggar. Lend me four bob in Noo Yark, 'e did.

DRISCOLL
*Warmly.*
A good shipmate he was and is, none better. Ye said no more than the truth, Cocky. Five years and more ut is since first I shipped wid him, and we've stuck together iver since through good luck and bad. Fights we've had, God help us, but 'twas only when we'd a bit av drink taken, and we always shook hands the nixt mornin'. Whativer was his was mine, and many's the toime I'd a been on the beach or worse, but for him. And now—
*His voice trembles as he fights to control his emotion.*
Divil take me if I'm not startin' to blubber loike an auld woman, and he not dead at all, but goin' to live many a long year yet, maybe.

DAVIS
The sleep'll do him good. He seems better now.

OLSON
If he wude eat something—

DRISCOLL

Wud ye have him be eatin' in his condishun? Sure it's hard enough
on the rest av us wid nothin' the matther wid our insides to be stom-
achin' the skoff on this rusty lime-juicer.

SCOTTY

*Indignantly.*
It's a starvation ship.

DAVIS

Plenty o' work and no food—and the owners ridin' around in car-
riages!

OLSON

Hash, hash! Stew, stew! Marmalade, py damn!
*He spits disgustedly.*

COCKY

Bloody swill! Fit only for swine is wot I say.

DRISCOLL

And the dishwather they disguise wid the name av tea! And the putty
they call bread! My belly feels loike I'd swalleyed a dozen rivets at
the thought av ut! And sea-biscuit that'd break the teeth av a lion if
he had the misfortune to take a bite at one!
*Unconsciously they have all raised their voices, forgetting the sick man in
their sailor's delight at finding something to grumble about.*

PAUL

*Swings his feet over the side of his bunk, stops playing his accordion, and
says slowly.*
And rot-ten po-tay-toes!
*He starts in playing again. The sick man gives a groan of pain.*

DRISCOLL

*Holding up his hand.*
Shut your mouths, all av you. 'Tis a hell av a thing for us to be com-
plainin' about our guts, and a sick man maybe dyin' listenin' to us.
*Gets up and shakes his fist at the Norwegian.*
God stiffen you, ye squarehead scut! Put down that organ av yours

or I'll break your ugly face for you. Is that banshee schreechin' fit music for a sick man?

*The Norwegian puts his accordion in the bunk and lies back and closes his eyes.* DRISCOLL *goes over and stands beside* YANK. *The steamer's whistle sounds particularly loud in the silence.*

DAVIS

Damn this fog!

*Reaches in under a bunk and yanks out a pair of seaboots, which he pulls on.*

My lookout next, too. Must be nearly eight bells, boys.

*With the exception of* OLSON, *all the men sitting up put on oilskins, sou'westers, seaboots, etc., in preparation for the watch on deck.* OLSON *crawls into a lower bunk on the right.*

SCOTTY

My wheel.

OLSON

*Disgustedly.*

Nothin' but yust dirty weather all dis voyage. I yust can't sleep when weestle blow.

*He turns his back to the light and is soon fast asleep and snoring.*

SCOTTY

If this fog keeps up, I'm tellin' ye, we'll no be in Carrdiff for a week or more.

DRISCOLL

'Twas just such a night as this the auld Dover wint down. Just about this toime ut was, too, and we all sittin' round in the fo'castle, Yank beside me, whin all av a suddint we heard a great slitherin' crash, and the ship heeled over till we was all in a heap on wan side. What came afther I disremimber exactly, except 'twas a hard shift to get the boats over the side before the auld teakittle sank. Yank was in the same boat wid me, and sivin morthal days we drifted wid scarcely a drop of wather or a bite to chew on. 'Twas Yank here that held me down whin I wanted to jump into the ocean, roarin' mad wid the thirst.

Picked up we were on the same day wid only Yank in his senses, and him steerin' the boat.

COCKY
*Protestingly.*
Blimey but you're a cheerful blighter, Driscoll! Talkin' abaht ship-wrecks in this 'ere blushin' fog.
YANK *groans and stirs uneasily, opening his eyes.* DRISCOLL *hurries to his side.*

DRISCOLL
Are ye feelin' any betther, Yank?

YANK
*In a weak voice.*
No.

DRISCOLL
Sure, you must be. You look as sthrong as an ox.
*Appealing to the others.*
Am I tellin' him a lie?

DAVIS
The sleep's done you good.

COCKY
You'll be 'avin your pint of beer in Cardiff this day week.

SCOTTY
And fish and chips, mon!

YANK
*Peevishly.*
What're yuh all lyin' fur? D'yuh think I'm scared to—
*He hesitates as if frightened by the word he is about to say.*

DRISCOLL
Don't be thinkin' such things!
*The ship's bell is heard heavily tolling eight times. From the forecastle head above the voice of the lookout rises in a long wail:* Aaall's welll. *The*

*men look uncertainly at* YANK *as if undecided whether to say good-by or not.*

YANK
*In an agony of fear.*
Don't leave me, Drisc! I'm dyin', I tell yuh. I won't stay here alone with every one snorin'. I'll go out on deck.
*He makes a feeble attempt to rise, but sinks back with a sharp groan. His breath comes in wheezy gasps.*
Don't leave me, Drisc!
*His face grows white and his head falls back with a jerk.*

DRISCOLL
Don't be worryin', Yank. I'll not move a step out av here—and let that divil av a bosun curse his black head off. You speak a word to the bosun, Cocky. Tell him that Yank is bad took and I'll be stayin' wid him a while yet.

COCKY
Right-o.
COCKY, DAVIS, *and* SCOTTY *go out quietly.*

COCKY
*From the alleyway.*
Gawd blimey, the fog's thick as soup.

DRISCOLL
Are ye satisfied now, Yank?
*Receiving no answer, he bends over the still form.*
He's fainted, God help him!
*He gets a tin dipper from the bucket and bathes* YANK's *forehead with the water.* YANK *shudders and opens his eyes.*

YANK
*Slowly.*
I thought I was goin' then. Wha' did yuh wanta wake me up fur?

DRISCOLL
*With forced gayety.*
Is it wishful for heaven ye are?

YANK
*Gloomily.*
Hell, I guess.

DRISCOLL
*Crossing himself involuntarily.*
For the love av the saints don't be talkin' loike that! You'd give a man
the creeps. It's chippin' rust on deck you'll be in a day or two wid
the best av us.
YANK *does not answer, but closes his eyes wearily. The seaman who has
been on lookout,* SMITTY, *a young Englishman, comes in and takes off
his dripping oilskins. While he is doing this the man whose turn at the
wheel has been relieved enters. He is a dark burly fellow with a round
stupid face. The Englishman steps softly over to* DRISCOLL. *The other
crawls into a lower bunk.*

SMITTY
*Whispering.*
How's Yank?

DRISCOLL
Betther. Ask him yourself. He's awake.

YANK
I'm all right, Smitty.

SMITTY
Glad to hear it, Yank.
*He crawls to an upper bunk and is soon asleep.*

IVAN
*The stupid-faced seaman who came in after* SMITTY *twists his head in
the direction of the sick man.*
You feel gude, Jank?

YANK
*Wearily.*
Yes, Ivan.

IVAN
Dot's gude.

*He rolls over on his side and falls asleep immediately.*

YANK

*After a pause broken only by snores—with a bitter laugh.*
Good-by and good luck to the lot of you!

DRISCOLL
Is ut painin' you again?

YANK
It hurts like hell—here.
*He points to the lower part of his chest on the left side.*
I guess my old pump's busted. Ooohh!
*A spasm of pain contracts his pale features. He presses his hand to his side and writhes on the thin mattress of his bunk. The perspiration stands out in beads on his forehead.*

DRISCOLL
*Terrified.*
Yank! Yank! What is ut?
*Jumping to his feet.*
I'll run for the captain.
*He starts for the doorway.*

YANK
*Sitting up in his bunk, frantic with fear.*
Don't leave me, Drisc! For God's sake don't leave me alone!
*He leans over the side of his bunk and spits.* DRISCOLL *comes back to him.*
Blood! Ugh!

DRISCOLL
Blood again! I'd best be gettin' the captain.

YANK
No, no, don't leave me! If yuh do I'll git up and follow you. I ain't no coward, but I'm scared to stay here with all of them asleep and snorin'.

DRISCOLL, *not knowing what to do, sits down on the bench beside him. He grows calmer and sinks back on the mattress.*

The captain can't do me no good, yuh know it yourself. The pain ain't so bad now, but I thought it had me then. It was like a buzzsaw cuttin' into me.

DRISCOLL
*Fiercely.*
God blarst ut!
*The captain and the second mate of the steamer enter the forecastle. The captain is an old man with gray mustache and whiskers. The mate is clean-shaven and middle-aged. Both are dressed in simple blue uniforms.*

THE CAPTAIN
*Taking out his watch and feeling* YANK's *pulse.*
And how is the sick man?

YANK
*Feebly.*
All right, sir.

THE CAPTAIN
And the pain in the chest?

YANK
It still hurts, sir, worse than ever.

THE CAPTAIN
*Taking a thermometer from his pocket and putting it into* YANK's *mouth.*
Here. Be sure and keep this in under your tongue, not over it.

THE MATE
*After a pause.*
Isn't this your watch on deck, Driscoll?

DRISCOLL
Yes, sorr, but Yank was fearin' to be alone, and—

THE CAPTAIN
That's all right, Driscoll.

DRISCOLL
Thank ye, sorr.

**THE CAPTAIN**

*Stares at his watch for a moment or so; then takes the thermometer from* YANK's *mouth and goes to the lamp to read it. His expression grows very grave. He beckons the* MATE *and* DRISCOLL *to the corner near the doorway.* YANK *watches them furtively. The* CAPTAIN *speaks in a low voice to the* MATE.

Way up, both of them.

*To* DRISCOLL.

Has he been spitting blood again?

**DRISCOLL**

Not much for the hour just past, sorr, but before that—

**THE CAPTAIN**

A great deal?

**DRISCOLL**

Yes, sorr.

**THE CAPTAIN**

He hasn't eaten anything?

**DRISCOLL**

No, sorr.

**THE CAPTAIN**

Did he drink that medicine I sent him?

**DRISCOLL**

Yes, sorr, but it didn't stay down.

**THE CAPTAIN**

*Shaking his head.*

I'm afraid—he's very weak. I can't do anything else for him. It's too serious for me. If this had only happened a week later we'd be in Cardiff in time to—

**DRISCOLL**

Plaze help him some way, sorr!

**THE CAPTAIN**

*Impatiently.*

But, my good man, I'm not a doctor.
*More kindly as he sees* DRISCOLL's *grief.*
You and he have been shipmates a long time?

DRISCOLL
Five years and more, sorr.

THE CAPTAIN
I see. Well, don't let him move. Keep him quiet and we'll hope for the best. I'll read the matter up and send him some medicine, something to ease the pain, anyway.
*Goes over to* YANK.
Keep up your courage! You'll be better to-morrow.
*He breaks down lamely before* YANK's *steady gaze.*
We'll pull you through all right—and—hm—well—coming. Robinson? Dammit!
*He goes out hurriedly, followed by the* MATE.

DRISCOLL
*Trying to conceal his anxiety.*
Didn't I tell you you wasn't half as sick as you thought you was? The Captain'll have you out on deck cursin' and swearin' loike a trooper before the week is out.

YANK
Don't lie, Drisc. I heard what he said, and if I didn't I c'd tell by the way I feel. I know what's goin' to happen. I'm goin' to—
*He hesitates for a second—then resolutely.*
I'm goin' to die, that's what, and the sooner the better!

DRISCOLL
*Wildly.*
No, and be damned to you, you're not. I'll not let you.

YANK
It ain't no use, Drisc. I ain't got a chance, but I ain't scared. Gimme a drink of water, will yuh, Drisc? My throat's burnin' up.
DRISCOLL *brings the dipper full of water and supports his head while he drinks in great gulps.*

**DRISCOLL**
*Seeking vainly for some word of comfort.*
Are ye feelin' more aisy loike now?

**YANK**
Yes—now—when I know it's all up.
*A pause.*
You must'nt take it so hard, Drisc. I was just thinkin' it ain't as bad as people think—dyin'. I ain't never took much stock in the truck them sky-pilots preach. I ain't never had religion; but I know whatever it is what comes after it can't be no worser'n this. I don't like to leave you, Drisc, but—that's all.

**DRISCOLL**
*With a groan.*
Lad, lad, don't be talkin'.

**YANK**
This sailor life ain't much to cry about leavin'—just one ship after another, hard work, small pay, and bum grub; and when we git into port, just a drunk endin' up in a fight, and all your money gone, and then ship away again. Never meetin' no nice people; never gittin' outa sailor town, hardly, in any port; travellin' all over the world and never seein' none of it; without no one to care whether you're alive or dead.
*With a bitter smile.*
There ain't much in all that that'd make yuh sorry to lose it, Drisc.

**DRISCOLL**
*Gloomily.*
It's a hell av a life, the sea.

**YANK**
*Musingly.*
It must be great to stay on dry land all your life and have a farm with a house of your own with cows and pigs and chickens, 'way in the middle of the land where yuh'd never smell the sea or see a ship. It must be great to have a wife, and kids to play with at night after sup-

per when your work was done. It must be great to have a home of your own, Drisc.

DRISCOLL
*With a great sigh.*
It must, surely; but what's the use av thinkin' av ut? Such things are not for the loikes av us.

YANK
Sea-farin' is all right when you're young and don't care, but we ain't chickens no more, and somehow, I dunno, this last year has seemed rotten, and I've had a hunch I'd quit—with you, of course—and we'd save our coin, and go to Canada or Argentine or some place and git a farm, just a small one, just enough to live on. I never told yuh this cause I thought you'd laugh at me.

DRISCOLL
*Enthusiastically.*
Laugh at you, is ut? When I'm havin' the same thoughts myself, toime afther toime. It's a grand idea and we'll be doin' ut sure if you'll stop your crazy notions—about—about bein' so sick.

YANK
*Sadly.*
Too late. We shouldn'ta made this trip, and then—How'd all the fog git in here?

DRISCOLL
Fog?

YANK
Everything looks misty. Must be my eyes gittin' weak, I guess. What was we talkin' of a minute ago? Oh, yes, a farm. It's too late.
*His mind wandering.*
Argentine, did I say? D'yuh remember the times we've had in Buenos Aires? The moving pictures in Barracas? Some class to them, d'yuh remember?

DRISCOLL
*With satisfaction.*

I do that; and so does the piany player. He'll not be forgettin' the black eye I gave him in a hurry.

YANK

Remember the time we was there on the beach and had to go to Tommy Moore's boarding house to git shipped? And he sold us rotten oilskins and seaboots full of holes, and shipped us on a skysail yarder round the Horn, and took two months' pay for it. And the days we used to sit on the park benches along the Paseo Colon with the vigilantes lookin' hard at us? And the songs at the Sailor's Opera where the guy played ragtime — d'yuh remember them?

DRISCOLL

I do, surely.

YANK

And La Plata — phew, the stink of the hides! I always liked Argentine — all except that booze, caña. How drunk we used to git on that, remember?

DRISCOLL

Cud I forget ut? My head pains me at the menshun av that divil's brew.

YANK

Remember the night I went crazy with the heat in Singapore? And the time you was pinched by the cops in Port Said? And the time we was both locked up in Sydney for fightin'?

DRISCOLL

I do so.

YANK

And that fight on the dock at Cape Town —
*His voice betrays great inward perturbation.*

DRISCOLL

*Hastily.*
Don't be thinkin' av that now. 'Tis past and gone.

YANK

D'yuh think He'll hold it up against me?

DRISCOLL

*Mystified.*

Who's that?

YANK

God. They say He sees everything. He must know it was done in fair fight, in self-defense, don't yuh think?

DRISCOLL

Av course. Ye stabbed him, and be damned to him, for the skulkin' swine he was, afther him tryin' to stick you in the back, and you not suspectin'. Let your conscience be aisy. I wisht I had nothin' blacker than that on my sowl. I'd not be afraid av the angel Gabriel himself.

YANK

*With a shudder.*

I c'd see him a minute ago with the blood spurtin' out of his neck. Ugh!

DRISCOLL

The fever, ut is, that makes you see such things. Give no heed to ut.

YANK

*Uncertainly.*

You don't think He'll hold it up agin me—God, I mean.

DRISCOLL

If there's justice in hiven, no!

YANK *seems comforted by this assurance.*

YANK

*After a pause.*

We won't reach Cardiff for a week at least. I'll be buried at sea.

DRISCOLL

*Putting his hands over his ears.*

Ssshh! I won't listen to you.

YANK

*As if he had not heard him.*

It's as good a place as any other, I s'pose—only I always wanted to be buried on dry land. But what the hell'll I care—then?

*Fretfully.*

Why should it be a rotten night like this with that damned whistle blowin' and people snorin' all round? I wish the stars was out, and the moon, too; I c'd lie out on deck and look at them, and it'd make it easier to go—somehow.

DRISCOLL

For the love av God don't be talkin' loike that!

YANK

Whatever pay's comin' to me yuh can divvy up with the rest of the boys; and you take my watch. It ain't worth much, but it's all I've got.

DRISCOLL

But have ye no relations at all to call your own?

YANK

No, not as I know of. One thing I forgot: You know Fanny the barmaid at the Red Stork in Cardiff?

DRISCOLL

Sure, and who doesn't?

YANK

She's been good to me. She tried to lend me half a crown when I was broke there last trip. Buy her the biggest box of candy yuh c'n find in Cardiff.

*Breaking down—in a choking voice.*

It's hard to ship on this voyage I'm goin' on—alone!

DRISCOLL *reaches out and grasps his hand. There is a pause, during which both fight to control themselves.*

My throat's like a furnace.

*He gasps for air.*

Gimme a drink of water, will yuh, Drisc?

DRISCOLL *gets him a dipper of water.*
I wish this was a pint of beer. Oooohh!
*He chokes, his face convulsed with agony, his hands tearing at his shirt front. The dipper falls from his nerveless fingers.*

DRISCOLL
For the love av God, what is ut, Yank?

YANK
*Speaking with tremendous difficulty.*
S'long, Drisc!
*He stares straight in front of him with eyes starting from their sockets.*
Who's that?

DRISCOLL
Who? What?

YANK
*Faintly.*
A pretty lady dressed in black.
*His face twitches and his body writhes in a final spasm, then straightens out rigidly.*

DRISCOLL
*Pale with horror.*
Yank! Yank! Say a word to me for the love av hiven!
*He shrinks away from the bunk, making the sign of the cross. Then comes back and puts a trembling hand on* YANK's *chest and bends closely over the body.*

COCKY
*From the alleyway.*
Oh, Driscoll! Can you leave Yank for arf a mo' and give me a 'and?

DRISCOLL
*With a great sob.*
Yank!
*He sinks down on his knees beside the bunk, his head on his hands. His lips move in some half-remembered prayer.*

COCKY

*Enters, his oilskins and sou'wester glistening with drops of water.*
The fog's lifted.
COCKY *sees* DRISCOLL *and stands staring at him with open mouth.*
DRISCOLL *makes the sign of the cross again.*

COCKY

*Mockingly.*
Sayin' 'is prayers!
*He catches sight of the still figure in the bunk and an expression of awed understanding comes over his face. He takes off his dripping sou'wester and stands, scratching his head.*

COCKY

*In a hushed whisper.*
Gawd blimey!

THE CURTAIN FALLS

*Fog*
A Play in One Act

# Characters

A POET

A MAN OF BUSINESS

A POLISH PEASANT WOMAN

A DEAD CHILD

THE THIRD OFFICER OF A STEAMER

SAILORS FROM THE STEAMER

# Fog

SCENE

*The lifeboat of a passenger steamer is drifting helplessly off the Grand Banks of Newfoundland. A dense fog lies heavily upon the still sea. There is no wind and the long swells of the ocean are barely perceptible. The surface of the water is shadowy and unreal in its perfect calmness. A menacing silence, like the genius of the fog, broods over everything.*

*Three figures in the boat are darkly outlined against the gray background of vapor. Two are seated close together on the thwarts in the middle. The other is huddled stiffly at one end. None of their faces can be distinguished.*

*Day is just about to break, and as the action progresses, the vague twilight of dawn creeps over the sea. This, in turn, is succeeded by as bright a semblance of daylight as can sift through the thick screen of fog.*

MAN'S VOICE
*Appallingly brisk and breezy under the circumstances.*
Brrr! I wish daylight would come. I'm beginning to feel pretty chilly. How about you?
*He receives no answer and raises his voice, the fear of solitude suddenly alive within him.*
Hello there! You havn't gone to sleep, have you?

ANOTHER MAN'S VOICE
*More refined than the first, clear and unobtrusively melancholy.*
No, I'm not asleep.

FIRST VOICE
*Complacently reassured.*
Thought you might have dozed off. I did a while ago—eyes refused

27

to stay open any longer—couldn't imagine where I was when I woke up—had forgotten all about the damned wreck.

SECOND VOICE
You are fortunate to be able to sleep. I wish I could go to sleep and forget—all this—

FIRST VOICE
Oh, come now! You mustn't keep thinking about it. That won't do any good. Brace up! We're sure to get out of this mess all right. I've figured it all out. You know how long a time it was between the time we hit the derelict—it was a derelict we hit, wasn't it?

SECOND VOICE
I believe so.

FIRST VOICE
Well, the wireless was going all the time, if you remember, and one of the officers told me we had lots of answers from ships saying they were on the way to help us. One of them is sure to pick us up.

SECOND VOICE
In this fog?

FIRST VOICE
Oh, this'll all go away as soon as the sun goes up. I've seen plenty like it at my country place on the Connecticut shore, maybe not as thick as this one but nearly as bad, and when the sun came up they always disappeared before the morning was over.

SECOND VOICE
You forget we are now near the Grand Banks, the home of fog.

FIRST VOICE
*With a laugh that is a bit troubled.*
I must say you aren't a very cheerful companion. Why don't you look at the bright side?
*A pause during which he is evidently thinking over what the other man has told him.*
The Grand Banks? Hmm, well, I refuse to be scared.

SECOND VOICE

I have no intention of making our situation seem worse than it really is. I have every hope that we will eventually be rescued, but it's better not to expect too much. It only makes disappointment more bitter when it comes.

FIRST VOICE

I suppose you're right, but I can't help being optimistic.

SECOND VOICE

You remember how downcast you were yesterday when we failed to hear any sound of a ship? Today is liable to be the same unless this fog lifts. So don't hope for too much.

FIRST VOICE

You're forgetting the fact that there was no sun yesterday. That kind of weather can't last forever.

SECOND VOICE
*Dryly.*
Perhaps we could not see the sun on account of the fog.

FIRST VOICE
*After a pause.*
I'll admit I did feel pretty dismal yesterday—after that terrible thing happened.

SECOND VOICE
*Softly.*
You mean after the child died?

FIRST VOICE
*Gloomily.*
Yes. I thought that woman would never stop crying. Ugh! It was awful—her cries, and the fog, and not another sound anywhere.

SECOND VOICE

It was the most horrible thing I have ever seen or even heard of. I never dreamed anything could be so full of tragedy.

FIRST VOICE

It was enough to give anyone the blues, that's sure. Besides, my clothes were wet and I was freezing cold and you can imagine how merry I felt.
*Grumbling.*
Not that they're any dryer now but somehow I feel warmer.

SECOND VOICE
*After a long pause.*
So you think the child's death was a terrible thing?

FIRST VOICE
*In astonishment.*
Of course. Why? Don't you?

SECOND VOICE
No.

FIRST VOICE
But you said just a minute ago that—

SECOND VOICE
I was speaking of the grief and despair of the mother. But death was kind to the child. It saved him many a long year of sordid drudgery.

FIRST VOICE
I don't know as I agree with you there. Everyone has a chance in this world; but we've all got to work hard, of course. That's the way I figure it out.

SECOND VOICE
What chance had that poor child? Naturally sickly and weak from underfeeding, transplanted to the stinking room of a tenement or the filthy hovel of a mining village, what glowing opportunities did life hold out that death should not be regarded as a blessing for him? I mean if he possessed the ordinary amount of ability and intelligence—considering him as the average child of ignorant Polish immigrants. Surely his prospects of ever becoming anything but a beast of burden were not bright, were they?

**FIRST VOICE**
Well, no, of course not, but—

**SECOND VOICE**
If you could bring him back to life would you do so? Could you conscientiously drag him away from that fine sleep of his to face what he would have to face? Leaving the joy you would give his mother out of the question, would you do it for him individually?

**FIRST VOICE**
*Doubtfully.*
Perhaps not, looking at it from that standpoint.

**SECOND VOICE**
There is no other standpoint. The child was diseased at birth, stricken with a hereditary ill that only the most vital men are able to shake off.

**FIRST VOICE**
You mean?

**SECOND VOICE**
I mean poverty—the most deadly and prevalent of all diseases.

**FIRST VOICE**
*Amused.*
Oh, that's it, eh? Well, it seems to be a pretty necessary sickness and you'll hardly find a cure for it. I see you're a bit of a reformer.

**SECOND VOICE**
Oh no. But there are times when the frightful injustice of it all sickens me with life in general.

**FIRST VOICE**
I find life pretty good. I don't know as I'd change it even if I could.

**SECOND VOICE**
Spoken like a successful man. For I'm sure you are a successful man, are you not? I mean in a worldly way.

FIRST VOICE
*Flattered.*
Yes, you might call me so, I guess. I've made my little pile but it was no easy time getting it, let me tell you.

SECOND VOICE
You had some advantages, did you not? Education and plenty to eat, and a clean home, and so forth?

FIRST VOICE
I went to high school and of course had the other things you mentioned. My people were not exactly what you could call poor but they were certainly not rich. Why do you ask?

SECOND VOICE
Do you think you would be as successful and satisfied with life if you had started with handicaps like those which that poor dead child would have had to contend with if he had lived?

FIRST VOICE
*Impatiently.*
Oh, I don't know! What's the use of talking about what might have happened? I'm not responsible for the way the world is run.

SECOND VOICE
But supposing you are responsible?

FIRST VOICE
What!

SECOND VOICE
I mean supposing we—the self-satisfied, successful members of society—are responsible for the injustice visited upon the heads of our less fortunate "brothers-in-Christ" because of our shameful indifference to it. We see misery all around us and we do not care. We do nothing to prevent it. Are we not then, in part at least, responsible for it? Have you ever thought of that?

FIRST VOICE
*In tones of annoyance.*
No, and I'm not going to start in thinking about it now.

SECOND VOICE
*Quietly.*
I see. It's a case of what is Hecuba to you that you should weep for her.

FIRST VOICE
*Blankly.*
Hecuba? Oh, you mean the woman. You can't accuse me of any heartlessness there. I never felt so sorry for anyone in my life. Why, I was actually crying myself at one time, I felt so sorry for her. By the way, she hasn't made a sound since it got dark last evening. Is she asleep? Can you see her? You're nearer to her than I am.

*It is becoming gradually lighter although the fog is as thick as ever. The faces of the two men in the boat can be dimly distinguished—one round, jowly, and clean-shaven; the other oval with big dark eyes and a black mustache and black hair pushed back from his high forehead. The huddled figure at the end of the boat is clearly that of a woman. One arm is flung over her face, concealing it. In the other she clutches something like a bundle of white clothes.*

DARK MAN
*He of the Second Voice, who is seated on the thwart nearer to the woman —turning round and peering in her direction.*
She is very still. She must be asleep. I hope so, poor woman!

OTHER MAN
Yes, a little sleep will do her a world of good.

DARK MAN
She still holds the body of the child close to her breast.
*He returns to his former position facing the* OTHER MAN.
I suppose you—

OTHER MAN
*Exultingly.*
Excuse my interrupting you, but have you noticed how light it's getting? It didn't strike me until you turned around just now. I can see your face plainly and a few minutes ago I couldn't tell whether you were a blond or brunette.

DARK MAN

Now if this fog would only lift—

OTHER MAN

It's going to lift. You wait and see. You'll find my optimism is justified. But what was it you started to say?

DARK MAN

I was saying that I supposed you had never seen this woman on board.

OTHER MAN

No. I was in the smoking room playing bridge most of the time. I'm not much of a sailor—don't care much about the water—just went over to Europe because the wife and the girls insisted. I was bored to death—made an excuse to get away as soon as I could. No, sir, you can't teach an old dog new tricks. I'm a businessman pure and simple and the farther I get away from that business the more dissatisfied I am. I've built that business up from nothing and it's sort of like a child of mine. It gives me pleasure to watch over it and when I'm away I'm uneasy. I don't like to leave it in strange hands. As for traveling, little old New York in the U.S.A. is good enough for me. *He pauses impressively, waiting for some word of approval for his sterling patriotic principles. The* DARK MAN *is silent and he of the U.S.A. continues, a bit disconcerted.*
But you asked me if I had seen the woman. I don't think so, because I never went down into the steerage. I know some of the first-class passengers did but I wasn't curious. It's a filthy sort of hole, isn't it?

DARK MAN

It's not so bad. I spent quite a good deal of my time down there.

BUSINESSMAN

*For he of the jowly, fat face and the bald spot is such by his own confession. Chuckling.*
In your role of reformer?

DARK MAN

No. Simply because I found the people in the steerage more interesting to talk to than the second-class passengers. I am not a re-former—at least not in the professional sense.

BUSINESSMAN
Do you mind my asking what particular line you are in?

DARK MAN
I am a writer.

BUSINESSMAN
I thought it was something of the kind. I knew you weren't in busi-ness when I heard those socialistic ideas of yours.
*Condescendingly.*
Beautiful idea—socialism—but too impractical—never come about—just a dream.

DARK MAN
I'm not a socialist—especially—just a humanist, that is all.

BUSINESSMAN
What particular kind of writing do you do?

DARK MAN
I write poetry.

BUSINESSMAN
*In a tone indicating that in his mind poets and harmless lunatics have more than one point in common.*
Oh, I see. Well, there's not much money in that, is there?

POET
No.

BUSINESSMAN
*After a long pause.*
I don't know about you but I'm beginning to feel hungry. Is that box of crackers near you?
*The POET reaches in under a thwart and pulls out a box of sea biscuits. The BUSINESSMAN takes a handful and munches greedily.*
Never thought hardtack could taste so good. Aren't you going to have any?

POET

No. I am not hungry. The thought of that poor woman takes all my hunger away. I used to watch her every day down in the steerage playing with her little son who is now dead. I think he must have been the only child she ever had, the look on her face was so wonderfully tender as she bent over him. What will her life be now that death has robbed her of the only recompense for her slavery? It seems such needless cruelty. Why was I not taken instead?—I, who have no family or friends to weep, and am not afraid to die.

BUSINESSMAN

*His mouth full.*

You take things to heart too much. That's just like a poet. She'll forget all about it—probably sooner than you will. One forgets everything in time. What a devil of a world it would be if we didn't.

*He takes another handful of sea biscuits and continues his munching. The* POET *turns away from him in disgust.*

Funny thing when you come to think of it—I mean how we happened to come together in this boat. It's a mystery to me how she ever got in here. And then, how is it there's no oars in this boat and still there's plenty of food? You remember there was no lack of lifeboats, and after the women and children were taken off I was ordered into one and we were rowed away. The damned thing must have gotten smashed somehow, for it leaked like a sieve and in spite of our bailing we were soon dumped in the water. I heard the noise of voices near us and tried to swim to one of the other boats, but I must have got twisted in the fog, for when I did find a boat—and let me tell you I was pretty nearly "all in" about then—it was this one and you and she were in it. Now what I want to know is—

POET

It is easily explained. Did you ever become so sick of disappointment and weary of life in general that death appeared to you the only way out?

BUSINESSMAN

Hardly. But what has that to do—

**POET**

Listen and you will see. That is the way I felt — sick and weary of soul and longing for sleep. When the ship struck the derelict it seemed to me providential. Here was the solution I had been looking for. I would go down with the ship, and that small part of the world which knew me would think my death an accident.

**BUSINESSMAN**

*Forgetting to eat in his amazement.*

You mean to say you were going to commit—

**POET**

I was going to die, yes. So I hid in the steerage fearing that some of the ship's officers would insist on saving my life in spite of me. Finally, when everyone had gone, I came out and walked around the main deck. I heard the sound of voices come from a dark corner and discovered that this woman and her child had been left behind. How that happened I don't know. Probably she hid because she was afraid the child would be crushed by the terror-stricken immigrants. At any rate there she was and I decided she was so happy in her love for her child that it would be wrong to let her die. I looked around and found this lifeboat had been lowered down to the main deck and left hanging there. The oars had been taken out — probably for extra rowers in some other boat. I persuaded the woman to climb in and then went up to the boat deck and lowered the boat the rest of the way to the water. This was not much of a task, for the steamer was settling lower in the water every minute. I then slid down one of the ropes to the boat and, cutting both of the lines that held her, pushed off. There was a faint breeze which blew us slowly away from the sinking ship until she was hidden in the fog. The suspense of waiting for her to go down was terrible. Even as it was we were nearly swamped by the waves when the steamer took her final plunge.

**BUSINESSMAN**

*Edges away from the* POET, *firmly convinced that his convictions regarding the similarity of poets and madmen are based upon fact.*

I hope you've abandoned that suicide idea.

POET

I have—absolutely. I think all that happened to me is an omen sent by the gods to convince me my past unhappiness is past and my fortune will change for the better.

BUSINESSMAN

That's the way to talk! Superstition is a good thing sometimes.

POET

But if I had known the sufferings that poor woman was to undergo as a result of my reckless life-saving, I would have let her go down with the ship and gone myself.

BUSINESSMAN

Don't think of it any longer. You couldn't help that. I wonder what it was the child died of? I thought it was asleep when I heard it choke and cough—and the next minute *she* commenced to scream. I won't forget those screams for the rest of my life.

POET

The child was naturally frail and delicate and I suppose the fright he received and the exposure combined to bring on some kind of convulsion. He was dead when I went over to see what was the matter.

BUSINESSMAN

*Peering upward through the fog.*
It's getting considerably lighter. It must be about time for the sun to rise—if we're going to have any sun.

POET

*Sadly.*
It was just about this time yesterday morning when the poor little fellow died.

BUSINESSMAN

*Looks apprehensively toward the huddled figure in the end of the boat. Now that it is lighter, what appeared before like a bundle of white clothes can be seen to be a child four or five years old with a thin, sallow face and long black curls. The body is rigid, wrapped in a white shawl, and the eyes are open and glassy.*

Let's not talk any more about it. She might wake up and start screaming again — and I can't stand that.

POET
She does not understand English.

BUSINESSMAN
*Shaking his head.*
She'd know we were talking about the kid just the same. Mothers have an instinct when it comes to that. I've seen that proved in my own family more than once.

POET
Have you ever lost any of your children?

BUSINESSMAN
No. Thank God!

POET
You may well thank God, even if people do, as you claimed a while ago, forget so easily.

BUSINESSMAN
You're not married, are you?

POET
No.

BUSINESSMAN
I didn't think you were.
*Jocularly.*
You people with artistic temperaments run more to affinities than to wives. I suppose you've lots of those?

POET
*Does not hear or will not notice this question. He is staring through the fog and speaks in excited tones.*
Did you hear that?

BUSINESSMAN
Hear what?

POET

Just now when you were talking. I thought I heard a sound like a steamer's whistle.

*They both listen intently. After a second or so the sound comes again, faint and far-off, wailing over the water.*

BUSINESSMAN

*Wildly elated.*

By God, it is a steamer!

POET

It sounded nearer that time. She must be coming this way.

BUSINESSMAN

Oh, if only this rotten fog would lift for a minute!

POET

Let's hope it will. We run as much risk of being run down as we do of being saved while this continues. They couldn't see us twenty feet away in this.

BUSINESSMAN

*Nervously.*

Can't we yell or make some kind of a noise?

POET

They couldn't hear us now. We can try when they get close to us.

*A pause during which they hear the steamer whistle again.*

How cold the air is! Or is it my imagination?

BUSINESSMAN

No, I notice it too. I've been freezing to death for the last five minutes. I wish we had the oars so we could row and keep warm.

POET

Sssh! Do you hear that?

BUSINESSMAN

What? The whistle? I heard it a moment ago.

**POET**

No. This is a sound like running water. There! Don't you hear it now?
*A noise as of water falling over rocks comes clearly through the fog.*

**BUSINESSMAN**

Yes, I hear it. What can it be? There isn't any water out here except
what's under us.
*With a shiver.*
Brrr, but it's chilly!

**POET**

That poor woman will be frozen when she wakes up.
*He takes off his ulster, and walking carefully to the end of the boat, covers
the form of the sleeping woman with it.*

**BUSINESSMAN**

It sounds louder every minute but I can't see anything. Damn this
fog!
*The noise of the falling water grows more and more distinct. At regular
intervals the steamer's whistle blows and that, too, seems to be drawing
nearer.*

**POET**

*Still bent over the sleeping woman.*
Perhaps it may be land but I hardly think we could have drifted that
far.

**BUSINESSMAN**

*In terrified tones.*
Good God, what's that?
*The POET turns quickly around. Something huge and white is loom-
ing up through the fog directly beside the boat. The boat drifts up to it
sideways and strikes against it with a slight jar. The BUSINESSMAN
shrinks away as far along the thwart as he can get, causing the boat to
tip a little to one side. The spattering splash of falling water sounds from
all around them.*

**POET**

*Looking at the white mass towering above them.*
An iceberg!

*Turning to the* BUSINESSMAN.

Steady there! You will be in the water in a minute if you're not careful. There is nothing to be frightened over. Lucky for us it's calm or we would be smashed to pieces.

BUSINESSMAN

*Reassured by finding out that what he took for some horrible phantom of the sea is an ice and water reality, he moves over to the center of his thwart and remarks sarcastically.*

As it is we'll only freeze to death. Is that what you mean?

POET

*Thumping his hands against his sides.*

It *is* cold. I wonder how big the berg is. Help me try to push the boat away from it.

*They push against the side of the berg. The boat moves away a little but drifts right back again.*

BUSINESSMAN

Ouch! My hands are freezing.

POET

No use wasting effort on that. The boat is too heavy and you can get no grip on the ice.

*A blast of the steamer's whistle shrills through the fog. It sounds very close to them.*

Oh God, I never thought of that.

*He sits down dejectedly opposite the* BUSINESSMAN.

BUSINESSMAN

Never thought of what?

POET

*Excitedly.*

The steamer, man, the steamer! Think of the danger she is in. If she were ever to hit this mass of ice she would sink before they could lower a boat.

BUSINESSMAN

Can't we do something? We'll yell to them when they get nearer.

POET

Oh my God, man, don't do that. This may be one of the rescue ships come to pick up the survivors from our boat, and if they heard any shouts they would think they were cries for help and come right in this direction. Not a sound if you have any regard for the lives of those on board.

BUSINESSMAN
*Almost whimpering.*
But if we don't let them know we're here they are liable to pass by us and never know it.

POET
*Sternly.*
We can die but we cannot risk the lives of others to save our own.
*The* BUSINESSMAN *does not reply to this but a look of sullen stubbornness comes over his face. There is a long pause. The silence is suddenly shattered by a deafening blast from the steamer's whistle.*

POET
God! She must be right on top of us.
*They both start to their feet and stand straining their eyes to catch some glimpse of the approaching vessel through the blinding mist. The stillness is so intense that the throb of the engines can be plainly heard. This sound slowly recedes and the next whistle indicates by its lack of volume that the steamer has passed and is proceeding on her way.*

BUSINESSMAN
*Furiously.*
She's going away. I'm not going to be left here to die on account of your damn-fool ideas.
*He turns in the direction he supposes the steamer to be and raises his hands to his mouth, shaping them like a megaphone.*

POET
*Jumping over and forcing his hand over the* BUSINESSMAN's *mouth in time to stifle his call for help.*
You damned coward! I might have known what to expect.
*The* BUSINESSMAN *struggles to free himself, rocking the boat from side*

*to side with his futile twistings, but he is finally forced down to a sitting position on the thwart. The* POET *then releases him. He opens his mouth as if to shout but the* POET *stands over him with his right fist drawn back threateningly and the* BUSINESSMAN *thinks better of it.*

BUSINESSMAN
*Snarling.*
I'll get even with you, you loafer, if we ever get on shore.
*The* POET *pays no attention to this threat but sits down opposite him. They hear the whistle again, seemingly no farther away than before. The* BUSINESSMAN *stirs uneasily. A rending, tearing crash cracks through the silence, followed a moment later by a tremendous splash. Great drops of water fall in the rocking boat.*

BUSINESSMAN
*Trembling with terror.*
She must have hit it after all.

POET
No. That can't be it. I don't hear any shouts.
*Suddenly smiling with relief as he guesses what has happened.*
I know what it is. The berg is melting and breaking up. That was a piece that fell in the water.

BUSINESSMAN
It almost landed on us.
*He becomes panic-stricken at this thought and jumps to his feet.*
I'm not going to stand this any longer. We'll be crushed like flies. I'll take a chance and swim for it. You can stay here and be killed if you want to.
*Insane with fear of this new menace he puts one foot on the gunwale of the boat and is about to throw himself into the water when the* POET *grabs him by the arm and pulls him back.*
Let me go! This is all right for you. You want to die. Do you want to kill me too, you murderer?
*He hides his face in his hands and weeps like a fat child in a fit of temper.*

POET
You fool! You could not swim for five minutes in this icy water.

*More kindly.*
Come! Be sensible! Act like a man!
*The* BUSINESSMAN *shakes with a combination of sigh and sob. The whistle blows again and seems once more to be in their immediate vicinity. The* BUSINESSMAN *takes a new lease on life at this favorable sign and raises his head.*

BUSINESSMAN
She seems to be getting quite near us again.

POET
Yes, and a moment ago I heard something like oars creaking in the oarlocks and striking the water.

BUSINESSMAN
*Hopefully.*
Maybe they've lowered a boat.
*Even as he is speaking the curtain of fog suddenly lifts. The sun has just risen over the horizon rim, and the berg behind them, its surface carved and fretted by the streams of water from the melting ice, its whiteness vivid above the blue-gray water, seems like the façade of some huge Viking temple.*

POET
*He and the* BUSINESSMAN, *their backs turned to the berg, are looking at something over the water as if they could hardly believe their good fortune.*
There's the steamer now and she can hardly be more than a quarter of a mile away. What luck!

BUSINESSMAN
And there's the boat you heard. Look! They were rowing straight toward us.

POET
*Half to himself, with a puzzled expression.*
I wonder how they knew we were here.

VOICE FROM OVER THE WATER
Hello there!

BUSINESSMAN
*Waving frantically.*
Hello!

VOICE
*Nearer—the creak of the oars can be clearly heard.*
Are you people off the *Starland?*

BUSINESSMAN
Yes.
*With the return of his courage he has regained all his self-assured urban-ity. He tries to pull his clothes into some semblance of their former im-maculateness, and his round face with its imposing double chin assumes an expression of importance. The* POET's *face is drawn and melancholy as if he were uncertain of the outcome of this unexpected return to life.*

BUSINESSMAN
*Turning to the* POET *with a smile.*
You see, my optimism was justified after all.
*Growing confused before the* POET's *steady glance.*
I wish you'd—er—forget all about the little unpleasantness between us. I must confess I was a bit—er—rattled and didn't exactly know what I was doing.
*He holds out his hand uncertainly. The* POET *takes it with a quiet smile.*

POET
*Simply.*
I had forgotten all about it.

BUSINESSMAN
Thank you.
*The voice that hailed them is heard giving some orders. The sound of the oars ceases and a moment later a lifeboat similar to the one they are in, but manned by a full crew of sailors, comes alongside of them. A young man in uniform, evidently the Third Officer of the ship, is in the stern steering.*

BUSINESSMAN
*Breezily.*
Hello! You certainly are a welcome sight.

OFFICER
*Looking up at the towering side of the berg.*
You picked out a funny island to land on. What made you cling so close to this berg? Cold, wasn't it?

POET
We drifted into it in the fog and having no oars could not get away. It was about the same time we first heard your whistle.

OFFICER
*Nodding toward the woman's figure.*
Woman sick?

POET
She has been asleep, poor woman.

OFFICER
Where's the kid?

POET
In her arms.
*Then, wonderingly.*
But how did you know—?

OFFICER
We'd never have found you but for that. Why didn't you give us a shout or make some kind of a racket?

BUSINESSMAN
*Eagerly.*
We were afraid you would come in our direction and hit this iceberg.

OFFICER
But we might have passed you and never had an inkling—

BUSINESSMAN
*Impressively.*
In a case of that kind one has to take chances.
*The* POET *smiles quietly. The* OFFICER *looks surprised.*

OFFICER
That was very fine of you, I must say. Most people would only have

thought of themselves. As it was, if it hadn't been for the kid crying
we would have missed you. I was on the bridge with the First Officer. We had been warned about this berg, and when the fog came
up we slowed down until we were barely creeping, and stopped al-
together every now and then. It was during one of these stops, when
everything was still, we heard the crying, and I said to the First Officer: "Sounds like a kid bawling, doesn't it?" And he thought it did
too. It kept getting plainer and plainer until there was no chance for
a mistake—weird too it sounded with everything so quiet and the
fog so heavy. I said to him again: "It's a kid sure enough, but how
in the devil did it get out here?" And then we both remembered we
had been ordered to keep a lookout for any of the survivors of the
*Starland* who hadn't been picked up yet, and the First Officer said:
"It's probably some of the poor devils from the *Starland*," and told
me to have a boat lowered. I grabbed a compass and jumped in. We
could hear the kid crying all the time, couldn't we, boys?
*He turns to the crew, who all answer: "Yes, sir."*
That's how I was able to shape such a direct course for you. I was
steering by the sound. It stopped just as the fog rose.
*During the* OFFICER's *story the* BUSINESSMAN *has been looking at
him with an expression of annoyed stupefaction on his face. He is unable
to decide whether the* OFFICER *is fooling or not and turns to the* POET
*for enlightenment. But the latter, after listening to the* OFFICER's *expla-
nation with intense interest, goes quickly to the side of the woman and,
removing his ulster from over her shoulders, attempts to awaken her.*

OFFICER
*Noticing what he is doing.*
That's right. Better wake her up. The steamer will be ready to pick
us up in a minute, and she must be stiff with the cold.
*He turns to one of his crew.*
Make a line fast to this boat and we'll tow her back to the ship.
*The sailor springs into the* Starland's *boat with a coil of rope in his hand.*

POET
*Failing to awaken the woman he feels for her pulse and then bends down
to listen for a heart beat, his ear against her breast. He straightens up*

*finally and stands looking down at the two bodies and speaks to himself half aloud.*

Poor happy woman.

*The OFFICER and the BUSINESSMAN are watching him.*

OFFICER
*Sharply.*
Well?

POET
*Softly.*
The woman is dead.

BUSINESSMAN
Dead!
*He casts a horrified glance at the still figures in the end of the boat—then clambers clumsily into the other boat and stands beside the officer.*

OFFICER
Too bad! But the child is all right, of course?

POET
The child has been dead for twenty-four hours. He died at dawn yesterday.
*It is the OFFICER's turn to be bewildered. He stares at the POET pityingly and then turns to the BUSINESSMAN.*

OFFICER
*Indicating the POET with a nod of his head.*
A bit out of his head, isn't he? Exposure affects a lot of them that way.

BUSINESSMAN
*Solemnly.*
He told you the exact truth of the matter.

OFFICER
*Concluding he has two madmen to deal with instead of one.*
Of course.
*To the sailor who has made fast the towing rope.*
All fast?

*The sailor jumps into his own boat with a brisk "Aye, aye, sir." The* OFFICER *turns to the* POET.

Coming in here or going to stay where you are?

POET
*Gently.*
I think I will stay with the dead.
*He is sitting opposite the two rigid figures, looking at their still white faces with eyes full of a great longing.*

OFFICER
*Mutters.*
Cheerful beggar!
*He faces the crew.*
Give way all.
*The oars take the water and the two boats glide swiftly away from the iceberg.*

*The fresh morning breeze ripples over the water bringing back to the attentive ear some words of the* MAN OF BUSINESS *spoken argumentatively, but in the decided accents of one who is rarely acknowledged to be wrong.*

BUSINESSMAN
—the exact truth. So you see that, if you will pardon my saying so, Officer, what you have just finished telling us is almost unbelievable.

CURTAIN

*Thirst*
A Play in One Act

# Characters

A GENTLEMAN

A DANCER

A WEST INDIAN MULATTO SAILOR

# Thirst

*A steamer's life raft rising and falling slowly on the long ground swell of a glassy tropic sea. The sky above is pitilessly clear, of a steel-blue color merging into black shadow on the horizon's rim. The sun glares down from straight overhead like a great angry eye of God. The heat is terrific. Writhing, fantastic heat waves rise from the white deck of the raft. Here and there on the still surface of the sea the fins of sharks may be seen slowly cutting the surface of the water in lazy circles.*

*Two men and a woman are on the raft. Seated at one end is a West Indian mulatto dressed in the blue uniform of a sailor. Across his jersey may be seen the words "Union Mail Line" in red letters. He has on rough sailor shoes. His head is bare. When he speaks it is in drawling sing-song tones as if he were troubled by some strange impediment of speech. He croons a monotonous Negro song to himself as his round eyes follow the shark fins in their everlasting circles.*

*At the other end of the raft sits a middle-aged white man in what was once evening dress; but sun and salt water have reduced it to the mere caricature of such a garment. His white shirt is stained and rumpled; his collar a formless pulp about his neck; his black tie a withered ribbon. Evidently he had been a first-class passenger. Just now he cuts a sorry and pitiful figure as he sits staring stupidly at the water with unseeing eyes. His scanty black hair is disheveled, revealing a bald spot burnt crimson by the sun. A mustache droops over his lips, and some of the dye has run off it making a black line down the side of his lean face, blistered with sunburn, haggard with hunger and thirst. From time to time he licks his swollen lips with his blackened tongue.*

*Between the two men a young woman lies with arms outstretched, face downward on the raft. She is an even more bizarre figure than the man in evening clothes, for she is dressed in a complete short-skirted danc-er's costume of black velvet covered with spangles. Her long blond hair streams down over her bare, unprotected shoulders. Her silk stockings are baggy and wrinkled and her dancing shoes swollen and misshapen. When she lifts her head a diamond necklace can be seen glittering coldly on the protruding collarbones of her emaciated shoulders. Continuous weeping has made a blurred smudge of her rouge and the black make-up of her eyes but one can still see that she must have been very beautiful before hunger and thirst had transformed her into a mocking specter of a dancer. She is sobbing endlessly, hopelessly.*

*In the eyes of all three the light of a dawning madness is shining.*

DANCER
*Raising herself to a sitting posture and turning piteously to the* GENTLE-MAN.
My God! My God! This silence is driving me mad! Why do you not speak to me? Is there no ship in sight yet?

GENTLEMAN
*Dully.*
No. I do not think so. At least I cannot see any.
*He tries to rise to his feet but finds himself too weak and sits down again with a groan.*
If I could only stand up I could tell better. I cannot see far from this position. I am so near the water. And then my eyes are like two balls of fire. They burn and burn until they feel as if they were boring into my brain.

DANCER
I know! I know! Everywhere I look I see great crimson spots. It is as if the sky were raining drops of blood. Do you see them too?

GENTLEMAN
Yesterday I did—or some day—I no longer remember days. But to-day everything is red. The very sea itself seems changed to blood.

*He licks his swollen, cracked lips — then laughs — the shrill cackle of madness.*

Perhaps it is the blood of all those who were drowned that night rising to the surface.

DANCER

Do not say such things. You are horrible. I do not care to listen to you.
*She turns away from him with a shudder.*

GENTLEMAN
*Sulkily.*
Very well. I will not speak.
*He covers his face with his hands.*
God! God! How my eyes ache! How my throat burns!
*He sobs heavily — there is a pause — suddenly he turns to the* DANCER *angrily.*
Why did you ask me to speak if you do not care to listen to me?

DANCER

I did not ask you to speak of blood. I did not ask you to mention that night.

GENTLEMAN

Well, I will say no more then. You may talk to him if you wish.
*He points to the* SAILOR *with a sneer. The Negro does not hear. He is crooning to himself and watching the sharks. There is a long pause. The raft slowly rises and falls on the long swells. The sun blazes down.*

DANCER
*Almost shrieking.*
Oh, this silence! I cannot bear this silence. Talk to me about anything you please but, for God's sake, talk to me! I must not think! I must not think!

GENTLEMAN
*Remorsefully.*
Your pardon, dear lady! I am afraid I spoke harshly. I am not myself. I think I am a little out of my head. There is so much sun and so

much sea. Everything gets vague at times. I am very weak. We have not eaten in so long—we have not even had a drink of water in so long.

*Then in tones of great anguish.*

Oh, if we only had some water!

DANCER

*Flinging herself on the raft and beating it with clenched fists.*

Please do not speak of water!

SAILOR

*Stopping his song abruptly and turning quickly around.*

Water? Who's got water?

*His swollen tongue shows between his dry lips.*

GENTLEMAN

*Turning to the* SAILOR.

You know no one here has any water. You stole the last drop we had yourself.

*Irritably.*

Why do you ask such questions?

*The* SAILOR *turns his back again and watches the shark fins. He does not answer nor does he sing any longer. There is a silence, profound and breathless.*

DANCER

*Creeping over to the* GENTLEMAN *and seizing his arm.*

Do you not notice how deep the silence is? The world seems emptier than ever. I am afraid. Tell me why it is.

GENTLEMAN

I, too, notice it. But I do not know why it is.

DANCER

Ah! I know now. He is silent. Do you not remember he was singing? A queer monotonous song it was—more of a dirge than a song. I have heard many songs in many languages in the places I have played, but never a song like that before. Why did he stop, do you think? Maybe something frightened him.

GENTLEMAN

I do not know. But I will ask him.

*To the* SAILOR.

Why have you stopped singing?

*The* SAILOR *looks at him with a strange expression in his eyes. He does not answer but turns to the circling fins again and takes up his song, dully, droningly, as if from some place he had left off. The* DANCER *and the* GENTLEMAN *listen in attitudes of strained attention for a long time.*

DANCER

*Laughing hysterically.*

What a song! There is no tune to it and I can understand no words. I wonder what it means.

GENTLEMAN

Who knows? It is doubtless some folk song of his people which he is singing.

DANCER

But I wish to find out. Sailor! Will you tell me what it means—that song you are singing?

*The Negro stares at her uneasily for a moment.*

SAILOR

*Drawlingly.*

It is a song of my people.

DANCER

Yes. But what do the words mean?

SAILOR

*Pointing to the shark fins.*

I am singing to them. It is a charm. I have been told it is very strong. If I sing long enough they will not eat us.

DANCER

*Terrified.*

Eat us? What will eat us?

GENTLEMAN
*Pointing to the moving fins in the still water.*
He means the sharks. Those pointed black things you see moving
through the water are their fins. Have you not noticed them before?

DANCER
Yes, yes. I have seen them. But I did not know they were sharks.
*Sobbing.*
Oh, it is horrible, all this!

GENTLEMAN
*To the Negro harshly.*
Why do you tell her such things? Do you not know you will frighten
her?

SAILOR
*Dully.*
She asked me what I was singing.

GENTLEMAN
*Trying to comfort the* DANCER, *who is still sobbing.*
At least tell her the truth about the sharks. That is all a children's tale
about them eating people.
*Raising his voice.*
You know they never eat anyone. And I know it.
*The Negro looks at him and his lips contract grotesquely. Perhaps he is
trying to smile.*

DANCER
*Raising her head and drying her eyes.*
You are sure of what you say?

GENTLEMAN
*Confused by the Negro's stare.*
Of course I am sure. Everyone knows that sharks are afraid to touch
a person. They are all cowards.
*To the Negro.*
You were just trying to frighten the lady, were you not?
*The Negro turns away from them and stares at the sea. He commences
to sing again.*

**DANCER**

I no longer like his song. It makes me dream of horrible things. Tell him to stop.

**GENTLEMAN**

Bah! You are nervous. Anything is better than dead silence.

**DANCER**

Yes. Anything is better than silence—even a song like that.

**GENTLEMAN**

He is strange—that sailor. I do not know what to think of him.

**DANCER**

It is a strange song he sings.

**GENTLEMAN**

He does not seem to want to speak to us.

**DANCER**

I have noticed that, too. When I asked him about the song he did not want to answer at all.

**GENTLEMAN**

Yet he speaks good English. It cannot be that he does not understand us.

**DANCER**

When he does speak, it is as if he had some impediment in his throat.

**GENTLEMAN**

Perhaps he has. If so, he is much to be pitied and we are wrong to speak of him so.

**DANCER**

I do not pity him. I am afraid of him.

**GENTLEMAN**

That is foolish. It is the sun which beats down so fiercely which makes you have such thoughts. I, also, have been afraid of him at times, but I know now that I had been gazing at the sea too long and listening to the great silence. Such things distort your brain.

DANCER

Then you no longer fear him?

GENTLEMAN

I no longer fear him now that I am quite sane. It clears my brain to talk to you. We must talk to each other all the time.

DANCER

Yes, we must talk to each other. I do not dream when I talk to you.

GENTLEMAN

I think at one time I was going mad. I dreamed he had a knife in his hand and looked at me. But it was all madness; I can see that now. He is only a poor Negro sailor—our companion in misfortune. God knows we are all in the same pitiful plight. We should not grow suspicious of one another.

DANCER

All the same, I am afraid of him. There is something in his eyes when he looks at me which makes me tremble.

GENTLEMAN

There is nothing, I tell you. It is all your imagination.
*There is a long pause.*

DANCER

Good God! Is there no ship in sight yet?

GENTLEMAN

*Attempting to rise but falling back weakly.*
I can see none. And I cannot stand to get a wider view.

DANCER

*Pointing to the Negro.*
Ask him. He is stronger than we are. He may be able to see one.

GENTLEMAN

Sailor!
*The Negro ceases his chant and turns to him with expressionless eyes.*
You are stronger than we are and can see farther. Stand up and tell me if there is any ship in sight.

SAILOR

*Rising slowly to his feet and looking at all points of the horizon.*
No. There is none.
*He sits down again and croons his dreary melody.*

DANCER

*Weeping hopelessly.*
My God, this is horrible. To wait and wait for something that never comes.

GENTLEMAN

It is indeed horrible. But it is to be expected.

DANCER

Why do you say it is to be expected? Have you no hopes, then, of being rescued?

GENTLEMAN

*Wearily.*
I have hoped for many things in my life. Always I have hoped in vain. We are far out of the beaten track of steamers. I know little of navigation, yet I heard those on board say that we were following a course but little used. Why we did so, I do not know. I suppose the Captain wished to make a quicker passage. He alone knows what was in his mind and he will probably never tell.

DANCER

No, he will never tell.

GENTLEMAN

Why do you speak so decidedly? He might have been among those who escaped in the boats.

DANCER

He did not escape. He is dead!

GENTLEMAN

Dead?

DANCER

Yes. He was on the bridge. I can remember seeing his face as he stood in under a lamp. It was pale and drawn like the face of a dead man. His eyes, too, seemed dead. He shouted some orders in a thin, trembling voice. No one paid any attention to him. And then he shot himself. I saw the flash, and heard the report above all the screams of the drowning. Someone grasped me by the arm and I heard a hoarse voice shouting in my ear. Then I fainted.

GENTLEMAN

Poor Captain! It is evident, then, that he felt himself guilty—since he killed himself. It must be terrible to hear the screams of the dying and know oneself to blame. I do not wonder that he killed himself.

DANCER

He was so kind and good-natured—the Captain. It was only that afternoon on the promenade deck that he stopped beside my chair. "I hear you are to entertain us this evening," he said. "That will be delightful, and it is very kind of you. I had promised myself the pleasure of seeing you in New York, but you have forestalled me."
*After a pause.*
How handsome and broad-shouldered he was—the Captain.

GENTLEMAN

I would have liked to have seen his soul.

DANCER

You would have found it no better and no worse than the souls of other men. If he was guilty he has paid with his life.

GENTLEMAN

No. He has avoided payment by taking his life. The dead do not pay.

DANCER

And the dead cannot answer when we speak evil of them. All we can know is that he is dead. Let us talk of other things.
*There is a pause.*

GENTLEMAN

*Fumbles in the inside pocket of his dress coat and pulls out a black object that looks like a large card case. He opens it and stares at it with perplexed*

*eyes. Then, giving a hollow laugh, he holds it over for the* DANCER *to see.*
Oh, the damned irony of it!

DANCER
What is it? I cannot read very well. My eyes ache so.

GENTLEMAN
*Still laughing mockingly.*
Bend closer! Bend closer! It is worth while understanding—the joke that has been played on me.

DANCER
*Reading slowly, her face almost touching the case.*
United States Club of Buenos Aires! I do not understand what the joke is.

GENTLEMAN
*Impatiently snatching the case from her hand.*
I will explain the joke to you then. Listen! M-e-n-u—menu. That is the joke. This is a souvenir menu of a banquet given in my honor by this club.
*Reading.*
"Martini cocktails, soup, sherry, fish, Burgundy, chicken, champagne"—and here we are dying for a crust of bread, for a drink of water!
*His mad laughter suddenly ceases and in a frenzy of rage he shakes his fist at the sky and screams.*
God! God! What a joke to play on us!
*After this outburst he sinks back dejectedly, his trembling hand still clutching the menu.*

DANCER
*Sobbing.*
This is too horrible. What have we done that we should suffer so? It is as if one misfortune after another happened to make our agony more terrible. Throw that thing away! The very sight of it is a mockery.
*The* GENTLEMAN *throws the menu into the sea, where it floats, a black spot on the glassy water.*

How do you happen to have that thing with you? It is ghastly for you to torment me by reading it.

GENTLEMAN
I am sorry to have hurt you. The jest was so grotesque I could not keep it to myself. You ask how I happen to have it with me? I will tell you. It gives the joke an even bitterer flavor. You remember when the crash came? We were all in the salon. You were singing—a Cockney song I think?

DANCER
Yes. It is one I first sang at the Palace in London.

GENTLEMAN
It was in the salon. You were singing. You were very beautiful. I remember a woman on my right saying: "How pretty she is! I wonder if she is married?" Strange how some idiotic remark like that will stick in one's brain when all else is vague and confused. A tragedy happens—we are in the midst of it—and one of our clearest remembrances afterwards is a remark that might have been overheard in any subway train.

DANCER
It is so with me. There was a fat, bald-headed, little man. It was on deck after the crash. Everywhere they were fighting to get into the boats. This poor little man stood by himself. His moon face was convulsed with rage. He kept repeating in loud angry tones: "I shall be late. I must cable! I can never make it!" He was still bewailing his broken appointment when a rush of the crowd swept him off his feet and into the sea. I can see him now. He is the only person besides the Captain I remember clearly.

GENTLEMAN
*Continuing his story in a dead voice.*
You were very beautiful. I was looking at you and wondering what kind of a woman you were. You know I had never met you personally—only seen you in my walks around the deck. Then came the crash—that horrible dull crash. We were all thrown forward on the floor of the salon; then screams, oaths, fainting women, the hollow

boom of a bulkhead giving way. I vaguely remember rushing to my stateroom and picking up my wallet. It must have been that menu that I took instead. Then I was on deck fighting in the midst of the crowd. Somehow I got into a boat—but it was overloaded and was swamped immediately. I swam to another boat. They beat me off with the oars. That boat too was swamped a moment later. And then the gurgling, choking cries of the drowning! Something huge rushed by me in the water, leaving a gleaming trail of phosphorescence. A woman near me with a life belt around her gave a cry of agony and disappeared—then I realized—sharks! I became frenzied with terror. I swam. I beat the water with my hands. The ship had gone down. I swam and swam with but one idea—to put all that horror behind me. I saw something white on the water before me. I clutched it—climbed on it. It was this raft. You and he were on it. I fainted. The whole thing is a horrible nightmare in my brain—but I remember clearly that idiotic remark of the woman in the salon. What pitiful creatures we are!

DANCER
When the crash came I also rushed to my stateroom. I took this, *Pointing to the diamond necklace.*
clasped it round my neck and ran on deck; the rest I have told you.

GENTLEMAN
Do you not remember how you came on this raft? It is strange that you and he should be on a raft alone when so many died for lack of a place. Were there ever any others on the raft with you?

DANCER
No, I am sure there were not. Everything in my memory is blurred. But I feel sure we were always the only ones—until you came. I was afraid of you—your face was livid with fear. You were moaning to yourself.

GENTLEMAN
It was the sharks. Until they came I kept a half-control over myself. But when I saw them even my soul quivered with terror.

DANCER

*Horror-stricken, looking at the circling fins.*

Sharks! Why they are all around us now.

*Frenziedly.*

You lied to me. You said they would not touch us. Oh, I am afraid, I am afraid!

*She covers her face with her hands.*

GENTLEMAN

If I lied to you it was because I wished to spare you. Be brave! We are safe from them as long as we stay on the raft. These things must be faced.

*Then in tones of utter despondency.*

Besides, what does it matter—sharks or no sharks—the end is the same.

DANCER

*Taking her hands away from her eyes and looking dully at the water.*

You are right. What does it matter?

GENTLEMAN

God! How still the sea is! How still the sky is! One would say the world was dead. I think the accursed humming of that nigger only makes one feel the silence more keenly. There is nothing—that seems to live.

DANCER

How the sun burns into me!

*Piteously.*

My poor skin that I was once so proud of!

GENTLEMAN

*Rousing himself with an effort.*

Come! Let us not think about it. It is madness to think about it so. How do you account for your being on the raft alone with this nigger? You have not yet told me.

DANCER

—How can I tell? The last thing I remember was that harsh voice in my ear shouting something—what, I cannot recollect.

**GENTLEMAN**
There was nothing else?

**DANCER**
Nothing.
*Pause.*
Stop! Yes, there was something I had forgotten. I think that some-
one kissed me. Yes, I am sure that someone kissed me. But no, I
am not sure. It may have all been a dream I dreamed. I have had so
many dreams during these awful days and nights—so many mad,
mad dreams.
*Her eyes begin to glaze, her lips to twitch. She murmurs to herself.*
Mad, mad dreams.

**GENTLEMAN**
*Reaching over and shaking her by the shoulder.*
Come! You said someone kissed you. You must be mistaken. I surely
did not, and it could hardly have been that sailor.

**DANCER**
Yet I am sure someone did. It was not since I have been on this raft.
It was on the deck of the ship just as I was fainting.

**GENTLEMAN**
Who could it have been, do you think?

**DANCER**
I hardly dare to say what I think. I might be wrong. You remember
the Second Officer—the young Englishman with the great dark eyes
who was so tall and handsome? All the women loved him. I, too, I
loved him—a little bit. He loved me—very much—so he said. Yes,
I know he loved me very much. I think it was he who kissed me. I
am almost sure it was he.

**GENTLEMAN**
Yes, he must have been the one. That would explain it all. He must
have sent away the raft when only you and this sailor were on it. He
probably did not let the others know of the existence of this raft. Indeed he must have loved you to disregard his duty so. I will ask the
sailor about it. Maybe he can clear away our doubts.

*To the Negro.*

Sailor!

*The Negro stops singing and looks at them with wide, bloodshot eyes.*

Did the Second Officer order you to take this lady from the ship?

SAILOR

*Sullenly.*

I do not know.

GENTLEMAN

Did he tell you to take no one else with you but this lady—and perhaps himself afterwards?

SAILOR

*Angrily.*

I do not know.

*He turns away again and commences to sing.*

DANCER

Do not speak to him any more. He is angry at something. He will not answer.

GENTLEMAN

He is going mad, I think. However, it seems certain that it was the Second Officer who kissed you and saved your life.

DANCER

He was kind and brave to me. He meant well. Yet I wish now he had let me die. I would have way down in the cold green water. I would have been sleeping, coldly sleeping. While now my brain is scorched with sun-fire and dream-fire. And I am going mad. We are all going mad. Your eyes shine with a wild flame at times—and that sailor's are horrible with strangeness—and mine see great drops of blood that dance upon the sea. Yes, we are all mad.

*Pause.*

God! Oh God! Must this be the end of all? I was coming home, home after years of struggling, home to success and fame and money. And I must die out here on a raft like a mad dog.

*She weeps despairingly.*

GENTLEMAN

Be still! You must not despair so. I, too, might whine a prayer of
protest: Oh God, God! After twenty years of incessant grind, day
after weary day, I started on my first vacation. I was going home.
And here I sit dying by slow degrees, desolate and forsaken. Is this
the meaning of all my years of labor? Is this the end, oh God? So I
might wail with equal justice. But the blind sky will not answer your
appeals or mine. Nor will the cruel sea grow merciful for any prayer
of ours.

DANCER

Have you no hope that one of the ship's boats may have reached land
and reported the disaster? They would surely send steamers out to
search for the other survivors.

GENTLEMAN

We have drifted far, very far, in these long, weary days. I am afraid
no steamer would find us.

DANCER

We are lost then!
*She falls face downward on the raft. A great sob shakes her thin bare
shoulders.*

GENTLEMAN

I have not given up hope. These seas, I have heard, are full of coral
islands and we surely ought to drift near one of them soon. It was
probably an uncharted coral reef that our steamer hit. I heard someone say "derelict" but I saw no sign of one in the water. With us it is
only a question of whether we can hold out until we sight land.
*His voice quivers; he licks his blackened lips. His eyes have grown very
mad and he is shaking spasmodically from head to foot.*
Water would save us—just a little water—even a few drops would
be enough.
*Intensely.*
God, if we only had a little water!

DANCER

Perhaps there will be water on the island. Look; look hard! An island or a ship may have come in sight while we were talking.

*There is a pause. Suddenly she rises to her knees and pointing straight in front of her, shouts.*

See! An island!

GENTLEMAN

*Shading his eyes with a trembling hand and peering wildly around him.*

I see nothing—nothing but a red sea and a red sky.

DANCER

*Still looking at some point far out over the water, speaks in disappointed tones.*

It is gone. Yet I am quite sure I saw one. It was right out there quite near to us. It was all green and cleanlooking with a clear stream that ran into the sea. I could hear the water running over the stones. You do not believe me. You, Sailor, you must have seen it too, did you not?

*The Negro does not answer.*

I cannot see it any more. Yet I must see it. I *will* see it!

GENTLEMAN

*Shaking her by the shoulder.*

What you say is nonsense. There is no island there, I tell you. There is nothing but sun and sky and sea around us. There are no green trees. There is no water.

*The SAILOR has stopped singing and turns and looks at them.*

DANCER

*Angrily.*

Do you mean to tell me I lie? Can I not believe my own eyes, then? I tell you I saw it—cool clear water. I heard it bubbling over the stones. But now I hear nothing, nothing at all.

*Turning suddenly to the SAILOR.*

Why have you stopped singing? Is not everything awful enough already that you should make it worse?

SAILOR

*Sticking out his swollen tongue and pointing to it with a long brown finger.*

Water! I want water! Give me some water and I will sing.

GENTLEMAN

*Furiously.*

We have no water, fool! It is your fault we have none. Why did you drink all that was left in the cask when you thought we were asleep? I would not give you any even if we had some. You deserve to suffer, you pig! If any one of the three of us has any water it is you who have hidden some out of what you stole.

*With a laugh of mad cunning.*

But you will get no chance to drink it, I promise you that. I am watching you.

*The Negro sullenly turns away from them.*

DANCER

*Taking hold of the* GENTLEMAN'*s arm and almost hissing into his ear. She is terribly excited and he is still chuckling crazily to himself.*

Do you really think he has some?

GENTLEMAN

*Chuckling.*

He may have. He may have.

DANCER

Why do you say that?

GENTLEMAN

He has been acting strangely. He has looked as if he wished to hide something. I was wondering what it could be. Then suddenly I thought to myself: "What if it should be some water?" Then I knew I had found him out. I will not let him get the best of me. I will watch him. He will not drink while I am watching him. I will watch him as long as I can see.

DANCER

What could he have put the water in? He has nothing that I can discover.

*She is rapidly falling in with this mad fixed idea of his.*

GENTLEMAN

Who knows? He may have a flask hidden in under his jersey. But he has something, that I am sure of. Why is it he is so much stronger than we are? He can stand up without effort and we can scarcely move. Why is that, I ask you?

DANCER

It is true. He stood up and looked for a ship as easily as if he had never known hunger and thirst. You are right. He must have something hidden — food or water.

GENTLEMAN

*With mad eagerness to prove his fixed idea.*

No, he has no food. There has never been any food. But there has been water. There was a whole small cask full of it on the raft when I came. On the second or third night, I do not remember which, I awoke and saw him draining the cask. When I reached it, it was empty.

*Furiously shaking his fist at the Negro's back.*

Oh, you pig! You rotten pig!

*The Negro does not seem to hear.*

DANCER

That water would have saved our lives. He is no better than a murderer.

GENTLEMAN

*With insane shrewdness.*

Listen. I think he must have poured some of the water into his flask. There was quite a little there. He could not have drunk it all. Oh, he is a cunning one! That song of his — it was only a blind. He drinks when we are not looking. But he will drink no more, for I will watch him. I will watch him!

DANCER

You will watch him? And what good will that do either of us? Will we die any the less soon for your watching? No! Let us get the water away from him in some way. That is the only thing to do.

**GENTLEMAN**

He will not give it to us.

**DANCER**

We will steal it while he sleeps.

**GENTLEMAN**

I do not think he sleeps. I have never seen him sleep. Besides, we should wake him.

**DANCER**

*Violently.*

We will kill him then. He deserves to be killed.

**GENTLEMAN**

He is stronger than we are—and he has a knife. No, we cannot do that. I would willingly kill him. As you say, he deserves it. But I cannot even stand. I have no strength left. I have no weapons. He would laugh at me.

**DANCER**

There must be some way. You would think even the most heartless savage would share at a time like this. We must get that water. It is horrible to be dying of thirst with water so near. Think! Think! Is there no way?

**GENTLEMAN**

You might buy it from him with that necklace of yours. I have heard his people are very fond of such things.

**DANCER**

This necklace? It is worth a thousand pounds. An English duke gave it to me. I will not part with it. Do you think I am a fool?

**GENTLEMAN**

Think of a drink of water!

*They both lick their dry lips feverishly.*

If we do not drink soon we will die.

*Laughing harshly.*

You will take your necklace to the sharks with you? Very well then,

I will say no more. For my part, I would sell my soul for a *drop* of water.

DANCER

*Shuddering with horror she glances instinctively at the moving shark fins.*
You are horrible. I had almost forgotten those monsters. It is not kind of you to be always bringing them back to my memory.

GENTLEMAN

It is well that you should not forget them. You will value your duke's present less when you look at them.
*Impatiently pounding the deck with one bony hand.*
Come, come, we shall both die of thirst while you are dreaming. Offer it to him! Offer it to him!

DANCER

*She takes off the necklace and, musing vacantly, turns it over in her hands watching it sparkle in the sun.*
It is beautiful, is it not? I hate to part with it. He was very much in love with me—the old duke. I think he would even have married me in the end. I did not like him. He was old, very old. Something came up—I forget what. I never saw him again. This is the only gift of his that I have left.

GENTLEMAN

*In a frenzy of impatience—the vision of the water clear before his glaring eyes.*
Damn it, why are you chattering so? Think of the water he has got. Offer it to him!

DANCER

Yes, yes, my throat is burning up; my eyes are on fire. I must have the water.
*She drags herself on hands and knees across the raft to where the Negro is sitting. He does not notice her approach. She reaches out a trembling hand and touches him on the back. He turns slowly and looks at her, his round, animal eyes dull and lusterless. She holds the necklace out in her right hand before his face and speaks hurriedly in a husky voice.*

Look, you have stolen our water. You deserve to be killed. We will forget all that. Look at this necklace. It was given to me by an English duke—a nobleman. It is worth a thousand pounds—five thousand dollars. It will provide for you for the rest of your life. You need not be a sailor any more. You need never work at all any more. Do you understand what that means?

*The Negro does not answer. The* DANCER *hurries on however, her words pouring out in a sing-song jumble.*

That water that you stole—well, I will give you this necklace—they are all real diamonds, you know—five thousand dollars—for that water. You need not give me all of it. I am not unreasonable. You may keep some for yourself. I would not have you die. I want just enough for myself and my friend—to keep us alive until we reach some island. My lips are cracked with heat! My head is bursting! Here, take the necklace. It is yours.

*She tries to force it into his hand. He pushes her hand away and the necklace falls to the deck of the raft, where it lies glittering among the heat waves.*

DANCER

*Her voice raised stridently.*

Give me the water! I have given you the necklace. Give me the water!

*The* GENTLEMAN, *who has been watching her with anxious eyes, also cries: "Yes. Give her the water!"*

SAILOR

*His voice drawling and without expression.*

I have no water.

DANCER

Oh, you are cruel! Why do you lie? You see me suffering so and you lie to me. I have given you the necklace. It is worth five thousand dollars, do you understand? Surely for five thousand dollars you will give me a drink of water!

SAILOR

I have no water, I tell you.

*He turns his back to her. She crawls over to the* GENTLEMAN *and lies beside him, sobbing brokenly.*

GENTLEMAN

*His face convulsed with rage, shaking both fists in the air.*
The pig! The pig! The black dog!

DANCER

*Sitting up and wiping her eyes.*
Well, you have heard him. He will not give it to us. Maybe he only has a little and is afraid to share it. What shall we do now? What can we do?

GENTLEMAN

*Despondently.*
Nothing. He is stronger than we are. There is no wind. We will never reach an island. We can die, that is all.
*He sinks back and buries his head in his hands. A great dry sob shakes his shoulders.*

DANCER

*Her eyes flaming with a sudden resolution.*
Ah, who is the coward now? You have given up hope, it seems. Well, I have not. I have still one chance. It has never failed me yet.

GENTLEMAN

*Raising his head and looking at her in amazement.*
You are going to offer him more money?

DANCER

*With a strange smile.*
No. Not that. I will offer more than money. We shall get our water.
*She tears a piece of crumpled lace off the front of her costume and carefully wipes her face with it as if she were using a powder puff.*

GENTLEMAN

*Watching her stupidly.*
I do not understand.

DANCER

*She pulls up her stockings—tries to smooth the wrinkles out of her dress —then takes her long hair and, having braided it, winds it into a coil around her head. She pinches her cheeks, already crimson with sunburn. Then turning coquettishly to the* GENTLEMAN, *she says.*

There! Do I not look better? How do I look?

GENTLEMAN
*Bursting into a mad guffaw.*
You look terrible! You are hideous!

DANCER
You lie! I am beautiful. Everyone knows I am beautiful. You yourself have said so. It is you who are hideous. You are jealous of me. I will not give you any water.

GENTLEMAN
You will get no water. You are frightful. What is it you would do—dance for him?
*Mockingly.*
Dance! Dance, Salome! I will be the orchestra. He will be the gallery. We will both applaud you madly.
*He leans on one elbow and watches her, chuckling to himself.*

DANCER
*Turning from him furiously and crawling on her knees over to the* SAILOR, *calls in her most seductive voice.*
Sailor! Sailor!
*He does not seem to hear—she takes his arm and shakes it gently—he turns around and stares wonderingly at her.*
Listen to me, Sailor. What is your name—your first name?
*She smiles enticingly at him. He does not answer.*
You will not tell me then? You are angry at me, are you not? I cannot blame you. I have called you bad names. I am sorry, very sorry.
*Indicating the* GENTLEMAN, *who has ceased to notice them and is staring at the horizon with blinking eyes.*
It was he who put such ideas into my head. He does not like you. Neither did I, but I see now that you are the better of the two. I hate him! He has said dreadful things which I cannot forgive.
*Putting her hand on his shoulder she bends forward with her golden hair almost in his lap and smiles up into his face.*

I like you, Sailor. You are big and strong. We are going to be great friends, are we not?

*The Negro is hardly looking at her. He is watching the sharks.*

Surely you will not refuse me a little sip of your water?

SAILOR

I have no water.

DANCER

Oh, why will you keep up this subterfuge? Am I not offering you price enough?

*Putting her arm around his neck and half whispering in his ear.*

Do you not understand? I will love you, Sailor! Noblemen and millionaires and all degrees of gentlemen have loved me, have fought for me. I have never loved any of them as I will love you. Look in my eyes, Sailor, look in my eyes!

*Compelled in spite of himself by something in her voice, the Negro gazes deep into her eyes. For a second his nostrils dilate—he draws in his breath with a hissing sound—his body grows tense and it seems as if he is about to sweep her into his arms. Then his expression grows apathetic again. He turns to the sharks.*

Oh, will you never understand? Are you so stupid that you do not know what I mean? Look! I am offering myself to you! I am kneeling before you—I who always had men kneel to me! I am offering my body to you—my body that men have called so beautiful. I have promised to love you—a Negro sailor—if you will give me one small drink of water. Is that not humiliation enough that you must keep me waiting so?

*Raising her voice.*

Answer me! Answer me! Will you give me that water?

SAILOR

*Without even turning to look at her.*

I have no water.

DANCER

*Shaking with fury.*

Great God, have I abased myself for this? Have I humbled myself before this black animal only to be spurned like a wench of the streets? It is too much! You lie, you dirty slave! You have water. You have stolen my share of the water.

*In a frenzy she clutches the* SAILOR *about the throat with both hands.* Give it to me! Give it to me!

SAILOR

*Takes her hands from his neck and pushes her roughly away. She falls face downward in the middle of the raft.*
Let me alone! I have no water.

GENTLEMAN

*Aroused from the stupor he has been in.*
What is it? I was dreaming I was sitting before great tumblers of ice water. They were just beyond my reach. I tried and tried to get one of them. It was horrible. But what has happened here? What is the matter?

*No one answers him. The Negro is watching the sharks again. The* DANCER *is lying in a huddled heap, moaning to herself. Suddenly she jumps to her feet. All her former weakness seems quite gone. She stands swaying a little with the roll of the raft. Her eyes have a terrible glare in them. They seem bursting out of her head. She mutters incoherently to herself. The last string has snapped. She is mad.*

DANCER

*Smoothing her dress over her hips and looking before her as if in a mirror.*
Quick, Marie! You are so slow tonight. I will be late. Did you not hear the bell? I am the next on. Did he send any flowers tonight, Marie? Good, he will be in a stage box. I will smile at him, the poor old fool. He will marry me some day and I will be a duchess. Think of that, Marie—a real duchess! Yes, yes, I am coming! You need not hold the curtain.

*She drops her head on her breast and mutters to herself. The* GENTLE-MAN *has been watching her, at first in astonishment, then in a sort of crazy appreciation. When she stops talking he claps his hands.*

GENTLEMAN

Go on! Go on! It is as good as a play.
*He bursts into cackling laughter.*

DANCER

They are laughing. It cannot be at me. How hot it is! How the foot-lights glare! I shall be glad to get away tonight. I am very thirsty.

*Passing her hand across her eyes.*

There he is in the box—the poor old duke. I will wave to him.

*She waves her hand in the air.*

He is kind to me. It is a pity he is so old. What song is it I am to sing? Oh yes.

*She sings the last few lines of some music hall ballad in a harsh cracked voice. The Negro turns and looks at her wonderingly. The* GENTLEMAN *claps his hands.*

They are applauding. I must dance for them!

*She commences to dance on the swaying surface of the raft, half-stumbling every now and then. Her hair falls down. She is like some ghastly marionette jerked by invisible wires. She dances faster and faster. Her arms and legs fly grotesquely around as if beyond control.*

Oh, how hot it is!

*She grasps the front of her bodice in both hands and rips it over her shoulders. It hangs down in back. She is almost naked to the waist. Her breasts are withered and shrunken by starvation. She kicks first one foot and then the other frenziedly in the air.*

Oh, it is hot! I am stifling. Bring me a drink of water! I am choking!

*She falls back on the raft. A shudder runs over her whole body. A little crimson foam appears on her lips. Her eyes glaze. The wild stare leaves them. She is dead.*

GENTLEMAN

*Laughing insanely and clapping his hands.*

Bravo! Bravo! Give us some more!

*There is no answer. A great stillness hangs over everything. The heat waves rising from the raft near the woman's body seem like her soul departing into the great unknown. A look of fear appears on the* GENTLE-MAN's *face. The Negro wears a strange expression. One might say he looks relieved, even glad, as if some perplexing problem has been solved for him.*

She does not answer me. She must be sick.

*He crawls over to her.*

She has fainted.

*He puts his hand on her left breast—then bends and rests his ear over her heart. His face grows livid in spite of the sunburn.*

My God! She is dead! Poor girl! Poor girl!

*He whimpers weakly to himself, mechanically running her long golden hair through his fingers with a caressing gesture. He is startled when he hears the Negro's voice.*

SAILOR
Is she dead?

GENTLEMAN
Yes. She is dead, poor girl. Her heart no longer beats.

SAILOR
She is better off. She does not suffer now. One of us had to die.
*After a pause.*
It is lucky for us she is dead.

GENTLEMAN
What do you mean? What good can her death do us?

SAILOR
We will live now.
*He takes his SAILOR's knife from its sheath and sharpens it on the sole of his shoe. While he is doing this he sings—a happy Negro melody that mocks the great silence.*

GENTLEMAN
*In hushed, frightened tones.*
I do not understand.

SAILOR
*His swollen lips parting in a grin as he points with his knife to the body of the DANCER.*
We shall eat. We shall drink.

GENTLEMAN
*For a moment struck dumb with loathing—then in tones of anguished horror.*
No! No! No! Good God, not that!

*With a swift movement he grasps the* DANCER's *body with both hands and, making a tremendous effort, pushes it into the water. There is a swift rush of waiting fins. The sea near the raft is churned into foam. The* DANCER's *body disappears in a swirling eddy; then all is quiet again. A black stain appears on the surface of the water.*

*The* SAILOR, *who has jumped forward to save the body, gives a harsh cry of disappointed rage and, knife in hand, springs on the* GENTLEMAN *and drives the knife in his breast. The* GENTLEMAN *rises to his feet with a shriek of agony. As he falls backward into the sea, one of his clutching hands fastens itself in the neck of the* SAILOR's *jersey. The* SAILOR *tries to force the hand away, stumbles, loses his balance, and plunges headlong after him. There is a great splash. The waiting fins rush in. The water is lashed into foam. The* SAILOR's *black head appears for a moment, his features distorted with terror, his lips torn with a howl of despair. Then he is drawn under.*

*The black stain on the water widens. The fins circle no longer. The raft floats in the midst of a vast silence. The sun glares down like a great angry eye of God. The eerie heat waves float upward in the still air like the souls of the drowned. On the raft a diamond necklace lies glittering in the blazing sunshine.*

CURTAIN

*The Long Voyage Home*
A Play in One Act

# Characters

FAT JOE, *proprietor of a dive.*

NICK, *a crimp.*

MAG, *a barmaid.*

OLSON

DRISCOLL

             } *Seamen of the British tramp steamer,* Glencairn.

COCKY

IVAN

KATE

FREDA

TWO ROUGHS

# The Long Voyage Home

SCENE

*The bar of a low dive on the London water front—a squalid, dingy room dimly lighted by kerosene lamps placed in brackets on the walls. On the left, the bar. In front of it, a door leading to a side room. On the right, tables with chairs around them. In the rear, a door leading to the street.*

*A slovenly barmaid with a stupid face sodden with drink is mopping off the bar. Her arm moves back and forth mechanically and her eyes are half shut as if she were dozing on her feet. At the far end of the bar stands* FAT JOE, *the proprietor, a gross bulk of a man with an enormous stomach. His face is red and bloated, his little piggish eyes being almost concealed by rolls of fat. The thick fingers of his big hands are loaded with cheap rings and a gold watch chain of cable-like proportions stretches across his checked waistcoat.*

*At one of the tables, front, a round-shouldered young fellow is sitting, smoking a cigarette. His face is pasty, his mouth weak, his eyes shifting and cruel. He is dressed in a shabby suit, which must have once been cheaply flashy, and wears a muffler and cap.*

*It is about nine o'clock in the evening.*

JOE
*Yawning.*
Blimey if bizness ain't 'arf slow to-night. I donnow wot's 'appened. The place is like a bleedin' tomb. Where's all the sailor men, I'd like to know?
*Raising his voice.*

Ho, you Nick!

NICK *turns around listlessly.*

Wot's the name o' that wessel put in at the dock below jest arter noon?

NICK
*Laconically.*
Glencairn—from Bewnezerry. (Buenos Aires).

JOE
Ain't the crew been paid orf yet?

NICK
Paid orf this arternoon, they tole me. I 'opped on board of 'er an' seen 'em. 'Anded 'em some o' yer cards, I did. They promised faithful they'd 'appen in tonight—them as whose time was done.

JOE
Any two-year men to be paid orf?

NICK
Four—three Britishers an' a square-'ead.

JOE
*Indignantly.*
An' yer popped orf an' left 'em? An' me a-payin' yer to 'elp an' bring 'em in 'ere!

NICK
*Grumblingly.*
Much you pays me! An' I ain't slingin' me 'ook abaht the 'ole bleedin' town fur now man. See?

JOE
I ain't speakin' on'y fur meself. Down't I always give yer yer share, fair an' square, as man to man?

NICK
*With a sneer.*
Yus—b'cause you 'as to.

**JOE**

'As to? Listen to 'im! There's many'd be 'appy to 'ave your berth, me man!

**NICK**

Yus? Wot wiv the peelers li'ble to put me away in the bloody jail fur crimpin', an' all?

**JOE**

*Indignantly.*

We down't do no crimpin'.

**NICK**

*Sarcastically.*

Ho, now! Not arf!

**JOE**

*A bit embarrassed.*

Well, on'y a bit now an' agen when there ain't no reg'lar trade.

*To hide his confusion he turns to the barmaid angrily. She is still mopping off the bar, her chin on her breast, halfasleep.*

'Ere, me gel, we've 'ad enough o' that. You been a-moppin', an' a-moppin', an' a-moppin' the blarsted bar fur a 'ole 'our. 'Op it aht o' this! You'd fair guv a bloke the shakes a-watchin' yer.

**MAG**

*Beginning to sniffle.*

Ow, you do frighten me when you 'oller at me, Joe. I ain't a bad gel, I ain't. Gawd knows I tries to do me best fur you.

*She bursts into a tempest of sobs.*

**JOE**

*Roughly.*

Stop yer grizzlin'! An' 'op it aht of 'ere!

**NICK**

*Chuckling.*

She's drunk, Joe. Been 'ittin' the gin, eh, Mag?

**MAG**

*Ceases crying at once and turns on him furiously.*

You little crab, you! Orter wear a muzzle, you ort! A-openin' of your ugly mouth to a 'onest woman what ain't never done you no 'arm. *Commencing to sob again.*
H'abusin' me like a dawg cos I'm sick an' orf me oats, an' all.

JOE

Orf yer go, me gel! Go hupstairs and 'ave a sleep. I'll wake yer if I wants yer. An' wake the two gels when yer goes hup. It's 'arpas' nine an' time as some one was a-comin' in, tell 'em. D'yer 'ear me?

MAG

*Stumbling around the bar to the door on left—sobbing.*
Yus, yus, I 'ears you. Gawd knows wot's goin' to 'appen to me, I'm that sick. Much you cares if I dies, down't you?
*She goes out.*

JOE

*Still brooding over* NICK's *lack of diligence—after a pause.*
Four two-year men paid orf wiv their bloody pockets full o' sover-eigns—an' yer lorst 'em.
*He shakes his head sorrowfully.*

NICK

*Impatiently.*
Stow it! They promised faithful they'd come, I tells yer. They'll be walkin' in in 'arf a mo'. There's lots o' time yet.
*In a low voice.*
'Ave yer got the drops? We might wanter use 'em.

JOE

*Taking a small bottle from behind the bar.*
Yus; 'ere it is.

NICK

*With satisfaction.*
Righto!
*His shifty eyes peer about the room searchingly. Then he beckons to* JOE, *who comes over to the table and sits down.*
Reason I arst yer about the drops was 'cause I seen the capt'n of the Amindra this arternoon.

**JOE**
The Amindra? Wot ship is that?

**NICK**
Bloody windjammer—skys'l yarder—full rigged—painted white—
been layin' at the dock above 'ere fur a month. You knows 'er.

**JOE**
Ho, yus. I knows now.

**NICK**
The capt'n says as 'e wants a man special bad—ternight. They sails
at daybreak termorrer.

**JOE**
There's plenty o' 'ands lyin' abaht waitin' fur ships, I should fink.

**NICK**
Not fur this ship, ole buck. The capt'n an' mate are bloody slave-
drivers, an' they're bound down round the 'Orn. They 'arf starved
the 'ands on the larst trip 'ere, an' no one'll dare ship on 'er.
*After a pause.*
I promised the capt'n faithful I'd get 'im one, and ternight.

**JOE**
*Doubtfully.*
An' 'ow are yer goin' to git 'im?

**NICK**
*With a wink.*
I was thinkin' as one of 'em from the Glencairn'd do—them as was
paid orf an' is comin' 'ere.

**JOE**
*With a grin.*
It'd be a good 'aul, that's the troof.
*Frowning.*
If they comes 'ere.

**NICK**
They'll come, an' they'll all be rotten drunk, wait an' see.

*There is the noise of loud, boisterous singing from the street.*

Sounds like 'em, now.

*He opens the street door and looks out.*

Gawd blimey if it ain't the four of 'em!

*Turning to* JOE *in triumph.*

Naw, what d'yer say? They're lookin' for the place. I'll go aht an' tell 'em.

*He goes out.* JOE *gets into position behind the bar, assuming his most oily smile. A moment later the door is opened, admitting* DRISCOLL, COCKY, IVAN *and* OLSON. DRISCOLL *is a tall, powerful Irishman;* COCKY, *a wizened runt of a man with a straggling gray mustache;* IVAN, *a hulking oaf of a peasant;* OLSON, *a stocky, middle-aged Swede with round, childish blue eyes. The first three are all very drunk, especially* IVAN, *who is managing his legs with difficulty.* OLSON *is perfectly sober. All are dressed in their ill-fitting shore clothes and look very uncomfortable.* DRISCOLL *has unbuttoned his stiff collar and its ends stick out sideways. He has lost his tie.* NICK *slinks into the room after them and sits down at a table in rear. The seamen come to the table, front.*

JOE

*With affected heartiness.*

Ship ahoy, mates! 'Appy to see yer 'ome safe an' sound.

DRISCOLL

*Turns round, swaying a bit, and peers at him across the bar.*

So ut's you, is ut?

*He looks about the place with an air of recognition.*

'An the same damn rat's-hole, sure enough. I remimber foive or six years back 'twas here I was sthripped av me last shillin' whin I was aslape.

*With sudden fury.*

God stiffen ye, come none av your dog's thricks on me this trip or I'll—

*He shakes his fist at* JOE.

JOE

*Hastily interrupting.*

Yer must be mistaiken. This is a 'onest place, this is.

COCKY
*Derisively.*
Ho, yus! An' you're a bleedin' angel, I s'pose?

IVAN
*Vaguely taking off his derby hat and putting it on again—plaintively.*
I don' li-ike dis place.

DRISCOLL
*Going over to the bar—as genial as he was furious a moment before.*
Well, no matther, 'tis all past an' gone an' forgot. I'm not the man
to be holdin' harrd feelin's on me first night ashore, an' me dhrunk
as a lord.
*He holds out his hand, which* JOE *takes very gingerly.*
We'll all be havin' a dhrink, I'm thinkin'. Whiskey for the three av
us—*Irish* whiskey!

COCKY
*Mockingly.*
An' a glarse o' ginger beer fur our blarsted love-child 'ere.
*He jerks his thumb at* OLSON.

OLSON
*With a good-natured grin.*
I bane a good boy dis night, for one time.

DRISCOLL
*Bellowing, and pointing to* NICK *as* JOE *brings the drinks to the table.*
An' see what that crimpin' son av a crimp'll be wantin'—an' have
your own pleasure.
*He pulls a sovereign out of his pocket and slams it on the bar.*

NICK
Guv me a pint o' beer, Joe.
JOE *draws the beer and takes it down to the far end of the bar.* NICK
*comes over to get it and* JOE *gives him a significant wink and nods
toward the door on the left.* NICK *signals back that he understands.*

COCKY
*Drink in hand—impatiently.*

I'm that bloody dry!
*Lifting his glass to* DRISCOLL.
Cheero, ole dear, cheero!

DRISCOLL
*Pocketing his change without looking at it.*
A toast for ye: Hell roast that divil av a bo'sun!
*He drinks.*

COCKY
Righto! Gawd strike 'im blind!
*He drains his glass.*

IVAN
*Half-asleep.*
Dot's gude.
*He tosses down his drink in one gulp.* OLSON *sips his ginger ale.* NICK
*takes a swallow of his beer and then comes round the bar and goes out
the door on left.*

COCKY
*Producing a sovereign.*
Ho there, you Fatty! Guv us another!

JOE
The saime, mates?

COCKY
Yus.

DRISCOLL
No, ye scut! I'll be havin' a pint av beer. I'm dhry as a loime kiln.

IVAN
*Suddenly getting to his feet in a befuddled manner and nearly upsetting
the table.*
I don' li-ike dis place! I wan' see girls—plenty girls.
*Pathetically.*
I don't li-ike dis place. I wan' dance with girl.

DRISCOLL

*Pushing him back on his chair with a thud.*

Shut up, ye Rooshan baboon! A foine Romeo you'd make in your condishun.

IVAN *blubbers some incoherent protest—then suddenly falls asleep.*

JOE

*Bringing the drinks—looks at* OLSON.

An' you, matey?

OLSON

*Shaking his head.*

Noting dis time, thank you.

COCKY

*Mockingly.*

A-saivin' of 'is money, 'e is! Goin' back to 'ome an' mother. Goin' to buy a bloomin' farm an' punch the blarsted dirt, that's wot 'e is!

*Spitting disgustedly.*

There's a funny bird of a sailor man for yer, Gawd blimey!

OLSON

*Wearing the same good-natured grin.*

Yust what I like, Cocky. I wus on farm long time when I wus kid.

DRISCOLL

Lave him alone, ye bloody insect! 'Tis a foine sight to see a man wid some sense in his head instead av a damn fool the loike av us. I only wisht I'd a mother alive to call me own. I'd not be dhrunk in this divil's hole this minute, maybe.

COCKY

*Commencing to weep dolorously.*

Ow, down't talk, Drisc! I can't bear to 'ear you. I ain't never 'ad no mother, I ain't—

DRISCOLL

Shut up, ye ape, an' don't be makin' that squealin'. If ye cud see your ugly face, wid the big red nose av ye all screwed up in a knot, ye'd never shed a tear the rist av your loife.

*Roaring into song.*

We ar-re the byes av We-e-exford who fought wid hearrt an' hand!

*Speaking.*

To hell wid Ulster!

*He drinks and the others follow his example.*

An' I'll strip to any man in the city av London won't dhrink to that toast.

*He glares truculently at* JOE, *who immediately downs his beer.* NICK *enters again from the door on the left and comes up to* JOE *and whispers in his ear. The latter nods with satisfaction.*

DRISCOLL

*Glowering at them.*

What divil's thrick are ye up to now, the two av ye?

*He flourishes a brawny fist.*

Play fair wid us or ye deal wid me!

JOE

*Hastily.*

No trick, shipmate! May Gawd kill me if that ain't troof!

NICK

*Indicating* IVAN, *who is snoring.*

On'y your mate there was arskin' fur gels an' I thorght as 'ow yer'd like 'em to come dawn and 'ave a wet wiv yer.

JOE

*With a smirking wink.*

Pretty, 'olesome gels they be, ain't they, Nick?

NICK

Yus.

COCKY

Aar! I knows the gels you 'as, not 'arf! They'd fair blind yer, they're that 'omely. None of yer bloomin' gels fur me, ole Fatty. Me an' Drisc knows a place, down't we, Drisc?

DRISCOLL

Divil a lie, we do. An' we'll be afther goin' there in a minute. There's music there an' a bit av a dance to liven a man.

JOE

Nick, 'ere, can play yer a tune, can't yer, Nick?

NICK

Yus.

JOE

An' yer can 'ave a dance in the side room 'ere.

DRISCOLL

Hurroo! Now you're talkin'.

*The two women,* FREDA *and* KATE, *enter from the left.* FREDA *is a little, sallow-faced blonde.* KATE *is stout and dark.*

COCKY

*In a loud aside to* DRISCOLL.

Gawd blimey, look at 'em! Ain't they 'orrible?

*The women come forward to the table, wearing their best set smiles.*

FREDA

*In a raspy voice.*

'Ullo, mates.

KATE

'Ad a good voyage?

DRISCOLL

Rotten; but no matther. Welcome, as the sayin' is, an' sit down, an' what'll ye be takin' for your thirst?

*To* KATE.

You'll be sittin' by me, darlin'—what's your name?

KATE

*With a stupid grin.*

Kate.

*She stands by his chair.*

DRISCOLL

*Putting his arm around her.*

A good Irish name, but you're English by the trim av ye, an' be damned to you. But no matther. Ut's fat ye are, Katy dear, an' I never cud endure skinny wimin.

FREDA *favors him with a viperish glance and sits down by* OLSON. What'll ye have?

OLSON

No, Drisc. Dis one bane on me.

*He takes out a roll of notes from his inside pocket and lays one on the table.* JOE, NICK, *and the women look at the money with greedy eyes.* IVAN *gives a particularly violent snore.*

FREDA

Waike up your fren'. Gawd, 'ow I 'ates to 'ear snorin'.

DRISCOLL

*Springing to action, smashes* IVAN's *derby over his ears.*

D'you hear the lady talkin' to ye, ye Rooshan swab?

*The only reply to this is a snore.* DRISCOLL *pulls the battered remains of the derby off* IVAN's *head and smashes it back again.*

Arise an' shine, ye dhrunken swine!

*Another snore. The women giggle.* DRISCOLL *throws the beer left in his glass into* IVAN's *face. The Russian comes to in a flash, spluttering. There is a roar of laughter.*

IVAN

*Indignantly.*

I tell you—dot's someting I don' li-ike!

COCKY

Down't waste good beer, Drisc.

IVAN

*Grumblingly.*

I tell you—dot is not ri-ight.

**DRISCOLL**

Ut's your own doin', Ivan. Ye was moanin' for girrls an' whin they come you sit gruntin' loike a pig in a sty. Have ye no manners?
IVAN *seems to see the women for the first time and grins foolishly.*

**KATE**

*Laughing at him.*
Cheero, old chum, 'ows Russha?

**IVAN**

*Greatly pleased—putting his hand in his pocket.*
I buy a drink.

**OLSON**

No; dis one bane on me.
*To* JOE.
Hey, you faller!

**JOE**

Wot'll it be, Kate?

**KATE**

Gin.

**FREDA**

Brandy.

**DRISCOLL**

An' Irish whiskey for the rist av us—wid the excipshun av our timperance friend, God pity him!

**FREDA**

*To* OLSON.
You ain't drinkin'?

**OLSON**

*Half-ashamed.*
No.

**FREDA**

*With a seductive smile.*

I down't blame yer. You got sense, you 'ave. I on'y tike a nip o' brandy now an' agen fur my 'ealth.

JOE *brings the drinks and* OLSON's *change.* COCKY *gets unsteadily to his feet and raises his glass in the air.*

COCKY
'Ere's a toff toast for yer: The ladies, Gawd—
*He hesitates—then adds in a grudging tone.*
—bless 'em.

KATE
*With a silly giggle.*
Oo-er! That wasn't what you was goin' to say, you bad Cocky, you!
*They all drink.*

DRISCOLL
*To* NICK.
Where's the tune ye was promisin' to give us?

NICK
Come ahn in the side 'ere an' you'll 'ear it.

DRISCOLL
*Getting up.*
Come on, all av ye. We'll have a tune an' a dance if I'm not too dhrunk to dance, God help me.
COCKY *and* IVAN *stagger to their feet.* IVAN *can hardly stand. He is leering at* KATE *and snickering to himself in a maudlin fashion. The three, led by* NICK, *go out the door on the left.* KATE *follows them.* OLSON *and* FREDA *remain seated.*

COCKY
*Calling over his shoulder.*
Come on an' dance, Ollie.

OLSON
Yes, I come.
*He starts to get up. From the side room comes the sound of an accordion and a boisterous whoop from* DRISCOLL, *followed by a heavy stamping of feet.*

FREDA

Ow, down't go in there. Stay 'ere an' 'ave a talk wiv me. They're all drunk an' you ain't drinkin'.

*With a smile up into his face.*

I'll think yer don't like me if yer goes in there.

OLSON

*Confused.*

You wus wrong, Miss Freda. I don't—I mean I do like you.

FREDA

*Smiling—puts her hand over his on the table.*

An' I likes you. Yer a genelman. You don't get drunk an' hinsult poor gels wot 'as a 'ard an' uneppy life.

OLSON

*Pleased but still more confused—wriggling his feet.*

I bane drunk many time, Miss Freda.

FREDA

Then why ain't yer drinkin' now?

*She exchanges a quick, questioning glance with* JOE, *who nods back at her—then she continues persuasively.*

Tell me somethin' abaht yeself.

OLSON

*With a grin.*

There ain't noting to say, Miss Freda. I bane poor devil sailor man, dat's all.

FREDA

Where was you born—Norway?

OLSON *shakes his head.*

Denmark?

OLSON

No. You guess once more.

FREDA

Then it must be Sweden.

OLSON

Yes. I wus born in Stockholm.

FREDA

*Pretending great delight.*
Ow, ain't that funny! I was born there, too — in Stockholm.

OLSON

*Astonished.*
You wus born in Sweden?

FREDA

Yes; you wouldn't think it, but it's Gawd's troof.
*She claps her hands delightedly.*

OLSON

*Beaming all over.*
You speak Swedish?

FREDA

*Trying to smile sadly.*
Now. Y'see my ole man an' woman come 'ere to England when I was on'y a baby an' they was speakin' English b'fore I was old enough to learn. Sow I never knew Swedish.
*Sadly.*
Wisht I 'ad!
*With a smile.*
We'd 'ave a bloomin' lark of it if I 'ad, wouldn't we?

OLSON

It sound nice to hear the old talk yust once in a time.

FREDA

Righto! No place like yer 'ome, I says. Are yer goin' up to — to Stockholm b'fore yer ships away agen?

OLSON

Yes. I go home from here to Stockholm.
*Proudly.*
As passenger!

**FREDA**

An' you'll git another ship up there arter you've 'ad a vacation?

**OLSON**

No. I don't never ship on sea no more. I got all sea I want for my life—too much hard work for little money. Yust work, work, work on ship. I don't want more.

**FREDA**

Ow, I see. That's why you give up drinkin'.

**OLSON**

Yes.
*With a grin.*
If I drink I yust get drunk and spend all money.

**FREDA**

But if you ain't gointer be a sailor no more, what'll yer do? You been a sailor all yer life, ain't yer?

**OLSON**

No. I work on farm till I am eighteen. I like it, too—it's nice—work on farm.

**FREDA**

But ain't Stockholm a city same's London? Ain't no farms there, is there?

**OLSON**

We live—my brother and mother live—my father iss dead—on farm yust a little way from Stockholm. I have plenty money, now. I go back with two years' pay and buy more land yet; work on farm.
*Grinning.*
No more sea, no more bum grub, no more storms—yust nice work.

**FREDA**

Ow, ain't that luv'ly! I s'pose you'll be gittin' married, too?

**OLSON**

*Very much confused.*
I don't know. I like to, if I find nice girl, maybe.

**FREDA**

Ain't yer got some gel back in Stockholm? I bet yer 'as.

**OLSON**

No. I got nice girl once before I go on sea. But I go on ship, and I don't come back, and she marry other faller.
*He grins sheepishly.*

**FREDA**

Well, it's nice for yer to be goin' 'ome, anyway.

**OLSON**

Yes. I tank so.
*There is a crash from the room on left and the music abruptly stops. A moment later* COCKY *and* DRISCOLL *appear, supporting the inert form of* IVAN *between them. He is in the last stage of intoxication, unable to move a muscle.* NICK *follows them and sits down at the table in rear.*

**DRISCOLL**

*As they zigzag up to the bar.*
Ut's dead he is, I'm thinkin', for he's as limp as a blarsted corpse.

**COCKY**

*Puffing.*
Gawd, 'e ain't 'arf 'eavy!

**DRISCOLL**

*Slapping* IVAN's *face with his free hand.*
Wake up, ye divil, ye. Ut's no use. Gabriel's trumpet itself cudn't rouse him.
*To* JOE.
Give us a dhrink for I'm perishing wid the thirst. 'Tis harrd worrk, this.

**JOE**

Whiskey?

**DRISCOLL**

*Irish* whiskey, ye swab.

*He puts down a coin on the bar.* JOE *serves* COCKY *and* DRISCOLL.
*They drink and then swerve over to* OLSON's *table.*

OLSON

Sit down and rest for time, Drisc.

DRISCOLL

No, Ollie, we'll be takin' this lad home to his bed. Ut's late for wan
so young to be out in the night. An' I'd not trust him in this hole as
dhrunk as he is, an' him wid a full pay day on him.
*Shaking his fist at* JOE.
Oho, I know your games, me sonny bye!

JOE
*With an air of grievance.*
There yer goes again—hinsultin' a 'onest man!

COCKY

Ho, listen to 'im! Guv 'im a shove in the marf, Drisc.

OLSON
*Anxious to avoid a fight—getting up.*
I help you take Ivan to boarding house.

FREDA
*Protestingly.*
Ow, you ain't gointer leave me, are yer? An' we 'avin' sech a nice talk,
an' all.

DRISCOLL
*With a wink.*
Ye hear what the lady says, Ollie. Ye'd best stay here, me timperance
lady's man. An' we need no help. 'Tis only a bit av a way and we're
two strong men if we are dhrunk. Ut's no hard shift to take the re-
mains home. But ye can open the door for us, Ollie.
OLSON *goes to the door and opens it.*
Come on, Cocky, an' don't be fallin' aslape yourself.
*They lurch toward the door. As they go out* DRISCOLL *shouts back over
his shoulder.*

We'll be comin' back in a short time, surely. So wait here for us, Ollie.

OLSON

All right. I wait here, Drisc.

*He stands in the doorway uncertainly.* JOE *makes violent signs to* FREDA *to bring him back. She goes over and puts her arm around* OLSON's *shoulder.* JOE *motions to* NICK *to come to the bar. They whisper together excitedly.*

FREDA

*Coaxingly.*

You ain't gointer leave me, are yer, dearie?

*Then irritably.*

Fur Gawd's sake, shet that door! I'm fair freezin' to death wiv the fog.

OLSON *comes to himself with a start and shuts the door.*

OLSON

*Humbly.*

Excuse me, Miss Freda.

FREDA

*Leading him back to the table—coughing.*

Buy me a drink o' brandy, will yer? I'm sow cold.

OLSON

All you want, Miss Freda, all you want.

*To* JOE, *who is still whispering instructions to* NICK.

Hey, Yoe! Brandy for Miss Freda.

*He lays a coin on the table.*

JOE

Righto!

*He pours out her drink and brings it to the table.*

'Avin' somethink yeself, shipmate?

OLSON

No. I don't tank so.

*He points to his glass with a grin.*
Dis iss only belly-wash, no?
*He laughs.*

JOE
*Hopefully.*
'Ave a man's drink.

OLSON
I would like to—but no. If I drink one I want drink one tousand.
*He laughs again.*

FREDA
*Responding to a vicious nudge from* JOE's *elbow.*
Ow, tike somethin'. I ain't gointer drink all be meself.

OLSON
Den give me a little yinger beer—small one.
JOE *goes back of the bar, making a sign to* NICK *to go to their table.*
NICK *does so and stands so that the sailor cannot see what* JOE *is doing.*

NICK
*To make talk.*
Where's yer mates popped orf ter?
JOE *pours the contents of the little bottle into* OLSON's *glass of ginger beer.*

OLSON
Dey take Ivan, dat drunk faller, to bed. They come back.
JOE *brings* OLSON's *drink to the table and sets it before him.*

JOE
*To* NICK—*angrily.*
'Op it, will yer? There ain't no time to be dawdlin'. See? 'Urry!

NICK
Down't worry, ole bird, I'm orf.
*He hurries out the door.* JOE *returns to his place behind the bar.*

OLSON

*After a pause—worriedly.*

I tank I should go after dem. Cocky iss very drunk, too, and Drisc—

FREDA

Aar! The big Irish is all right. Don't yer 'ear 'im say as 'ow they'd surely come back 'ere, an' fur you to wait fur 'em?

OLSON

Yes; but if dey don't come soon I tank I go see if dey are in boarding house all right.

FREDA

Where is the boardin' 'ouse?

OLSON

Yust little way back from street here.

FREDA

You stayin' there, too?

OLSON

Yes—until steamer sail for Stockholm—in two day.

FREDA

*She is alternately looking at* JOE *and feverishly trying to keep* OLSON *talking so he will forget about going away after the others.*

Yer mother won't be arf glad to see yer agen, will she?

OLSON *smiles.*

Does she know yer comin'?

OLSON

No. I tought I would yust give her surprise. I write to her from Bonos Eres but I don't tell her I come home.

FREDA

Must be old, ain't she, yer ole lady?

OLSON

She iss eighty-two.

*He smiles reminiscently.*

You know, Miss Freda, I don't see my mother or my brother in—let me tank—

*He counts laboriously on his fingers.*

must be more than ten year. I write once in while and she write many time; and my brother he write me, too. My mother say in all letter I should come home right away. My brother he write same ting, too. He want me to help him on farm. I write back always I come soon; and I mean all time to go back home at end of voyage. But I come ashore, I take one drink, I take many drinks, I get drunk, I spend all money, I have to ship away for other voyage. So dis time I say to myself: Don't drink one drink, Ollie, or, sure, you don't get home. And I want go home dis time. I feel homesick for farm and to see my people again.

*He smiles.*

Yust like little boy, I feel homesick. Dat's why I don't drink noting tonight but dis—belly-wash!

*He roars with childish laughter, then suddenly becomes serious.*

You know, Miss Freda, my mother get very old, and I want see her. She might die and I would never—

FREDA

*Moved a lot in spite of herself.*

Ow, don't talk like that! I just 'ates to 'ear any one speakin' abaht dyin'.

*The door to the street is opened and* NICK *enters, followed by two rough-looking, shabbily-dressed men, wearing mufflers, with caps pulled down over their eyes. They sit at the table nearest to the door.* JOE *brings them three beers, and there is a whispered consultation, with many glances in the direction of* OLSON.

OLSON

*Starting to get up—worriedly.*

I tank I go round to boarding house. I tank someting go wrong with Drisc and Cocky.

FREDA

Ow, down't go. They kin take care of theyselves. They ain't babies. Wait 'arf a mo'. You ain't 'ad yer drink yet.

JOE

*Coming hastily over to the table, indicates the men in the rear with a jerk of his thumb.*

One of them blokes wants yer to 'ave a wet wiv 'im.

FREDA

Righto!

*To* OLSON.

Let's drink this.

*She raises her glass. He does the same.*

'Ere's a toast fur yer: Success to yer bloomin' farm an' may yer live long an' 'appy on it. Skoal!

*She tosses down her brandy. He swallows half his glass of ginger beer and makes a wry face.*

OLSON

Skoal!

*He puts down his glass.*

FREDA

*With feigned indignation.*

Down't yer like my toast?

OLSON

*Grinning.*

Yes. It iss very kind, Miss Freda.

FREDA

Then drink it all like I done.

OLSON

Well—

*He gulps down the rest.*

Dere!

*He laughs.*

FREDA

Done like a sport!

ONE OF THE ROUGHS
*With a laugh.*
Amindra, ahoy!

NICK
*Warningly.*
Sssshh!

OLSON
*Turns around in his chair.*
Amindra? Iss she in port? I sail on her once long time ago—three mast, full rig, skys'l yarder? Iss dat ship you mean?

THE ROUGH
*Grinning.*
Yus; right you are.

OLSON
*Angrily.*
I know dat damn ship—worst ship dat sail to sea. Rotten grub and dey make you work all time—and the Captain and Mate wus Bluenose devils. No sailor who know anyting ever ship on her. Where iss she bound from here?

THE ROUGH
Round Cape 'Orn—sails at daybreak.

OLSON
Py yingo, I pity poor fallers make dat trip round Cape Stiff dis time year. I bet you some of dem never see port once again.
*He passes his hand over his eyes in a dazed way. His voice grows weaker.*
Py golly, I feel dizzy. All the room go round and round like I wus drunk.
*He gets weakly to his feet.*
Good night, Miss Freda. I bane feeling sick. Tell Drisc—I go home.
*He takes a step forward and suddenly collapses over a chair, rolls to the floor, and lies there unconscious.*

JOE

*From behind the bar.*

Quick, nawh!

NICK *darts forward with* JOE *following.* FREDA *is already beside the unconscious man and has taken the roll of money from his inside pocket. She strips off a note furtively and shoves it into her bosom, trying to conceal her action, but* JOE *sees her. She hands the roll to* JOE, *who pockets it.* NICK *goes through all the other pockets and lays a handful of change on the table.*

JOE

*Impatiently.*

'Urry, 'urry, can't yer? The other blokes'll be 'ere in 'arf a mo'.
*The two roughs come forward.*
'Ere, you two, tike 'im in under the arms like 'e was drunk.
*They do so.*
Tike 'im to the Amindra—yer knows that, don't yer?—two docks above. Nick'll show yer. An' you, Nick, down't yer leave the bleedin' ship till the capt'n guvs yer this bloke's advance—full month's pay— five quid, d'yer 'ear?

NICK

I knows me bizness, ole bird.
*They support* OLSON *to the door.*

THE ROUGH

*As they are going out.*

This silly bloke'll 'ave the s'prise of 'is life when 'e wakes up on board of 'er.
*They laugh. The door closes behind them.* FREDA *moves quickly for the door on the left but* JOE *gets in her way and stops her.*

JOE

*Threateningly.*

Guv us what yer took!

FREDA

Took? I guv yer all 'e 'ad.

JOE

Yer a liar! I seen yer a-playin' yer sneakin' tricks, but yer can't fool
Joe. I'm too old a 'and.
*Furiously.*
Guv it to me, yer bloody cow!
*He grabs her by the arm.*

FREDA

Lemme alone! I ain't got no—

JOE

*Hits her viciously on the side of the jaw. She crumples up on the floor.*
That'll learn yer!
*He stoops down and fumbles in her bosom and pulls out the banknote,
which he stuffs into his pocket with a grunt of satisfaction.* KATE *opens
the door on the left and looks in—then rushes to* FREDA *and lifts her
head up in her arms.*

KATE

*Gently.*
Pore dearie!
*Looking at* JOE *angrily.*
Been 'ittin' 'er agen, 'ave yer, yer cowardly swine!

JOE

Yus; an' I'll 'it you, too, if yer don't keep yer marf shut. Tike 'er aht
of 'ere!
KATE *carries* FREDA *into the next room.* JOE *goes behind the bar. A
moment later the outer door is opened and* DRISCOLL *and* COCKY
*come in.*

DRISCOLL

Come on, Ollie.
*He suddenly sees that* OLSON *is not there, and turns to* JOE.
Where is ut he's gone to?

JOE

*With a meaning wink.*
'E an' Freda went aht t'gether 'bout five minutes past. 'E's fair gone
on 'er, 'e is.

DRISCOLL

*With a grin.*

Oho, so that's ut, is ut? Who'd think Ollie'd be sich a divil wid the wimin? 'Tis lucky he's sober or she'd have him stripped to his last ha'penny.

*Turning to* COCKY, *who is blinking sleepily.*

What'll ye have, ye little scut?

*To* JOE.

Give me whiskey, *Irish* whiskey!

THE CURTAIN FALLS

*Ile*
A Play in One Act

# Characters

BEN, *the cabin boy*

THE STEWARD

CAPTAIN KEENEY

SLOCUM, *second mate*

MRS. KEENEY

JOE, *a harpooner*

*Members of the crew of the steam whaler* Atlantic Queen.

# Ile

CAPTAIN KEENEY's *cabin on board the steam whaling ship* Atlantic Queen — *a small, square compartment about eight feet high with a skylight in the center looking out on the poop deck. On the left [the stern of the ship] a long bench with rough cushions is built in against the wall. In front of the bench, a table. Over the bench, several curtained portholes.*

*In the rear, left, a door leading to the captain's sleeping quarters. To the right of the door a small organ, looking as if it were brand new, is placed against the wall.*

*On the right, to the rear, a marble-topped sideboard. On the sideboard, a woman's sewing basket. Farther forward, a doorway leading to the companion way, and past the officer's quarters to the main deck.*

*In the center of the room, a stove. From the middle of the ceiling a hanging lamp is suspended. The walls of the cabin are painted white.*

*There is no rolling of the ship, and the light which comes through the skylight is sickly and faint, indicating one of those gray days of calm when ocean and sky are alike dead. The silence is unbroken except for the measured tread of some one walking up and down on the poop deck overhead.*

*It is nearing two bells — one o'clock — in the afternoon of a day in the year 1895.*

*At the rise of the curtain there is a moment of intense silence. Then the* STEWARD *enters and commences to clear the table of the few dishes which still remain on it after the* CAPTAIN's *dinner. He is an old, griz-*

zled man dressed in dungaree pants, a sweater, and a woolen cap with ear flaps. His manner is sullen and angry. He stops stacking up the plates and casts a quick glance upward at the skylight; then tiptoes over to the closed door in rear and listens with his ear pressed to the crack. What he hears makes his face darken and he mutters a furious curse. There is a noise from the doorway on the right and he darts back to the table.

BEN enters. He is an over-grown, gawky boy with a long, pinched face. He is dressed in sweater, fur cap, etc. His teeth are chattering with the cold and he hurries to the stove, where he stands for a moment shivering, blowing on his hands, slapping them against his sides, on the verge of crying.

THE STEWARD
In relieved tones—seeing who it is.
Oh, 'tis you, is it? What're ye shiverin' 'bout? Stay by the stove where ye belong and ye'll find no need of chatterin'.

BEN
It's c-c-cold.
Trying to control his chattering teeth—derisively.
Who d'ye think it were—the Old Man?

THE STEWARD
Makes a threatening move—BEN shrinks away.
None o' your lip, young un, or I'll learn ye.
More kindly.
Where was it ye've been all o' the time—the fo'c's'tle?

BEN
Yes.

THE STEWARD
Let the Old Man see ye up for'ard monkeyshinin' with the hands and ye'll get a hidin' ye'll not forget in a hurry.

BEN
Aw, he don't see nothin'.
A trace of awe in his tones—he glances upward.

He just walks up and down like he didn't notice nobody—and stares at the ice to the no'the'ard.

THE STEWARD
*The same tone of awe creeping into his voice.*
He's always starin' at the ice.
*In a sudden rage, shaking his fist at the skylight.*
Ice, ice, ice! Damn him and damn the ice! Holdin' us in for nigh on a year—nothin' to see but ice—stuck in it like a fly in molasses!

BEN
*Apprehensively.*
Ssshh! He'll hear ye.

THE STEWARD
*Raging.*
Aye, damn him, and damn the Arctic seas, and damn this stinkin' whalin' ship of his, and damn me for a fool to ever ship on it!
*Subsiding as if realizing the uselessness of this outburst—shaking his head—slowly, with deep conviction.*
He's a hard man—as hard a man as ever sailed the seas.

BEN
*Solemnly.*
Aye.

THE STEWARD
The two years we all signed up for are done this day. Blessed Christ! Two years o' this dog's life, and no luck in the fishin', and the hands half starved with the food runnin' low, rotten as it is; and not a sign of him turnin' back for home!
*Bitterly.*
Home! I begin to doubt if ever I'll set foot on land again.
*Excitedly.*
What is it he thinks he' goin' to do? Keep us all up here after our time is worked out till the last man of us is starved to death or frozen? We've grub enough hardly to last out the voyage back if we started now. What are the men goin' to do 'bout it? Did ye hear any talk in the fo'c's'tle?

**BEN**
*Going over to him—in a half whisper.*
They said if he don't put back south for home today they're goin' to mutiny.

**THE STEWARD**
*With grim satisfaction.*
Mutiny? Aye, 'tis the only thing they can do; and serve him right after the manner he's treated them—'s if they wern't no better nor dogs.

**BEN**
The ice is all broke up to s'uth'ard. They's clear water 's far 's you can see. He ain't got no excuse for not turnin' back for home, the men says.

**THE STEWARD**
*Bitterly.*
He won't look nowheres but no'the'ard where they's only the ice to see. He don't want to see no clear water. All he thinks on is gittin' the ile—'s if it was our fault he ain't had good luck with the whales. *Shaking his head.*
I think the man's mighty nigh losin' his senses.

**BEN**
*Awed.*
D'you really think he's crazy?

**THE STEWARD**
Aye, it's the punishment o' God on him. Did ye ever hear of a man who wasn't crazy do the things he does?
*Pointing to the door in rear.*
Who but a man that's mad would take his woman—and as sweet a woman as ever was—on a stinkin' whalin' ship to the Arctic seas to be locked in by the rotten ice for nigh on a year, and maybe lose her senses forever—for it's sure she'll never be the same again.

**BEN**
*Sadly.*
She useter be awful nice to me before—

*His eyes grow wide and frightened.*
she got—like she is.

THE STEWARD
Aye, she was good to all of us. 'Twould have been hell on board without her; for he's a hard man—a hard, hard man—a driver if there
ever was one.
*With a grim laugh.*
I hope he's satisfied now—drivin' her on till she's near lost her mind.
And who could blame her? 'Tis a God's wonder we're not a ship full
of crazed people—with the damned ice all the time, and the quiet
so thick you're afraid to hear your own voice.

BEN
*With a frightened glance toward the door on right.*
She don't never speak to me no more—jest looks at me 's if she didn't
know me.

THE STEWARD
She don't know no one—but him. She talks to him—when she does
talk—right enough.

BEN
She does nothin' all day long now but sit and sew—and then she
cries to herself without makin' no noise. I've seen her.

THE STEWARD
Aye, I could hear her through the door a while back.

BEN
*Tiptoes over to the door and listens.*
She's cryin' now.

THE STEWARD
*Furiously—shaking his fist.*
God send his soul to hell for the devil he is!
*There is the noise of some one coming slowly down the companionway
stairs.* THE STEWARD *hurries to his stacked up dishes. He is so nervous from fright that he knocks off the top one, which falls and breaks
on the floor. He stands aghast, trembling with dread.* BEN *is violently*

*rubbing off the organ with a piece of cloth which he has snatched from his pocket.* CAPTAIN KEENEY *appears in the doorway on right and comes into the cabin, removing his fur cap as he does so. He is a man of about forty, around five-ten in height but looking much shorter on account of the enormous proportions of his shoulders and chest. His face is massive and deeply lined, with gray-blue eyes of a bleak hardness, and a tightly clenched, thin-lipped mouth. His thick hair is long and gray. He is dressed in a heavy blue jacket and blue pants stuffed into his seaboots.*

*He is followed into the cabin by the* SECOND MATE, *a rangy six-footer with a lean weather-beaten face. The* MATE *is dressed about the same as the captain. He is a man of thirty or so.*

KEENEY
*Comes toward the* STEWARD—*with a stern look on his face. The* STEWARD *is visibly frightened and the stack of dishes rattles in his trembling hands.* KEENEY *draws back his fist and the* STEWARD *shrinks away. The fist is gradually lowered and* KEENEY *speaks slowly.*
'Twould be like hitting a worm. It is nigh on two bells, Mr. Steward, and this truck not cleared yet.

THE STEWARD
*Stammering.*
Y-y-yes, sir.

KEENEY
Instead of doin' your rightful work ye've been below here gossipin' old woman's talk with that boy.
*To* BEN, *fiercely.*
Get out o' this, you! Clean up the chart room.
BEN *darts past the* MATE *to the open doorway.*
Pick up that dish, Mr. Steward!

THE STEWARD
*Doing so with difficulty.*
Yes, sir.

KEENEY

The next dish you break, Mr. Steward, you take a bath in the Bering
Sea at the end of a rope.

THE STEWARD

*Tremblingly.*

Yes, sir.

*He hurries out. The* SECOND MATE *walks slowly over to the* CAPTAIN.

MATE

I warn't 'specially anxious the man at the wheel should catch what I
wanted to say to you, sir. That's why I asked you to come below.

KEENEY

*Impatiently.*

Speak your say, Mr. Slocum.

MATE

*Unconsciously lowering his voice.*

I'm afeard there'll be trouble with the hands by the look o' things.
They'll likely turn ugly, every blessed one o' them, if you don't put
back. The two years they signed up for is up to-day.

KEENEY

And d'you think you're tellin' me somethin' new, Mr. Slocum? I've
felt it in the air this long time past. D'you think I've not seen their
ugly looks and the grudgin' way they worked?

*The door in rear is opened and* MRS. KEENEY *stands in the doorway.
She is a slight, sweet-faced little woman primly dressed in black. Her eyes
are red from weeping and her face drawn and pale. She takes in the cabin
with a frightened glance and stands as if fixed to the spot by some name-
less dread, clasping and unclasping her hands nervously. The two men
turn and look at her.*

KEENEY

*With rough tenderness.*

Well, Annie?

MRS. KEENEY

*As if awakening from a dream.*

David, I—
*She is silent. The* MATE *starts for the doorway.*

KEENEY
*Turning to him — sharply.*
Wait!

MATE
Yes, sir.

KEENEY
D'you want anything, Annie?

MRS. KEENEY
*After a pause, during which she seems to be endeavoring to collect her thoughts.*
I thought maybe — I'd go up on deck, David, to get a breath of fresh air.
*She stands humbly awaiting his permission. He and the* MATE *exchange a significant glance.*

KEENEY
It's too cold, Annie. You'd best stay below today. There's nothing to look at on deck — but ice.

MRS. KEENEY
*Monotonously.*
I know — ice, ice, ice! But there's nothing to see down here but these walls.
*She makes a gesture of loathing.*

KEENEY
You can play the organ, Annie.

MRS. KEENEY
*Dully.*
I hate the organ. It puts me in mind of home.

KEENEY
*A touch of resentment in his voice.*
I got it jest for you.

MRS. KEENEY

*Dully.*

I know.

*She turns away from them and walks slowly to the bench on left. She lifts up one of the curtains and looks through a porthole; then utters an exclamation of joy.*

Ah, water! Clear water! As far as I can see! How good it looks after all these months of ice!

*She turns round to them, her face transfigured with joy.*

Ah, now I must go upon deck and look at it, David.

KEENEY

*Frowning.*

Best not today, Annie. Best wait for a day when the sun shines.

MRS. KEENEY

*Desperately.*

But the sun never shines in this terrible place.

KEENEY

*A tone of command in his voice.*

Best not today, Annie.

MRS. KEENEY

*Crumbling before this command—abjectly.*

Very well, David.

*She stands there staring straight before her as if in a daze. The two men look at her uneasily.*

KEENEY

*Sharply.*

Annie!

MRS. KEENEY

*Dully.*

Yes, David.

KEENEY

Me and Mr. Slocum has business to talk about—ship's business.

MRS. KEENEY
Very well, David.
*She goes slowly out, rear, and leaves the door three-quarters shut behind her.*

KEENEY
Best not have her on deck if they's goin' to be any trouble.

MATE
Yes, sir.

KEENEY
And trouble they's goin' to be. I feel it in my bones.
*Takes a revolver from the pocket of his coat and examines it.*
Got your'n?

MATE
Yes, sir.

KEENEY
Not that we'll have to use 'em—not if I know their breed of dog—jest to frighten 'em up a bit.
*Grimly.*
I ain't never been forced to use one yit; and trouble I've had by land and by sea 's long as I kin remember, and will have till my dyin' day, I reckon.

MATE
*Hesitatingly.*
Then you ain't goin'—to turn back?

KEENEY
Turn back! Mr. Slocum, did you ever hear 'o me pointin' s'uth for home with only a measly four hundred barrel of ile in the hold?

MATE
*Hastily.*
No, sir—but the grub's gittin' low.

KEENEY

They's enough to last a long time yit, if they're careful with it; and they's plenty o' water.

MATE

They say it's not fit to eat—what's left; and the two years they signed on fur is up today. They might make trouble for you in the courts when we git home.

KEENEY

To hell with 'em! Let them make what law trouble they kin. I don't give a damn 'bout the money. I've got to git the ile!
*Glancing sharply at the* MATE.
You ain't turnin' no damned sea lawyer, be you, Mr. Slocum?

MATE

*Flushing.*
Not by a hell of a sight, sir.

KEENEY

What do the fools want to go home fur now? Their share o' the four hundred barrel wouldn't keep 'em in chewin' terbacco.

MATE

*Slowly.*
They wants to git back to their folks an' things, I s'pose.

KEENEY

*Looking at him searchingly.*
'N you want to turn back, too.
THE MATE *looks down confusedly before his sharp gaze.*
Don't lie, Mr. Slocum. It's writ down plain in your eyes.
*With grim sarcasm.*
I hope, Mr. Slocum, you ain't agoin' to jine the men agin me.

MATE

*Indignantly.*
That ain't fair, sir, to say sich things.

KEENEY

*With satisfaction.*

I warn't much afeard o' that, Tom. You been with me nigh on ten year and I've learned ye whalin'. No man kin say I ain't a good master, if I be a hard one.

MATE

I warn't thinkin' of myself, sir—'bout turnin' home, I mean.

*Desperately.*

But Mrs. Keeney, sir—seems like she ain't jest satisfied up here, ailin' like—what with the cold an' bad luck an' the ice an' all.

KEENEY

*His face clouding—rebukingly but not severely.*

That's my business, Mr. Slocum. I'll thank you to steer a clear course o' that.

*A pause.*

The ice'll break up soon to no'th'ard. I could see it startin' today. And when it goes and we git some sun Annie'll perk up.

*Another pause—then he bursts forth.*

It ain't the damned money what's keepin' me up in the Northern seas, Tom. But I can't go back to Homeport with a measly four hundred barrel of ile. I'd die fust. I ain't never come back home in all my days without a full ship. Ain't that truth?

MATE

Yes, sir; but this voyage you been ice-bound, an'—

KEENEY

*Scornfully.*

And d'you s'pose any of 'em would believe that—any o' them skippers I've beaten voyage after voyage? Can't you hear 'em laughin' and sneerin'—Tibbots 'n' Harris 'n' Simms and the rest—and all o' Homeport makin' fun o' me? "Dave Keeney what boasts he's the best whalin' skipper out o' Homeport comin' back with a measly four hundred barrel of ile?"

*The thought of this drives him into a frenzy, and he smashes his fist down on the marble top of the sideboard.*

Hell! I got to git the ile, I tell you. How could I figger on this ice?

It's never been so bad before in the thirty year I been acomin' here. And now it's breakin' up. In a couple o' days it'll be all gone. And they's whale here, plenty of 'em. I know they is and I ain't never gone wrong yit. I got to git the ile! I got to git it in spite of all hell, and by God, I ain't agoin' home till I do git it!

*There is the sound of subdued sobbing from the door in rear. The two men stand silent for a moment, listening. Then* KEENEY *goes over to the door and looks in. He hesitates for a moment as if he were going to enter—then closes the door softly.* JOE, *the harpooner, an enormous six-footer with a battered, ugly face, enters from right and stands waiting for the captain to notice him.*

KEENEY
*Turning and seeing him.*
Don't be standin' there like a gawk, Harpooner. Speak up!

JOE
*Confusedly.*
We want—the men, sir—they wants to send a depitation aft to have a word with you.

KEENEY
*Furiously.*
Tell 'em to go to—
*Checks himself and continues grimly.*
Tell 'em to come. I'll see 'em.

JOE
Aye, aye, sir.
*He goes out.*

KEENEY
*With a grim smile.*
Here it comes, the trouble you spoke of, Mr. Slocum, and we'll make short shift of it. It's better to crush such things at the start than let them make headway.

MATE
*Worriedly.*
Shall I wake up the First and Fourth, sir? We might need their help.

**KEENEY**

No, let them sleep. I'm well able to handle this alone, Mr. Slocum.
*There is the shuffling of footsteps from outside and five of the crew crowd
into the cabin, led by* JOE. *All are dressed alike—sweaters, seaboots, etc.
They glance uneasily at the* CAPTAIN, *twirling their fur caps in their
hands.*

**KEENEY**
*After a pause.*
Well? Who's to speak fur ye?

**JOE**
*Stepping forward with an air of bravado.*
I be.

**KEENEY**
*Eyeing him up and down coldly.*
So you be. Then speak your say and be quick about it.

**JOE**
*Trying not to wilt before the* CAPTAIN's *glance and avoiding his eyes.*
The time we signed up for is done today.

**KEENEY**
*Icily.*
You're tellin' me nothin' I don't know.

**JOE**
You ain't pintin' fur home yit, far 's we kin see.

**KEENEY**
No, and I ain't agoin' to till this ship is full of ile.

**JOE**
You can't go no further no'the with the ice afore ye.

**KEENEY**
The ice is breaking up.

**JOE**
*After a slight pause during which the others mumble angrily to one an-
other.*

The grub we're gittin' now is rotten.

KEENEY

It's good enough fur ye. Better men than ye are have eaten worse.
*There is a chorus of angry exclamations from the crowd.*

JOE

*Encouraged by this support.*
We ain't agoin' to work no more less you puts back for home.

KEENEY

*Fiercely.*
You ain't, ain't you?

JOE

No; and the law courts'll say we was right.

KEENEY

To hell with your law courts! We're at sea now and I'm the law on
this ship.
*Edging up toward the harpooner.*
And every mother's son of you what don't obey orders goes in irons.
*There are more angry exclamations from the crew.* MRS. KEENEY *appears in the doorway in rear and looks on with startled eyes. None of the men notice her.*

JOE

*With bravado.*
Then we're agoin' to mutiny and take the old hooker home ourselves.
Ain't we, boys?
*As he turns his head to look at the others,* KEENEY's *fist shoots out to the side of his jaw.* JOE *goes down in a heap and lies there.* MRS. KEENEY *gives a shriek and hides her face in her hands. The men pull out their sheath knives and start a rush, but stop when they find themselves confronted by the revolvers of* KEENEY *and the* MATE.

KEENEY

*His eyes and voice snapping.*
Hold still!

*The men stand huddled together in a sullen silence.* KEENEY'*s voice is full of mockery.*

You've found out it ain't safe to mutiny on this ship, ain't you? And now git for'ard where ye belong, and—

*He gives* JOE'*s body a contemptuous kick.*

Drag him with you. And remember the first man of ye I see shirkin' I'll shoot dead as sure as there's a sea under us, and you can tell the rest the same. Git for'ard now! Quick!

*The men leave in cowed silence, carrying* JOE *with them.* KEENEY *turns to the* MATE *with a short laugh and puts his revolver back in his pocket.*

Best get up on deck, Mr. Slocum, and see to it they don't try none of their skulkin' tricks. We'll have to keep an eye peeled from now on. I know 'em.

MATE
Yes, sir.

*He goes out, right.* KEENEY *hears his wife's hysterical weeping and turns around in surprise—then walks slowly to her side.*

KEENEY
*Putting an arm around her shoulder—with gruff tenderness.*
There, there, Annie. Don't be afeard. It's all past and gone.

MRS. KEENEY
*Shrinking away from him.*
Oh, I can't bear it! I can't bear it any longer!

KEENEY
*Gently.*
Can't bear what, Annie?

MRS. KEENEY
*Hysterically.*
All this horrible brutality, and these brutes of men, and this terrible ship, and this prison cell of a room, and the ice all around, and the silence.

*After this outburst she calms down and wipes her eyes with her handkerchief.*

KEENEY

*After a pause during which he looks down at her with a puzzled frown.*
Remember, I warn't hankerin' to have you come on this voyage,
Annie.

MRS. KEENEY

I wanted to be with you, David, don't you see? I didn't want to wait
back there in the house all alone as I've been doing these last six years
since we were married—waiting, and watching, and fearing—with
nothing to keep my mind occupied—not able to go back teaching
school on account of being Dave Keeney's wife. I used to dream of
sailing on the great, wide, glorious ocean. I wanted to be by your
side in the danger and vigorous life of it all. I wanted to see you the
hero they make you out to be in Homeport. And instead—
*Her voice grows tremulous.*
All I find is ice and cold—and brutality!
*Her voice breaks.*

KEENEY

I warned you what it'd be, Annie. "Whalin' ain't no ladies' tea party,"
I says to you, and "you better stay to home where you've got all your
woman's comforts."
*Shaking his head.*
But you was so set on it.

MRS. KEENEY

*Wearily.*
Oh, I know it isn't your fault, David. You see, I didn't believe you. I
guess I was dreaming about the old Vikings in the story books and
I thought you were one of them.

KEENEY

*Protestingly.*
I done my best to make it as cozy and comfortable as could be.
MRS. KEENEY *looks around her in wild scorn.*
I even sent to the city for that organ for ye, thinkin' it might be
soothin' to ye to be playin' it times when they was calms and things
was dull like.

MRS. KEENEY

*Wearily.*

Yes, you were very kind, David. I know that.

*She goes to left and lifts the curtains from the porthole and looks out—then suddenly bursts forth.*

I won't stand it—I can't stand it—pent up by these walls like a prisoner.

*She runs over to him and throws her arms around him, weeping. He puts his arm protectingly over her shoulders.*

Take me away from here, David! If I don't get away from here, out of this terrible ship, I'll go mad! Take me home, David! I can't think any more. I feel as if the cold and the silence were crushing down on my brain. I'm afraid. Take me home!

KEENEY

*Holds her at arm's length and looks at her face anxiously.*

Best go to bed, Annie. You ain't yourself. You got fever. Your eyes look so strange like. I ain't never seen you look this way before.

MRS. KEENEY

*Laughing hysterically.*

It's the ice and the cold and the silence—they'd make any one look strange.

KEENEY

*Soothingly.*

In a month or two, with good luck, three at the most, I'll have her filled with ile and then we'll give her everything she'll stand and pint for home.

MRS. KEENEY

But we can't wait for that—I can't wait. I want to get home. And the men won't wait. They want to get home. It's cruel, it's brutal for you to keep them. You must sail back. You've got no excuse. There's clear water to the south now. If you've a heart at all you've got to turn back.

KEENEY

*Harshly.*

I can't, Annie.

MRS. KEENEY
Why can't you?

KEENEY
A woman couldn't rightly understand my reason.

MRS. KEENEY
*Wildly.*
Because it's a stupid, stubborn reason. Oh, I heard you talking with
the second mate. You're afraid the other captains will sneer at you
because you didn't come back with a full ship. You want to live up
to your silly reputation even if you do have to beat and starve men
and drive me mad to do it.

KEENEY
*His jaw set stubbornly.*
It ain't that, Annie. Them skippers would never dare sneer to my
face. It ain't so much what any one'd say—but—
*He hesitates, struggling to express his meaning.*
You see—I've always done it—since my first voyage as skipper. I
always come back—with a full ship—and—it don't seem right not
to—somehow. I been always first whalin' skipper out o' Homeport,
and—Don't you see my meanin', Annie?
*He glances at her. She is not looking at him but staring dully in front of
her, not hearing a word he is saying.*
Annie!
*She comes to herself with a start.*
Best turn in, Annie, there's a good woman. You ain't well.

MRS. KEENEY
*Resisting his attempts to guide her to the door in rear.*
David! Won't you please turn back?

KEENEY
*Gently.*
I can't, Annie—not yet awhile. You don't see my meanin'. I got to
git the ile.

MRS. KEENEY

It'd be different if you needed the money, but you don't. You've got more than plenty.

KEENEY

*Impatiently.*

It ain't the money I'm thinkin' of. D'you think I'm as mean as that?

MRS. KEENEY

*Dully.*

No—I don't know—I can't understand—

*Intensely.*

Oh, I want to be home in the old house once more and see my own kitchen again, and hear a woman's voice talking to me and be able to talk to her. Two years! It seems so long ago—as if I'd been dead and could never go back.

KEENEY

*Worried by her strange tone and the far-away look in her eyes.*

Best go to bed, Annie. You ain't well.

MRS. KEENEY

*Not appearing to hear him.*

I used to be lonely when you were away. I used to think Homeport was a stupid, monotonous place. Then I used to go down on the beach, especially when it was windy and the breakers were rolling in, and I'd dream of the fine free life you must be leading.

*She gives a laugh which is half a sob.*

I used to love the sea then.

*She pauses; then continues with slow intensity.*

But now—I don't ever want to see the sea again.

KEENEY

*Thinking to humor her.*

'Tis no fit place for a woman, that's sure. I was a fool to bring ye.

MRS. KEENEY

*After a pause—passing her hand over her eyes with a gesture of pathetic weariness.*

How long would it take us to reach home—if we started now?

KEENEY

*Frowning.*

'Bout two months, I reckon, Annie, with fair luck.

MRS. KEENEY

*Counts on her fingers—then murmurs with a rapt smile.*

That would be August, the latter part of August, wouldn't it? It was on the twenty-fifth of August we were married, David, wasn't it?

KEENEY

*Trying to conceal the fact that her memories have moved him—gruffly.*

Don't *you* remember?

MRS. KEENEY

*Vaguely—again passes her hand over her eyes.*

My memory is leaving me—up here in the ice. It was so long ago.

*A pause—then she smiles dreamily.*

It's June now. The lilacs will be all in bloom in the front yard—and the climbing roses on the trellis to the side of the house—they're budding.

*She suddenly covers her face with her hands and commences to sob.*

KEENEY

*Disturbed.*

Go in and rest, Annie. You're all wore out cryin' over what can't be helped.

MRS. KEENEY

*Suddenly throwing her arms around his neck and clinging to him.*

You love me, don't you, David?

KEENEY

*In amazed embarrassment at this outburst.*

Love you? Why d'you ask me such a question, Annie?

MRS. KEENEY

*Shaking him—fiercely.*

But you do, don't you, David? Tell me!

KEENEY

I'm your husband, Annie, and you're my wife. Could there be aught but love between us after all these years?

MRS. KEENEY

*Shaking him again—still more fiercely.*
Then you do love me. Say it!

KEENEY

*Simply.*
I do, Annie.

MRS. KEENEY

*Gives a sigh of relief—her hands drop to her sides.* KEENEY *regards her anxiously. She passes her hand across her eyes and murmurs half to herself.*
I sometimes think if we could only have had a child.
KEENEY *turns away from her, deeply moved. She grabs his arm and turns him around to face her—intensely.*
And I've always been a good wife to you, haven't I, David?

KEENEY

*His voice betraying his emotion.*
No man has ever had a better, Annie.

MRS. KEENEY

And I've never asked for much from you, have I, David? Have I?

KEENEY

You know you could have all I got the power to give ye, Annie.

MRS. KEENEY

*Wildly.*
Then do this this once for my sake, for God's sake—take me home! It's killing me, this life—the brutality and cold and horror of it. I'm going mad. I can feel the threat in the air. I can hear the silence threatening me—day after gray day and every day the same. I can't bear it.
*Sobbing.*

I'll go mad, I know I will. Take me home, David, if you love me as you say. I'm afraid. For the love of God, take me home!

*She throws her arms around him, weeping against his shoulder. His face betrays the tremendous struggle going on within him. He holds her out at arm's length, his expression softening. For a moment his shoulders sag, he becomes old, his iron spirit weakens as he looks at her tear-stained face.*

KEENEY
*Dragging out the words with an effort.*
I'll do it, Annie—for your sake—if you say it's needful for ye.

MRS. KEENEY
*With wild joy—kissing him.*
God bless you for that, David!
*He turns away from her silently and walks toward the companionway. Just at that moment there is a clatter of footsteps on the stairs and the* SECOND MATE *enters the cabin.*

MATE
*Excitedly.*
The ice is breakin' up to no'the'ard, sir. There's a clear passage through the floe, and clear water beyond, the lookout says.
KEENEY *straightens himself like a man coming out of a trance.* MRS. KEENEY *looks at the* MATE *with terrified eyes.*

KEENEY
*Dazedly—trying to collect his thoughts.*
A clear passage? To no'the'ard?

MATE
Yes, sir.

KEENEY
*His voice suddenly grim with determination.*
Then get her ready and we'll drive her through.

MATE
Aye, aye, sir.

MRS. KEENEY
*Appealingly.*
David!

KEENEY
*Not heeding her.*
Will the men turn to willin' or must we drag 'em out?

MATE
They'll turn to willin' enough. You put the fear o' God into 'em, sir.
They're meek as lambs.

KEENEY
Then drive 'em—both watches.
*With grim determination.*
They's whale t'other side o' this floe and we're going to git 'em.

MATE
Aye, aye, sir.
*He goes out hurriedly. A moment later there is the sound of scuffling feet from the deck outside and the* MATE's *voice shouting orders.*

KEENEY
*Speaking aloud to himself—derisively.*
And I was agoin' home like a yaller dog!

MRS. KEENEY
*Imploringly.*
David!

KEENEY
*Sternly.*
Woman, you ain't adoin' right when you meddle in men's business
and weaken 'em. You can't know my feelin's. I got to prove a man
to be a good husband for ye to take pride in. I got to git the ile, I
tell ye.

MRS. KEENEY
*Supplicatingly.*
David! Aren't you going home?

KEENEY

*Ignoring this question—commandingly.*

You ain't well. Go and lay down a mite.

*He starts for the door.*

I got to git on deck.

*He goes out. She cries after him in anguish.*

David!

*A pause. She passes her hand across her eyes—then commences to laugh hysterically and goes to the organ. She sits down and starts to play wildly an old hymn.* KEENEY *reenters from the doorway to the deck and stands looking at her angrily. He comes over and grabs her roughly by the shoulder.*

KEENEY

Woman, what foolish mockin' is this?

*She laughs wildly and he starts back from her in alarm.*

Annie! What is it?

*She doesn't answer him.* KEENEY's *voice trembles.*

Don't you know me, Annie?

*He puts both hands on her shoulders and turns her around so that he can look into her eyes. She stares up at him with a stupid expression, a vague smile on her lips. He stumbles away from her, and she commences softly to play the organ again.*

KEENEY

*Swallowing hard—in a hoarse whisper, as if he had difficulty in speaking.*

You said—you was a-goin' mad—God!

*A long wail is heard from the deck above.*

Ah bl-o-o-o-ow!

*A moment later the* MATE's *face appears through the skylight. He cannot see* MRS. KEENEY.

MATE

*In great excitement.*

Whales, sir—a whole school of 'em—off the star'b'd quarter 'bout five mile away—big ones!

KEENEY
*Galvanized into action.*
Are you lowerin' the boats?

MATE
Yes, sir.

KEENEY
*With grim decision.*
I'm a-comin' with ye.

MATE
Aye, aye, sir.
*Jubilantly.*
You'll git the ile now right enough, sir.
*His head is withdrawn and he can be heard shouting orders.*

KEENEY
*Turning to his wife.*
Annie! Did you hear him? I'll git the ile.
*She doesn't answer or seem to know he is there. He gives a hard laugh, which is almost a groan.*
I know you're foolin' me, Annie. You ain't out of your mind—
*Anxiously.*
be you? I'll git the ile now right enough—jest a little while longer, Annie—then we'll turn hom'ard. I can't turn back now, you see that, don't ye? I've got to git the ile.
*In sudden terror.*
Answer me! You ain't mad, be you?
*She keeps on playing the organ, but makes no reply. The* MATE's *face appears again through the skylight.*

MATE
All ready, sir.
KEENEY *turns his back on his wife and strides to the doorway, where he stands for a moment and looks back at her in anguish, fighting to control his feelings.*

MATE
Comin', sir?

KEENEY

*His face suddenly grown hard with determination.*

Aye.

*He turns abruptly and goes out.* MRS. KEENEY *does not appear to notice his departure. Her whole attention seems centered in the organ. She sits with half-closed eyes, her body swaying a little from side to side to the rhythm of the hymn. Her fingers move faster and faster and she is playing wildly and discordantly as*

THE CURTAIN FALLS

*The Moon of the Caribbees*
A Play in One Act

# Characters

YANK

DRISCOLL

OLSON

DAVIS                    *Seamen of the British tramp steamer,* Glencairn.

COCKY

SMITTY

PAUL

LAMPS, *the lamptrimmer.*

CHIPS, *the carpenter.*

OLD TOM, *the donkeyman.*

BIG FRANK

DICK
                        *Firemen on the* Glencairn.
MAX

PADDY

BELLA

SUSIE
} *West Indian Negresses.*
VIOLET

PEARL

THE FIRST MATE

*Two other seamen—*SCOTTY *and* IVAN*—and several
other members of the stokehole-engine-room crew.*

# The Moon of the Caribbees

*A forward section of the main deck of the British tramp steamer* Glencairn, *at anchor off an island in the West Indies. The full moon, half-way up the sky, throws a clear light on the deck. The sea is calm and the ship motionless.*

*On the left two of the derrick booms of the foremast jut out at an angle of forty-five degrees, black against the sky. In the rear the dark outline of the port bulwark is sharply defined against a distant strip of coral beach, white in the moonlight, fringed with coco palms whose tops rise clear of the horizon. On the right is the forecastle with an open doorway in the center leading to the seamen's and firemen's compartments. On either side of the doorway are two closed doors opening on the quarters of the Bo'sun, the ship's carpenter, the messroom steward, and the donkeyman—what might be called the petty officers of the ship. Near each bulwark there is also a short stairway, like a section of fire escape, leading up to the forecastle head (the top of the forecastle)—the edge of which can be seen on the right.*

*In the center of the deck, and occupying most of the space, is the large, raised square of the number one hatch, covered with canvas, battened down for the night.*

*A melancholy negro chant, faint and far-off, drifts, crooning, over the water.*

*Most of the seamen and firemen are reclining or sitting on the hatch.* PAUL *is leaning against the port bulwark, the upper part of his stocky figure outlined against the sky.* SMITTY *and* COCKY *are sitting on the edge of the forecastle head with their legs dangling over. Nearly all are smoking pipes or cigarettes. The majority are dressed in patched suits of dungaree. Quite a few are in their bare feet and some of them, especially the firemen, have nothing on but a pair of pants and an undershirt. A good many wear caps.*

*There is the low murmur of different conversations going on in the separate groups as the curtain rises. This is followed by a sudden silence in which the singing from the land can be plainly heard.*

DRISCOLL
*A powerfully built Irishman who is sitting on the edge of the hatch, front—irritably.*
Will ye listen to them naygurs? I wonder now, do they call that keenin' a song?

SMITTY
*A young Englishman with a blond mustache. He is sitting on the forecastle head looking out over the water with his chin supported on his hands.*
It doesn't make a chap feel very cheerful, does it?
*He sighs.*

COCKY
*A wizened runt of a man with a straggling gray mustache—slapping* SMITTY *on the back.*
Cheero, ole dear! Down't be ser dawhn in the marf, Duke. She loves yer.

SMITTY
*Gloomily.*
Shut up, Cocky!
*He turns away from* COCKY *and falls to dreaming again, staring toward the spot on shore where the singing seems to come from.*

BIG FRANK
*A huge fireman sprawled out on the right of the hatch—waving a hand toward the land.*

They bury somebody—py chiminy Christmas, I tink so from way it sound.

YANK

*A rather good-looking rough who is sitting beside* DRISCOLL.
What d'yuh mean, bury? They don't plant 'em down here, Dutchy. They eat 'em to save fun'ral expenses. I guess this guy went down the wrong way an' they got indigestion.

COCKY

Indigestion! Ho yus, not 'arf! Down't yer know as them blokes 'as two stomacks like a bleedin' camel?

DAVIS

*A short, dark man seated on the right of hatch.*
An' you seen the two, I s'pect, ain't you?

COCKY

*Scornfully.*
Down't be showin' yer igerance be tryin' to make a mock o' me what has seen more o' the world than yeself ever will.

MAX

*A Swedish fireman—from the rear of hatch.*
Spin dat yarn, Cocky.

COCKY

It's Gawd's troof, what I tole yer. I 'eard it from a bloke what was captured pris'ner by 'em in the Solomon Islands. Shipped wiv 'im one voyage. 'Twas a rare treat to 'ear 'im tell what 'appened to 'im among 'em.
*Musingly.*
'E was a funny bird, 'e was—'ailed from Mile End, 'e did.

DRISCOLL

*With a snort.*
Another lyin' Cockney, the loike av yourself!

LAMPS

*A fat Swede who is sitting on a camp stool in front of his door talking with* CHIPS.

Where you meet up with him, Cocky?

CHIPS
*A lanky Scotchman—derisively.*
In New Guinea, I'll lay my oath!

COCKY
*Defiantly.*
Yus! It *was* in New Guinea, time I was shipwrecked there.
*There is a perfect storm of groans and laughter at this speech.*

YANK
*Getting up.*
Yuh know what we said yuh'd get if yuh sprung any of that lyin' New
Guinea dope on us again, don't yuh? Close that trap if yuh don't
want a duckin' over the side.

COCKY
Ow, I was on'y tryin' to edicate yer a bit.
*He sinks into dignified silence.*

YANK
*Nodding toward the shore.*
Don't yuh know this is the West Indies, yuh crazy mut? There ain't
no cannibals here. They're only common niggers.

DRISCOLL
*Irritably.*
Whativir they are, the divil take their cryin'. It's enough to give a
man the jigs listenin' to 'em.

YANK
*With a grin.*
What's the matter, Drisc? Yuh're as sore as a boil about somethin'.

DRISCOLL
I'm dyin' wid impatience to have a dhrink; an' that blarsted bumboat naygur woman took her oath she'd bring back rum enough for
the lot av us whin she came back on board tonight.

**BIG FRANK**

*Overhearing this—in a loud eager voice.*

You say the bumboat voman vill bring booze?

**DRISCOLL**

*Sarcastically.*

That's right—tell the Old Man about ut, an' the Mate, too.
*All of the crew have edged nearer to* DRISCOLL *and are listening to the conversation with an air of suppressed excitement.* DRISCOLL *lowers his voice impressively and addresses them all.*

She said she cud snake ut on board in the bottoms av thim baskets av fruit they're goin' to bring wid 'em to sell to us for'ard.

**THE DONKEYMAN**

*An old gray-headed man with a kindly, wrinkled face. He is sitting on a camp stool in front of his door, right front.*

She'll be bringin' some black women with her this time—or times has changed since I put in here last.

**DRISCOLL**

She said she wud—two or three—more, maybe, I dunno.
*This announcement is received with great enthusiasm by all hands.*

**COCKY**

Wot a bloody lark!

**OLSON**

Py yingo, we have one hell of a time!

**DRISCOLL**

*Warningly.*

Remimber ye must be quiet about ut, ye scuts—wid the dhrink, I mane—ivin if the bo'sun is ashore. The Old Man ordered her to bring no booze on board or he wudn't buy a thing off av her for the ship.

**PADDY**

*A squat, ugly Liverpool Irishman.*

To the divil wid him!

BIG FRANK
*Turning on him.*
Shud up, you tamn fool, Paddy! You vant make trouble?
*To* DRISCOLL.
You und me, ve keep dem quiet, Drisc.

DRISCOLL
Right ye are, Dutchy. I'll split the skull av the first wan av ye starts
to foight.
*Three bells are heard striking.*

DAVIS
Three bells. When's she comin', Drisc?

DRISCOLL
She'll be here any minute now, surely.
*To* PAUL, *who has returned to his position by the bulwark after hearing*
DRISCOLL's *news.*
D'you see 'em comin', Paul?

PAUL
I don't see anyting like bumboat.
*They all set themselves to wait, lighting pipes, cigarettes, and making*
*themselves comfortable. There is a silence broken only by the mournful*
*singing of the negroes on shore.*

SMITTY
*Slowly—with a trace of melancholy.*
I wish they'd stop that song. It makes you think of—well—things
you ought to forget. Rummy go, what?

COCKY
*Slapping him on the back.*
Cheero, ole love! We'll be 'avin our rum in arf a mo', Duke.
*He comes down to the deck, leaving* SMITTY *alone on the forecastle*
*head.*

BIG FRANK
Sing someting, Drisc. Den ve don't hear dot yelling.

**DAVIS**
Give us a chanty, Drisc.

**PADDY**
Wan all av us knows.

**MAX**
We all sing in on chorus.

**OLSON**
"Rio Grande," Drisc.

**BIG FRANK**
No, ve don't know dot. Sing "Viskey Johnny."

**CHIPS**
"Flyin' Cloud."

**COCKY**
Now! Guv us "Maid o' Amsterdam."

**LAMPS**
"Santa Anna" iss good one.

**DRISCOLL**
Shut your mouths, all av you.
*Scornfully.*
A chanty is ut ye want? I'll bet me whole pay day there's not wan in the crowd 'ceptin' Yank here, an' Ollie, an' meself, an' Lamps an' Cocky, maybe, wud be sailors enough to know the main from the mizzen on a windjammer. Ye've heard the names av chanties but divil a note av the tune or a loine av the words do ye know. There's hardly a rale deep-water sailor lift on the seas, more's the pity.

**YANK**
Give us "Blow The Man Down." We all know some of that.
*A chorus of assenting voices.* Yes!—Righto!—Let 'er drive! Start 'er, Drisc! *etc.*

**DRISCOLL**
Come in then, all av ye.

*He sings.*

As I was a-roamin' down Paradise Street—

ALL

Wa-a-ay, blow the man down!

DRISCOLL

As I was a-roamin' down Paradise Street—

ALL

Give us some time to blow the man down!

CHORUS

Blow the man down, boys, oh, blow the man down!

Wa-a-ay, blow the man down!

As I was a-roamin' down Paradise Street—

Give us some time to blow the man down!

DRISCOLL

A pretty young maiden I chanced for to meet.

ALL

Wa-a-ay, blow the man down!

DRISCOLL

A pretty young maiden I chanced for to meet.

ALL

Give us some time to blow the man down!

CHORUS

Blow the man down, boys, oh, blow the man down!

Wa-a-ay, blow the man down!

A pretty young maiden I chanced for to meet.

Give us some time to blow the man down!

PAUL

*Just as Driscoll is clearing his throat preparatory to starting the next verse.*
Hay, Drisc! Here she come, I tink. Some bumboat comin' dis way.
*They all rush to the side and look toward the land.*

YANK

There's five or six of them in it—and they paddle like skirts.

**DRISCOLL**
*Wildly elated.*
Hurroo, ye scuts! 'Tis thim right enough.
*He does a few jig steps on the deck.*

**OLSON**
*After a pause during which all are watching the approaching boat.*
Py yingo, I see six in boat, yes, sir.

**DAVIS**
I kin make out the baskets. See 'em there amidships?

**BIG FRANK**
Vot kind booze dey bring—viskey?

**DRISCOLL**
Rum, foine West Indy rum wid a kick in ut loike a mule's hoind leg.

**LAMPS**
Maybe she don't bring any; maybe skipper scare her.

**DRISCOLL**
Don't be throwin' cold water, Lamps. I'll skin her black hoide off av her if she goes back on her worrd.

**YANK**
Here they come. Listen to 'em gigglin'.
*Calling.*
Oh, you kiddo!
*The sound of women's voices can be heard talking and laughing.*

**DRISCOLL**
*Calling.*
Is ut you, Mrs. Old Black Joe?

**A WOMAN'S VOICE**
Ullo, Mike!
*There is loud feminine laughter at this retort.*

**DRISCOLL**
Shake a leg an' come abord thin.

THE WOMAN'S VOICE
We're a-comin'.

DRISCOLL
Come on, Yank. You an' me'd best be goin' to give 'em a hand wid their truck. 'Twill put 'em in good spirits.

COCKY
*As they start off left.*
Ho, you ain't 'arf a fox, Drisc. Down't drink it all afore we sees it.

DRISCOLL
*Over his shoulder.*
You'll be havin' yours, me sonny bye, don't fret.
*He and Yank go off left.*

COCKY
*Licking his lips.*
Gawd blimey, I can do wiv a wet.

DAVIS
Me, too!

CHIPS
I'll bet there ain't none of us'll let any go to waste.

BIG FRANK
I could trink a whole barrel mineself, py chimminy Christmas!

COCKY
I 'opes all the gels ain't as bloomin' ugly as 'er. Looked like a bloody organ-grinder's monkey, she did. Gawd, I couldn't put up wiv the likes of 'er!

PADDY
Ye'll be lucky if any of thim looks at ye, ye squint-eyed runt.

COCKY
*Angrily.*
Ho, yus? You ain't no bleedin' beauty prize yeself, me man. A 'airy ape, I calls yer.

PADDY

*Walking toward him—truculently.*

Whot's thot? Say ut again if ye dare.

COCKY

*His hand on his sheath knife—snarling.*

'Airy ape! That's wot I says!

PADDY *tries to reach him but the others keep them apart.*

BIG FRANK

*Pushing* PADDY *back.*

Vot's the matter mit you, Paddy. Don't you hear vat Driscoll say—
no fighting?

PADDY

*Grumblingly.*

I don't take no back talk from that deck-scrubbin' shrimp.

COCKY

Blarsted coal-puncher!

DRISCOLL *appears wearing a broad grin of satisfaction. The fight is
immediately forgotten by the crowd who gather around him with exclamations of eager curiosity.* How is it, Drisc? Any luck? Vot she bring,
Drisc? Where's the gels? *etc.*

DRISCOLL

*With an apprehensive glance back at the bridge.*

Not so loud, for the love av hivin!

*The clamor dies down.*

Yis, she has ut wid her. She'll be here in a minute wid a pint bottle
or two for each wan av ye—three shillin's a bottle. So don't be im-
pashunt.

COCKY

*Indignantly.*

Three bob! The bloody cow!

SMITTY

*With an ironic smile.*

Grand larceny, by God!

*They all turn and look up at him, surprised to hear him speak.*

OLSON

Py yingo, we don't pay so much.

BIG FRANK

Tamn black tief!

PADDY

We'll take ut away from her and give her nothin'.

THE CROWD

*Growling.*

Dirty thief! Dot's right! Give her nothin'! Not a bloomin' 'apenny!
*etc.*

DRISCOLL

*Grinning.*

Ye can take ut or lave ut, me sonny byes.

*He casts a glance in the direction of the bridge and then reaches inside
his shirt and pulls out a pint bottle.*

'Tis foine rum, the rale stuff.

*He drinks.*

I slipped this wan out av wan av the baskets whin they wasn't lookin'.

*He hands the bottle to* OLSON *who is nearest him.*

Here ye are, Ollie. Take a small sup an' pass ut to the nixt. 'Tisn't
much but 'twill serve to take the black taste out av your mouths if
ye go aisy wid ut. An' there's buckets more av ut comin'.

*The bottle passes from hand to hand, each man taking a sip and smack-
ing his lips with a deep "Aaah" of satisfaction.*

DAVIS

Where's she now, Drisc?

DRISCOLL

Up havin' a worrd wid the skipper, makin' arrangements about the
money, I s'pose.

DAVIS

An' where's the other gels?

DRISCOLL

Wid her. There's foive av thim she took aboard—two swate little slips av things, near as white as you an' me are, for that gray-whiskered auld fool, an' the mates—an' the engineers too, maybe. The rist av thim'll be comin' for'ard whin she comes.

COCKY

'E ain't 'arf a funny ole bird, the skipper. Gawd blimey! 'Member when we sailed from 'ome 'ow 'e stands on the bridge lookin' like a bloody ole sky pilot? An' 'is missus dawn on the bloomin' dock 'owlin' fit to kill 'erself? An' 'is kids 'owlin' an' wavin' their 'andkerchiefs?
*With great moral indignation.*
An' 'ere 'e is makin' up to a bleedin' nigger! There's a captain for yer! Gawd blimey! Bloody crab, I calls 'im!

DRISCOLL

Shut up, ye insect! Sure, it's not you should be talkin', an' you wid a woman an' childer weepin' for ye in iviry divil's port in the wide worrld, if we can believe your own tale av ut.

COCKY
*Still indignant.*
I ain't no bloomin' captain, I ain't. I ain't got no missus—reg'lar married, I means. I ain't——

BIG FRANK
*Putting a huge paw over Cocky's mouth.*
You ain't going talk so much, you hear?
COCKY *wriggles away from him.*
Say, Drisc, how ve pay dis voman for booze? Ve ain't got no cash.

DRISCOLL

It's aisy enough. Each girl'll have a slip av paper wid her an' whin you buy anythin' you write ut down and the price beside ut and sign your name. If ye can't write have some one who can do ut for ye. An' rimimber this: Whin ye buy a bottle av dhrink or
*With a wink.*

somethin' else forbid, ye must write down tobaccy or fruit or somethin' the loike av that. Whin she laves the skipper'll pay what's owin'
on the paper an' take ut out av your pay. Is ut clear to ye now?

ALL
Yes—Clear as day—Aw right, Drisc—Righto—Sure. *etc.*

DRISCOLL
An' don't forgit what I said about bein' quiet wid the dhrink, or the
Mate'll be down on our necks an' spile the fun.
*A chorus of assent.*

DAVIS
*Looking aft.*
Ain't this them comin'?
*They all look in that direction. The silly laughter of a woman is heard.*

DRISCOLL
Look at Yank, wud ye, wid his arm around the middle av wan av
thim. That lad's not wastin' any toime.
*The four women enter from the left, giggling and whispering to each
other. The first three carry baskets on their heads. The youngest and best-
looking comes last.* YANK *has his arm about her waist and is carrying her basket in his other hand. All four are distinct negro types. They
wear light-colored, loose-fitting clothes and have bright bandana hand-
kerchiefs on their heads. They put down their baskets on the hatch and
sit down beside them. The men crowd around, grinning.*

BELLA
*She is the oldest, stoutest, and homeliest of the four—grinning back at
them.*
'Ullo, boys.

THE OTHER GIRLS
'Ullo, boys.

THE MEN
Hello, yourself—Evenin'—Hello—How are you? *etc.*

BELLA

*Genially.*

Hope you had a nice voyage. My name's Bella, this here's Susie, yander's Violet, and her there

*Pointing to the girl with* YANK.

is Pearl. Now we all knows each other.

PADDY

*Roughly.*

Never mind the girls. Where's the dhrink?

BELLA

*Tartly.*

You're a hawg, ain't you? Don't talk so loud or you don't git any— you nor no man. Think I wants the ole captain to put me off the ship, do you?

YANK

Yes, nix on hollerin', you! D'yuh wanta queer all of us?

BELLA

*Casting a quick glance over her shoulder.*

Here! Some of you big strapping boys sit back of us on the hatch there so's them officers can't see what we're doin'.

DRISCOLL *and several of the others sit and stand in back of the girls on the hatch.* BELLA *turns to* DRISCOLL.

Did you tell 'em they gotter sign for what they gits—and *how* to sign?

DRISCOLL

I did—what's your name again—oh, yis—Bella, darlin'.

BELLA

Then it's all right; but you boys has gotter go inside the fo'castle when you gits your bottle. No drinkin' out here on deck. I ain't takin' no chances.

*An impatient murmur of assent goes up from the crowd.*

Ain't that right, Mike?

**DRISCOLL**
Right as rain, darlin'.
BIG FRANK *leans over and says something to him in a low voice.* DRIS-
COLL *laughs and slaps his thigh.*
Listen, Bella, I've somethin' to ask ye for my little friend here who's
bashful. Ut has to do wid the ladies so I'd best be whisperin' ut to ye
meself to kape them from blushin.
*He leans over and asks her a question.*

**BELLA**
*Firmly.*
Four shillin's.

**DRISCOLL**
*Laughing.*
D'you hear that, all av ye? Four shillin's ut is.

**PADDY**
*Angrily.*
To hell wid this talkin'. I want a dhrink.

**BELLA**
Is everything all right, Mike?

**DRISCOLL**
*After a look back at the bridge.*
Sure. Let her droive!

**BELLA**
All right, girls.
*The girls reach down in their baskets in under the fruit which is on top
and each pulls out a pint bottle. Four of the men crowd up and take the
bottles.*
Fetch a light, Lamps, that's a good boy.
LAMPS *goes to his room and returns with a candle. This is passed from
one girl to another as the men sign the sheets of paper for their bottles.*
Don't you boys forget to mark down cigarettes or tobacco or fruit,
remember! Three shillin's is the price. Take it into the fo'castle. For
Gawd's sake, don't stand out here drinkin' in the moonlight.

*The four go into the forecastle. Four more take their places.* PADDY *plants himself in front of* PEARL *who is sitting by* YANK *with his arm still around her.*

PADDY
*Gruffly.*
Gimme thot!
*She holds out a bottle which he snatches from her hand. He turns to go away.*

YANK
*Sharply.*
Here, you! Where d'yuh get that stuff? You ain't signed for that yet.

PADDY
*Sullenly.*
I can't write me name.

YANK
Then I'll write it for yuh.
*He takes the paper from* PEARL *and writes.*
There ain't goin' to be no welchin' on little Bright Eyes here—not when I'm around, see? Ain't I right, kiddo?

PEARL
*With a grin.*
Yes, suh.

BELLA
*Seeing all four are served.*
Take it into the fo'castle, boys.
PADDY *defiantly raises his bottle and gulps down a drink in the full moonlight.* BELLA *sees him.*
Look at 'im! Look at the dirty swine!
PADDY *slouches into the forecastle.*
Wants to git me in trouble. That settles it! We all got to git inside, boys, where we won't git caught. Come on, girls.
*The girls pick up their baskets and follow* BELLA. YANK *and* PEARL *are the last to reach the doorway. She lingers behind him, her eyes fixed on*

SMITTY, *who is still sitting on the forecastle head, his chin on his hands, staring off into vacancy.*

PEARL
*Waving a hand to attract his attention.*
Come ahn in, pretty boy. Ah likes you.

SMITTY
*Coldly.*
Yes; I want to buy a bottle, please.
*He goes down the steps and follows her into the forecastle. No one remains on deck but the* DONKEYMAN, *who sits smoking his pipe in front of his door. There is the subdued babble of voices from the crowd inside but the mournful cadence of the song from the shore can again be faintly heard.* SMITTY *reappears and closes the door to the forecastle after him. He shudders and shakes his shoulders as if flinging off something which disgusted him. Then he lifts the bottle which is in his hand to his lips and gulps down a long drink.* THE DONKEYMAN *watches him impassively.* SMITTY *sits down on the hatch facing him. Now that the closed door has shut off nearly all the noise the singing from shore comes clearly over the moonlit water.*

SMITTY
*Listening to it for a moment.*
Damn that song of theirs.
*He takes another big drink.*
What do you say, Donk?

THE DONKEYMAN
*Quietly.*
Seems nice an' sleepy-like.

SMITTY
*With a hard laugh.*
Sleepy! If I listened to it long—sober—I'd never go to sleep.

THE DONKEYMAN
'Tain't sich bad music, is it? Sounds kinder pretty to me—low an' mournful—same as listenin' to the organ outside o' church of a Sunday.

SMITTY

*With a touch of impatience.*

I didn't mean it was bad music. It isn't. It's the beastly memories the
damn thing brings up—for some reason.

*He takes another pull at the bottle.*

THE DONKEYMAN

Ever hear it before?

SMITTY

No; never in my life. It's just a something about the rotten thing
which makes me think of—well—oh, the devil!

*He forces a laugh.*

THE DONKEYMAN

*Spitting placidly.*

Queer things, mem'ries. I ain't ever been bothered much by 'em.

SMITTY

*Looking at him fixedly for a moment—with quiet scorn.*

No, you wouldn't be.

THE DONKEYMAN

Not that I ain't had my share o' things goin' wrong; but I puts 'em
out o' me mind, like, an' fergets 'em.

SMITTY

But suppose you couldn't put them out of your mind? Suppose they
haunted you when you were awake and when you were asleep—what
then?

THE DONKEYMAN

*Quietly.*

I'd git drunk, same's you're doin'.

SMITTY

*With a harsh laugh.*

Good advice.

*He takes another drink. He is beginning to show the effects of the liquor.
His face is flushed and he talks rather wildly.*

We're poor little lambs who have lost our way, eh, Donk? Damned from here to eternity, what? God have mercy on such as we! True, isn't it, Donk?

THE DONKEYMAN
Maybe; I dunno.
*After a slight pause.*
Whatever set you goin' to sea? You ain't made for it.

SMITTY
*Laughing wildly.*
My old friend in the bottle here, Donk.

THE DONKEYMAN
I done my share o' drinkin' in my time.
*Regretfully.*
Them was good times, those days. Can't hold up under drink no more. Doctor told me I'd got to stop or die.
*He spits contentedly.*
So I stops.

SMITTY
*With a foolish smile.*
Then I'll drink one for you. Here's your health, old top!
*He drinks.*

THE DONKEYMAN
*After a pause.*
S'pose there's a gel mixed up in it someplace, ain't there?

SMITTY
*Stiffly.*
What makes you think so?

THE DONKEYMAN
Always is when a man lets music bother 'im.
*After a few puffs at his pipe.*
An' she said she threw you over 'cause you was drunk; an' you said you was drunk 'cause she threw you over.
*He spits leisurely.*
Queer thing, love, ain't it?

SMITTY

*Rising to his feet with drunken dignity.*

I'll trouble you not to pry into my affairs, Donkeyman.

THE DONKEYMAN

*Unmoved.*

That's everybody's affair, what I said. I been through it many's the time.

*Genially.*

I always hit 'em a whack on the ear an' went out and got drunker'n ever. When I come home again they always had somethin' special nice cooked fur me to eat.

*Puffing at his pipe.*

That's the on'y way to fix 'em when they gits on their high horse. I don't s'pose you ever tried that?

SMITTY

*Pompously.*

Gentlemen don't hit women.

THE DONKEYMAN

*Placidly.*

No; that's why they has mem'ries when they hears music.

SMITTY *does not deign to reply to this but sinks into a scornful silence.* DAVIS *and the girl* VIOLET *come out of the forecastle and close the door behind them. He is staggering a bit and she is laughing shrilly.*

DAVIS

*Turning to the left.*

This way, Rose, or Pansy, or Jessamine, or black Tulip, or Violet, or whatever the hell flower your name is. No one'll see us back here.

*They go off left.*

THE DONKEYMAN

There's love at first sight for you—an' plenty more o' the same in the fo'c's'tle. No mem'ries jined with that.

SMITTY

*Really repelled.*

Shut up, Donk. You're disgusting.

*He takes a long drink.*

THE DONKEYMAN
*Philosophically.*
All depends on how you was brung up, I s'pose.
PEARL *comes out of the forecastle. There is a roar of voices from inside. She shuts the door behind her, sees* SMITTY *on the hatch, and comes over and sits beside him and puts her arm over his shoulder.*

THE DONKEYMAN
*Chuckling.*
There's love for you, Duke.

PEARL
*Patting* SMITTY'S *face with her hand.*
'Ullo, pretty boy.
SMITTY *pushes her hand away coldly.*
What you doin' out here all alone by yourself?

SMITTY
*With a twisted grin.*
Thinking and,—
*He indicates the bottle in his hand.*
—drinking to stop thinking.
*He drinks and laughs maudlinly. The bottle is three-quarters empty.*

PEARL
You oughtn't drink so much, pretty boy. Don' you know dat? You have big, big headache come mawnin'.

SMITTY
*Dryly.*
Indeed?

PEARL
That's true. Ah knows what Ah say.
*Cooingly.*
Why you run 'way from me, pretty boy? Ah likes you. Ah don' like them other fellahs. They act too rough. You ain't rough. You're a genelman. Ah knows. Ah can tell a genelman fahs Ah can see 'im.

SMITTY

Thank you for the compliment; but you're wrong, you see. I'm merely—a ranker.

*He adds bitterly.*

And a rotter.

PEARL

*Patting his arm.*

No, you ain't. Ah knows better. You're a genelman.

*Insinuatingly.*

Ah wouldn't have nothin' to do with them other men, but

*She smiles at him enticingly.*

you is diff'rent.

*He pushes her away from him disgustedly. She pouts.*

Don' you like me, pretty boy?

SMITTY

*A bit ashamed.*

I beg your pardon. I didn't mean to be rude, you know, really.

*His politeness is drunkenly exaggerated.*

I'm a bit off color.

PEARL

*Brightening up.*

Den you do like me—little ways?

SMITTY

*Carelessly.*

Yes, yes, why shouldn't I?

*He suddenly laughs wildly and puts his arm around her waist and presses her to him.*

Why not?

*He pulls his arm back quickly with a shudder of disgust, and takes a drink.* PEARL *looks at him curiously, puzzled by his strange actions. The door from the forecastle is kicked open and* YANK *comes out. The uproar of shouting, laughing and singing voices has increased in violence.* YANK *staggers over toward* SMITTY *and* PEARL.

YANK

*Blinking at them.*

What the hell—oh, it's you, Smitty the Duke. I was goin' to turn one loose on the jaw of any guy'd cop my dame, but seein' it's you—

*Sentimentally.*

Pals is pals and any pal of mine c'n have anythin' I got, see?

*Holding out his hand.*

Shake, Duke.

SMITTY *takes his hand and he pumps it up and down.*

You'n me's frens. Ain't I right?


SMITTY

Right it is, Yank. But you're wrong about this girl. She isn't with me. She was just going back to the fo'c's'tle to you.

PEARL *looks at him with hatred gathering in her eyes.*


YANK

Tha' right?


SMITTY

On my word!


YANK

*Grabbing her arm.*

Come on then, you, Pearl! Le's have a drink with the bunch.

*He pulls her to the entrance where she shakes off his hand long enough to turn on* SMITTY *furiously.*


PEARL

You swine! You can go to hell!

*She goes in the forecastle, slamming the door.*


THE DONKEYMAN

*Spitting calmly.*

There's love for you. They're all the same—white, brown, yeller 'n' black. A whack on the ear's the only thing'll learn 'em.

SMITTY *makes no reply but laughs harshly and takes another drink; then sits staring before him, the almost empty bottle tightly clutched in one hand. There is an increase in volume of the muffled clamor from the forecastle and a moment later the door is thrown open and the whole mob, led by Driscoll, pours out on deck. All of them are very drunk and several of them carry bottles in their hands.* BELLA *is the only one of the women who is absolutely sober. She tries in vain to keep the men quiet.* PEARL *drinks from* YANK's *bottle every moment or so, laughing shrilly, and leaning against* YANK, *whose arm is about her waist.* PAUL *comes out last carrying an accordion. He staggers over and stands on top of the hatch, his instrument under his arm.*

DRISCOLL
Play us a dance, ye square-head swab!—a rale, Godforsaken son av a turkey trot wid guts to ut.

YANK
Straight from the old Barbary Coast in Frisco!

PAUL
I don' know. I try.
*He commences tuning up.*

YANK
Ataboy! Let 'er rip!
DAVIS *and* VIOLET *come back and join the crowd.* THE DONKEY-MAN *looks on them all with a detached, indulgent air.* SMITTY *stares before him and does not seem to know there is any one on deck but himself.*

BIG FRANK
Dance? I don't dance. I trink!
*He suits the action to the word and roars with meaningless laughter.*

DRISCOLL
Git out av the way thin, ye big hulk, an' give us some room.
BIG FRANK *sits down on the hatch, right. All of the others who are not going to dance either follow his example or lean against the port bulwark.*

BELLA
*On the verge of tears at her inability to keep them in the forecastle or make them be quiet now they are out.*
For Gawd's sake, boys, don't shout so loud! Want to git me in trouble?

DRISCOLL

*Grabbing her.*

Dance wid me, me cannibal quane.

*Someone drops a bottle on deck and it smashes.*

BELLA

*Hysterically.*

There they goes! There they goes! Captain'll hear that! Oh, my
Lawd!

DRISCOLL

Be damned to him! Here's the music! Off ye go!

PAUL *starts playing "You Great Big Beautiful Doll" with a note left
out every now and then. The four couples commence dancing—a jerk-
shouldered version of the old Turkey Trot as it was done in the sailor-
town dives, made more grotesque by the fact that all the couples are
drunk and keep lurching into each other every moment. Two of the men
start dancing together, intentionally bumping into the others.* YANK
*and* PEARL *come around in front of* SMITTY *and, as they pass him,*
PEARL *slaps him across the side of the face with all her might, and laughs
viciously. He jumps to his feet with his fists clenched but sees who hit him
and sits down again smiling bitterly.* YANK *laughs boisterously.*

YANK

Wow! Some wallop! One on you, Duke.

DRISCOLL

*Hurling his cap at* PAUL.

Faster, ye toad!

PAUL *makes frantic efforts to speed up and the music suffers in the process.*

BELLA

*Puffing.*

Let me go. I'm wore out with you steppin' on my toes, you clumsy
Mick.

*She struggles but Driscoll holds her tight.*

DRISCOLL

God blarst you for havin' such big feet, thin. Aisy, aisy, Mrs. Old Black Joe! 'Tis dancin'll take the blubber off ye.

*He whirls her around the deck by main force.* COCKY, *with* SUSIE, *is dancing near the hatch, right, when* PADDY, *who is sitting on the edge with* BIG FRANK, *sticks his foot out and the wavering couple stumble over it and fall flat on the deck. A roar of laughter goes up.* COCKY *rises to his feet, his face livid with rage, and springs at* PADDY, *who promptly knocks him down.* DRISCOLL *hits* PADDY *and* BIG FRANK *hits* DRISCOLL. *In a flash a wholesale fight has broken out and the deck is a surging crowd of drink-maddened men hitting out at each other indiscriminately, although the general idea seems to be a battle between seamen and firemen. The women shriek and take refuge on top of the hatch, where they huddle in a frightened group. Finally there is the flash of a knife held high in the moonlight and a loud yell of pain.*

DAVIS

*Somewhere in the crowd.*

Here's the Mate comin'! Let's git out o' this!

*There is a general rush for the forecastle. In a moment there is no one left on deck but the little group of women on the hatch;* SMITTY, *still dazedly rubbing his cheek;* THE DONKEYMAN *quietly smoking on his stool; and* YANK *and* DRISCOLL, *their faces battered up considerably, their undershirts in shreds, bending over the still form of* PADDY, *which lies stretched out on the deck between them. In the silence the mournful chant from the shore creeps slowly out to the ship.*

DRISCOLL

*Quickly—in a low voice.*

Who knoifed him?

YANK

*Stupidly.*

I didn't see it. How do I know? Cocky, I'll bet.

*The* FIRST MATE *enters from the left. He is a tall, strongly-built man.*

THE MATE

*Angrily.*

What's all this noise about?

*He sees the man lying on the deck dressed in a plain blue uniform.*
Hello! What's this?
*He bends down on one knee beside* PADDY.

DRISCOLL
*Stammering.*
All av us—was in a bit av a harmless foight, sir,—an'—I dunno—
*The* MATE *rolls* PADDY *over and sees a knife wound on his shoulder.*

THE MATE
Knifed, by God.
*He takes an electric flash from his pocket and examines the cut.*
Lucky it's only a flesh wound. He must have hit his head on deck
when he fell. That's what knocked him out. This is only a scratch.
Take him aft and I'll bandage him up.

DRISCOLL
Yis, sor.
*They take* PADDY *by the shoulders and feet and carry him off left. The*
MATE *looks up and sees the women on the hatch for the first time.*

THE MATE
*Surprised.*
Hello!
*He walks over to them.*
Go to the cabin and get your money and clear off. If I had my way,
you'd never——
*His foot hits a bottle. He stoops down and picks it up and smells of it.*
Rum, by God! So that's the trouble! I thought their breaths smelled
damn queer.
*To the women, harshly.*
You needn't go to the skipper for any money. You won't get any.
That'll teach you to smuggle rum on a ship and start a riot.

BELLA
But, Mister——

THE MATE
*Sternly.*
You know the agreement—rum—no money.

**BELLA**
*Indignantly.*
Honest to Gawd, Mister, I never brung no——

**THE MATE**
*Fiercely.*
You're a liar! And none of your lip or I'll make a complaint ashore tomorrow and have you locked up.

**BELLA**
*Subdued.*
Please, Mister—

**THE MATE**
Clear out of this, now! Not another word out of you! Tumble over the side damn quick! The two others are waiting for you. Hop, now! *They walk quickly—almost run—off to the left.* THE MATE *follows them, nodding to* THE DONKEYMAN, *and ignoring the oblivious* SMITTY.

*There is absolute silence on the ship for a few moments. The melancholy song of the negroes drifts crooning over the water.* SMITTY *listens to it intently for a time; then sighs heavily, a sigh that is half a sob.*

**SMITTY**
God!
*He drinks the last drop in the bottle and throws it behind him on the hatch.*

**THE DONKEYMAN**
*Spitting tranquilly.*
More mem'ries?
SMITTY *does not answer him. The ship's bell tolls four bells.* THE DONKEYMAN *knocks out his pipe.*
I think I'll turn in.
*He opens the door to his cabin, but turns to look at* SMITTY—*kindly.*
You can't hear it in the fo'c's'tle—the music, I mean—an' there'll likely be more drink in there, too. Good night.
*He goes in and shuts the door.*

SMITTY

Good night, Donk.

*He gets wearily to his feet and walks with bowed shoulders, staggering a bit, to the forecastle entrance and goes in. There is silence for a second or so, broken only by the haunted, saddened voice of that brooding music, faint and far-off, like the mood of the moonlight made audible.*

THE CURTAIN FALLS

*In the Zone*
A Play in One Act

# Characters

SMITTY

DAVIS

SWANSON

SCOTTY

IVAN          } *Seamen on the British Tramp Steamer* Glencairn

PAUL

JACK

DRISCOLL

COCKY

# In the Zone

*The seamen's forecastle. On the right above the bunks three or four port-holes covered with black cloth can be seen. On the floor near the doorway is a pail with a tin dipper. A lantern in the middle of the floor, turned down very low, throws a dim light around the place. Five men,* SCOTTY, IVAN, SWANSON, SMITTY *and* PAUL, *are in their bunks apparently asleep. It is about ten minutes of twelve on a night in the fall of the year 1915.*

SMITTY *turns slowly in his bunk and, leaning out over the side, looks from one to another of the men as if to assure himself that they are asleep. Then he climbs carefully out of his bunk and stands in the middle of the forecastle fully dressed, but in his stocking feet, glancing around him suspiciously. Reassured, he leans down and cautiously pulls out a suit-case from under the bunks in front of him.*

*Just at this moment* DAVIS *appears in the doorway, carrying a large steaming coffee-pot in his hand. He stops short when he sees* SMITTY. *A puzzled expression comes over his face, followed by one of suspicion, and he retreats farther back in the alleyway, where he can watch* SMITTY *without being seen.*

*All the latter's movements indicate a fear of discovery. He takes out a small bunch of keys and unlocks the suit-case, making a slight noise as he does so.* SCOTTY *wakes up and peers at him over the side of the bunk.* SMITTY *opens the suit-case and takes out a small black tin box, carefully places this under his mattress, shoves the suit-case back under the bunk, climbs into his bunk again, closes his eyes and begins to snore loudly.*

DAVIS *enters the forecastle, places the coffee-pot beside the lantern, and goes from one to the other of the sleepers and shakes them vigorously, saying to each in a low voice:* Near eight bells, Scotty. Arise and shine, Swanson. Eight bells, Ivan. SMITTY *yawns loudly with a great pretense of having been dead asleep. All of the rest of the men tumble out of their bunks, stretching and gaping, and commence to pull on their shoes. They go one by one to the cupboard near the open door, take out their cups and spoons, and sit down together on the benches. The coffee-pot is passed around. They munch their biscuits and sip their coffee in dull silence.*

DAVIS
*Suddenly jumping to his feet—nervously.*
Where's that air comin' from?
*All are startled and look at him wonderingly.*

SWANSON
*A squat, surly-faced Swede—grumpily.*
What air? I don't feel nothing.

DAVIS
*Excitedly.*
I kin feel it—a draft.
*He stands on the bench and looks around—suddenly exploding.*
Damn fool square-head!
*He leans over the upper bunk in which* PAUL *is sleeping and slams the porthole shut.*
I got a good notion to report him. Serve him bloody well right! What's the use o' blindin' the ports when that thickhead goes an' leaves 'em open?

SWANSON
*Yawning—too sleepy to be aroused by anything—carelessly.*
Dey don't see what little light go out yust one port.

SCOTTY
*Protestingly.*
Dinna be a loon, Swanson! D'ye no ken the dangerr o' showin' a licht wi' a pack o' submarines lyin' aboot?

IVAN

*Shaking his shaggy ox-like head in an emphatic affirmative.*
Dot's right, Scotty. I don' li-ike blow up, no, by devil!

SMITTY

*His manner slightly contemptuous.*
I don't think there's much danger of meeting any of their submarines, not until we get into the War Zone, at any rate.

DAVIS

*He and* SCOTTY *look at* SMITTY *suspiciously—harshly.*
You don't, eh?
*He lowers his voice and speaks slowly.*
Well, we're in the war zone right this minit if you wants to know.
*The effect of this speech is instantaneous. All sit bolt upright on their
benches and stare at Davis.*

SMITTY

How do you know, Davis?

DAVIS

*Angrily.*
'Cos Drisc heard the First send the Third below to wake the skipper
when we fetched the zone—bout five bells, it was. Now whata y' got
to say?

SMITTY

*Conciliatingly.*
Oh, I wasn't doubting your word, Davis; but you know they're not
pasting up bulletins to let the crew know when the zone is reached—
especially on ammunition ships like this.

IVAN

*Decidedly.*
I don't li-ike dees voyage. Next time I ship on windjammer Boston
to River Plate, load with wood only so it float, by golly!

SWANSON

*Fretfully.*
I hope British navy blow 'em to hell, those submarines, py damn!

SCOTTY

*Looking at* SMITTY, *who is staring at the doorway in a dream, his chin on his hands. Meaningly.*

It is no the submarrines only we've to fear, I'm thinkin'.

DAVIS

*Assenting eagerly.*

That's no lie, Scotty.

SWANSON

You mean the mines?

SCOTTY

I wasna thinkin' o' mines eitherr.

DAVIS

There's many a good ship blown up and at the bottom of the sea, what never hit no mine or torpedo.

SCOTTY

Did ye neverr read of the German spies and the dirrty work they're doin' all the war?

*He and* DAVIS *both glance at* SMITTY, *who is deep in thought and is not listening to the conversation.*

DAVIS

An' the clever way they fool you!

SWANSON

Sure; I read it in paper many time.

DAVIS

Well—

*He is about to speak but hesitates and finishes lamely.*

you got to watch out, that's all I says.

IVAN

*Drinking the last of his coffee and slamming his fist on the bench explosively.*

I tell you dis rotten coffee give me belly-ache, yes!

*They all look at him in amused disgust.*

Barnes & Noble Booksellers #2252
Bascom Avenue Ste 240
Campbell, CA 95008
408 559 8101

CO TRAV6295 CSHR JOSE M

MEMBER EXP 08/31/2009

Subtotal                                    35
Sales Tax (9                                36
TOTAL                                    15.71
MASTERCARD                               15.71
        #: XXXXXXXXXXXXX1087
        XX/XX
        92342
    Entry Method: Swiped

MEMBER SAVINGS                            1.50

            Thanks for shopping at
               Barnes & Noble

V101.18                  05/11/2009  03:32PM

        CUSTOMER COPY

With a sales receipt, a full refund in the original form of payment will be issued from any Barnes & Noble store for returns of new and unread books (except textbooks) and unopened music/DVDs/audio made within (i) 14 days of purchase from a Barnes & Noble retail store (except for purchases made by check less than 7 days prior to the date of return) or (ii) 14 days of delivery date for Barnes & Noble.com purchases (except for purchases made via PayPal). A store credit for the purchase price will be issued for (i) purchases made by check less than 7 days prior to the date of return, (ii) when a gift receipt is presented within 60 days of purchase, (iii) textbooks returned with a receipt within 14 days of purchase, or (iv) original purchase was made through Barnes & Noble.com via PayPal. Opened music/DVDs/audio may not be returned, but can be exchanged only for the same title if defective.

After 14 days or without a sales receipt, returns or exchanges will not be permitted.

Magazines, newspapers, and used books are not returnable. *Product not carried by Barnes & Noble or Barnes & Noble.com will not be accepted for return.*

*Policy on receipt may appear in two sections.*

### Return Policy

With a sales receipt, a full refund in the original form of payment will be issued from any Barnes & Noble store for returns of new and unread books (except textbooks) and unopened music/DVDs/audio made within (i) 14 days of purchase from a Barnes & Noble retail store (except for purchases made by check less than 7 days prior to the date of return) or (ii) 14 days of delivery date for Barnes & Noble.com purchases (except for purchases made via PayPal). A store credit for the purchase price will be issued for (i) purchases made by check less than 7 days prior to the date of return, (ii) when a gift receipt is presented within 60 days of purchase, (iii) textbooks returned with a receipt within 14 days of purchase, or (iv) original purchase was made through Barnes & Noble.com via PayPal. Opened music/DVDs/audio may not be returned, but can be exchanged only for the same title if defective.

After 14 days or without a sales receipt, returns or exchanges will not be permitted.

SCOTTY
*Sardonically.*
Dinna fret about it, Ivan. If we blow up ye'll no be mindin' the pain in your middle.
JACK *enters. He is a young American with a tough, good-natured face. He wears dungarees and a heavy jersey.*

JACK
Eight bells, fellers.

IVAN
*Stupidly.*
I don' hear bell ring.

JACK
No, and yuh won't hear any ring, yuh boob—
*Lowering his voice unconsciously.*
now we're in the war zone.

SWANSON
*Anxiously.*
Is the boats all ready?

JACK
Sure; we can lower 'em in a second.

DAVIS
A lot o' good the boats'll do, with us loaded deep with all kinds o' dynamite and stuff the like o' that! If a torpedo hits this hooker we'll all be in hell b'fore you could wink your eye.

JACK
They ain't goin' to hit us, see? That's my dope. Whose wheel is it?

IVAN
*Sullenly.*
My wheel.
*He lumbers out.*

JACK
And whose lookout?

SWANSON
Mine, I tink.
*He follows* IVAN.

JACK
*Scornfully.*
A hell of a lot of use keepin' a lookout! We couldn't run away or fight
if we wanted to.
*To* SCOTTY *and* SMITTY.
Better look up the bo'sun or the Fourth, you two, and let 'em see
you're awake.
SCOTTY *goes to the doorway and turns to wait for* SMITTY, *who is
still in the same position, head on hands, seemingly unconscious of every-
thing.* JACK *slaps him roughly on the shoulder and he comes to with a
start.*
Aft and report, Duke! What's the matter with yuh—in a dope
dream?
SMITTY *goes out after* SCOTTY *without answering.* JACK *looks after
him with a frown.*
He's a queer guy. I can't figger him out.

DAVIS
Nor no one else.
*Lowering his voice—meaningly.*
An' he's liable to turn out queerer than any of us think if we ain't
careful.

JACK
*Suspiciously.*
What d'yuh mean?
*They are interrupted by the entrance of* DRISCOLL *and* COCKY.

COCKY
*Protestingly.*
Blimey if I don't fink I'll put in this 'ere watch ahtside on deck.
*He and* DRISCOLL *go over and get their cups.*
I down't want to be caught in this 'ole if they 'its us.
*He pours out coffee.*

DRISCOLL
*Pouring his.*
Divil a bit ut wud matther where ye arre. Ye'd be blown to smither-
eens b'fore ye cud say your name.
*He sits down, overturning as he does so the untouched cup of coffee which*
SMITTY *had forgotten and left on the bench. They all jump nervously*
*as the tin cup hits the floor with a bang.* DRISCOLL *flies into an un-*
*reasoning rage.*
Who's the dirty scut left this cup where a man 'ud sit on ut?

DAVIS
It's Smitty's.

DRISCOLL
*Kicking the cup across the forecastle.*
Does he think he's too much av a bloody gentleman to put his own
away loike the rist av us? If he does I'm the bye'll beat that noshun
out av his head.

COCKY
Be the airs 'e puts on you'd think 'e was the Prince of Wales. Wot's
'e doin' on a ship, I arsks yer? 'E ain't now good as a sailor, is 'e?—
dawdlin' abaht on deck like a chicken wiv 'is 'ead cut orf!

JACK
*Good-naturedly.*
Aw, the Duke's all right. S'posin' he did ferget his cup—what's the
dif?
*He picks up the cup and puts it away—with a grin.*
This war zone stuff's got yer goat, Drisc—and yours too, Cocky—
and I ain't cheerin' much fur it myself, neither.

COCKY
*With a sigh.*
Blimey, it ain't no bleedin' joke, yer first trip, to know as there's a
ship full of shells li'ble to go orf in under your bloomin' feet, as you
might say, if we gets 'it be a torpedo or mine.
*With sudden savagery.*
Calls theyselves 'uman bein's, too! Blarsted 'Uns!

DRISCOLL

*Gloomily.*

'Tis me last trip in the bloody zone, God help me. The divil take their twenty-foive percent bonus—and be drowned like a rat in a trap in the bargain, maybe.

DAVIS

Wouldn't be so bad if she wasn't carryin' ammunition. Them's the kind the subs is layin' for.

DRISCOLL

*Irritably.*

Fur the love av hivin, don't be talkin' about ut. I'm sick wid thinkin' and jumpin' at iviry bit av a noise.

*There is a pause during which they all stare gloomily at the floor.*

JACK

Hey, Davis, what was you sayin' about Smitty when they come in?

DAVIS

*With a great air of mystery.*

I'll tell you in a minit. I want to wait an' see if he's comin' back.

*Impressively.*

You won't be callin' him all right when you hears what I seen with my own eyes.

*He adds with an air of satisfaction.*

An' you won't be feelin' no safer, neither.

*They all look at him with puzzled glances full of a vague apprehension.*

DRISCOLL

God blarst ut!

*He fills his pipe and lights it. The others, with an air of remembering something they had forgotten, do the same.* SCOTTY *enters.*

SCOTTY

*In awed tones.*

Mon, but it's clear outside the nicht! Like day.

**DAVIS**
*In low tones.*
Where's Smitty, Scotty?

**SCOTTY**
Out on the hatch starin' at the moon like a mon half-daft.

**DAVIS**
Kin you see him from the doorway?

**SCOTTY**
*Goes to doorway and carefully peeks out.*
Aye; he's still there.

**DAVIS**
Keep your eyes on him for a moment. I've got something I wants to tell the boys and I don't want him walkin' in in the middle of it. Give a shout if he starts this way.

**SCOTTY**
*With suppressed excitement.*
Aye, I'll watch him. And I've somethin' myself to tell aboot his Lordship.

**DRISCOLL**
*Impatiently.*
Out wid ut! You're talkin' more than a pair av auld women wud be standin' in the road, and gittin' no further along.

**DAVIS**
Listen! You 'member when I went to git the coffee, Jack?

**JACK**
Sure, I do.

**DAVIS**
Well, I brings it down here same as usual and got as far as the door there when I sees him.

**JACK**
Smitty?

DAVIS

Yes, Smitty! He was standin' in the middle of the fo'c's'tle there
*Pointing.*
lookin' around sneakin'-like at Ivan and Swanson and the rest 's if
he wants to make certain they're asleep.
*He pauses significantly, looking from one to the other of his listeners.*
SCOTTY *is nervously dividing his attention between* SMITTY *on the
hatch outside and* DAVIS' *story, fairly bursting to break in with his own
revelations.*

JACK
*Impatiently.*
What of it?

DAVIS

Listen! He was standin' right there —
*Pointing again.*
in his stockin' feet — no shoes on, mind, so he wouldn't make no
noise!

JACK
*Spitting disgustedly.*
Aw!

DAVIS
*Not heeding the interruption.*
I seen right away somethin' on the queer was up so I slides back into
the alleyway where I kin see him but he can't see me. After he makes
sure they're all asleep he goes in under the bunks there — bein' careful not to raise a noise, mind! — an' takes out his bag there.
*By this time every one,* JACK *included, is listening breathlessly to his
story.*
Then he fishes in his pocket an' takes out a bunch o' keys an' kneels
down beside the bag an' opens it.

SCOTTY
*Unable to keep silent longer.*
Mon, didn't I see him do that same thing wi' these two eyes. 'Twas
just that moment I woke and spied him.

DAVIS

*Surprised, and a bit nettled to have to share his story with any one.*

Oh, you seen him, too, eh?

*To the others.*

Then Scotty kin tell you if I'm lyin' or not.

DRISCOLL

An' what did he do whin he'd the bag opened?

DAVIS

He bends down and reaches out his hand sort o' scared-like, like it was somethin' dang'rous he was after, an' feels round in under his duds—hidden in under his duds an' wrapped up in 'em, it was—an' he brings out a black iron box!

COCKY

*Looking around him with a frightened glance.*

Gawd blimey!

*The others likewise betray their uneasiness, shuffling their feet nervously.*

DAVIS

Ain't that right, Scotty?

SCOTTY

Right as rain, I'm tellin' ye'!

DAVIS

*To the others with an air of satisfaction.*

There you are!

*Lowering his voice.*

An' then what d'you suppose he did? Sneaks to his bunk an' slips the black box in under his mattress—in under his mattress, mind!—

JACK

And it's there now?

DAVIS

Course it is!

JACK *starts toward* SMITTY's *bunk.* DRISCOLL *grabs him by the arm.*

DRISCOLL

Don't be touchin' ut, Jack!

JACK

Yuh needn't worry. I ain't goin' to touch it.

*He pulls up* SMITTY'S *mattress and looks down. The others stare at him, holding their breaths. He turns to them, trying hard to assume a careless tone.*

It's there, aw right.

COCKY

*Miserably upset.*

I'm gointer 'op it aht on deck.

*He gets up but* DRISCOLL *pulls him down again.* COCKY *protests.*

It fair guvs me the trembles sittin' still in 'ere.

DRISCOLL

*Scornfully.*

Are ye frightened, ye toad? 'Tis a hell av a thing fur grown men to be shiverin' loike childer at a bit av a black box.

*Scratching his head in uneasy perplexity.*

Still, ut's damn queer, the looks av ut.

DAVIS

*Sarcastically.*

A bit of a black box, eh? How big d'you think them—

*He hesitates.*

—things has to be—big as this fo'c's'tle?

JACK

*In a voice meant to be reassuring.*

Aw, hell! I'll bet it ain't nothin' but some coin he's saved he's got locked up in there.

DAVIS

*Scornfully.*

That's likely, ain't it? Then why does he act so s'picious? He's been on ship near two year, ain't he? He knows damn well there ain't no thiefs in this fo'c's'tle, don't he? An' you know 's well 's I do he didn't have no money when he came on board an' he ain't saved none since. Don't you?

JACK *doesn't answer.*

Listen! D'you know what he done after he put that thing in under his mattress?—an' Scotty'll tell you if I ain't speakin' truth. He looks round to see if any one's woke up—

SCOTTY

I clapped my eyes shut when he turned round.

DAVIS

An' then he crawls into his bunk an' shuts his eyes, an' starts in *snorin', pretendin'* he was asleep; mind!

SCOTTY

Aye, I could hear him.

DAVIS

An' when I goes to call him I don't even shake him. I just says, "Eight bells, Smitty," in a'most a whisper-like, an' up he gets yawnin' an' stretchin' fit to kill hisself 's if he'd been dead asleep.

COCKY

Gawd blimey!

DRISCOLL

*Shaking his head.*

Ut looks bad, divil a doubt av ut.

DAVIS

*Excitedly.*

An' now I come to think of it, there's the porthole. How'd it come to git open, tell me that? I know'd well Paul never opened it. Ain't he grumblin' about bein' cold all the time?

SCOTTY

The mon that opened it meant no good to this ship, whoever he was.

JACK

*Sourly.*

What porthole? What're yuh talkin' about?

**DAVIS**

*Pointing over* PAUL's *bunk.*

There. It was open when I come in. I felt the cold air on my neck an' shut it. It would'a been clear's a lighthouse to any sub that was watchin'—an' we s'posed to have all the ports blinded! Who'd do a dirty trick like that? It wasn't none of us, nor Scotty here, nor Swanson, nor Ivan. Who would it be, then?

**COCKY**

*Angrily.*

Must'a been 'is bloody Lordship.

**DAVIS**

For all's we know he might'a been signallin' with it. They does it like that by winkin' a light. Ain't you read how they gets caught doin' it in London an' on the coast?

**COCKY**

*Firmly convinced now.*

An' wots 'e doin' aht alone on the 'atch—keepin' 'isself clear of us like 'e was afraid?

**DRISCOLL**

Kape your eye on him, Scotty.

**SCOTTY**

There's no a move oot o' him.

**JACK**

*In irritated perplexity.*

But, hell, ain't he an Englishman? What'd he wanta—

**DAVIS**

English? How d'we know he's English? Cos he talks it? That ain't no proof. Ain't you read in the papers how all them German spies they been catchin' in England has been livin' there for ten, often as not twenty years, an' talks English as good's any one? An' look here, ain't you noticed he don't talk natural? He talks it too damn good, that's what I mean. He don't talk exactly like a toff, does he, Cocky?

**COCKY**

Not like any toff as I ever met up wiv.

**DAVIS**

No; an' he don't talk it like us, that's certain. An' he don't look English. An' what d'we know about him when you come to look at it? Nothin'! He ain't ever said where he comes from or why. All we knows is he ships on here in London 'bout a year b'fore the war starts, as an A. B.—stole his papers most lik'ly—when he don't know how to box the compass, hardly. Ain't that queer in itself? An' was he ever open with us like a good shipmate? No; he's always had that sly air about him 's if he was hidin' somethin'.

**DRISCOLL**

*Slapping his thigh—angrily.*

Divil take me if I don't think ye have the truth av ut, Davis.

**COCKY**

*Scornfully.*

Lettin' on be 'is silly airs, and all, 'e's the son of a blarsted earl or somethink!

**DAVIS**

An' the name he calls hisself—Smith! I'd risk a quid of my next pay day that his real name is Schmidt, if the truth was known.

**JACK**

*Evidently fighting against his own conviction.*

Aw, say, you guys give me a pain! What'd they want puttin' a spy on this old tub for?

**DAVIS**

*Shaking his head sagely.*

They're deep ones, an' there's a lot o' things a sailor'll see in the ports he puts in ought to be useful to 'em. An' if he kin signal to 'em an' they blows us up it's one ship less, ain't it?

*Lowering his voice and indicating* SMITTY's *bunk.*

Or if he blows us up hisself.

SCOTTY

*In alarmed tones.*

Hush, mon! Here he comes!

SCOTTY *hurries over to a bench and sits down. A thick silence settles over the forecastle. The men look from one to another with uneasy glances.* SMITTY *enters and sits down beside his bunk. He is seemingly unaware of the dark glances of suspicion directed at him from all sides. He slides his hand back stealthily over his mattress and his fingers move, evidently feeling to make sure the box is still there. The others follow this movement carefully with quick looks out of the corners of their eyes. Their attitudes grow tense as if they were about to spring at him. Satisfied the box is safe,* SMITTY *draws his hand away slowly and utters a sigh of relief.*

SMITTY

*In a casual tone which to them sounds sinister.*

It's a good light night for the subs if there's any about.

*For a moment he sits staring in front of him. Finally he seems to sense the hostile atmosphere of the forecastle and looks from one to the other of the men in surprise. All of them avoid his eyes. He sighs with a puzzled expression and gets up and walks out of the doorway. There is silence for a moment after his departure and then a storm of excited talk breaks loose.*

DAVIS

Did you see him feelin' if it was there?

COCKY

'E ain't arf a sly one wiv 'is talk of submarines, Gawd blind 'im!

SCOTTY

Did ve see the sneakin' looks he gave us?

DRISCOLL

If ivir I saw black shame on a man's face 'twas on his whin he sat there!

JACK

*Thoroughly convinced at last.*

He looked bad to me. He's a crook, aw right.

DAVIS
*Excitedly.*
What'll we do? We gotter do somethin' quick or —
*He is interrupted by the sound of something hitting against the port side of the forecastle with a dull, heavy thud. The men start to their feet in wild-eyed terror and turn as if they were going to rush for the deck. They stand that way for a strained moment, scarcely breathing and listening intently.*

JACK
*With a sickly smile.*
Hell! It's on'y a piece of driftwood or a floatin' log.
*He sits down again.*

DAVIS
*Sarcastically.*
Or a mine that didn't go off — that time — or a piece o' wreckage from some ship they've sent to Davy Jones.

COCKY
*Mopping his brow with a trembling hand.*
Blimey!
*He sinks back weakly on a bench.*

DRISCOLL
*Furiously.*
God blarst ut! No man at all cud be puttin' up wid the loike av this — an' I'm not wan to be fearin' anything or any man in the worrld'll stand up to me face to face; but this divil's trickery in the darrk —
*He starts for* SMITTY's *bunk.*
I'll throw ut out wan av the portholes an' be done wid ut.
*He reaches toward the mattress.*

SCOTTY
*Grabbing his arm — wildly.*
Arre ye daft, mon?

DAVIS
Don't monkey with it, Drisc. I knows what to do. Bring the bucket o' water here, Jack, will you?

JACK *gets it and brings it over to* DAVIS.

An' you, Scotty, see if he's back on the hatch.

SCOTTY

*Cautiously peering out.*

Aye, he's sittin' there the noo.

DAVIS

Sing out if he makes a move. Lift up the mattress, Drisc—careful now!

DRISCOLL *does so with infinite caution.*

Take it out, Jack—careful—don't shake it now, for Christ's sake! Here—put it in the water—easy! There, that's fixed it!

*They all sit down with great sighs of relief.*

The water'll git in and spoil it.

DRISCOLL

*Slapping* DAVIS *on the back.*

Good wurrk for ye, Davis, ye scut!

*He spits on his hands aggressively.*

An' now what's to be done wid that black-hearted thraitor?

COCKY

*Belligerently.*

Guv 'im a shove in the marf and 'eave 'im over the side!

DAVIS

An' serve him right!

JACK

Aw, say, give him a chance. Yuh can't prove nothin' till yuh find out what's in there.

DRISCOLL

*Heatedly.*

Is ut more proof ye'd be needin' afther what we've seen an' heard? Then listen to me—an' ut's Driscoll talkin'—if there's divilmint in that box an' we see plain 'twas his plan to murrdher his own ship-mates that have served him fair—

*He raises his fist.*

I'll choke his rotten hearrt out wid me own hands, an' over the side wid him, and one man missin' in the mornin'.

DAVIS
An' no one the wiser. He's the balmy kind what commits suicide.

COCKY
They 'angs spies ashore.

JACK
*Resentfully.*
If he's done what yuh think I'll croak him myself. Is that good enough for yuh?

DRISCOLL
*Looking down at the box.*
How'll we be openin' this, I wonder?

SCOTTY
*From the doorway—warningly.*
He's standin' up.

DAVIS
We'll take his keys away from him when he comes in. Quick, Drisc! You an' Jack get beside the door and grab him.
*They get on either side of the door.* DAVIS *snatches a small coil of rope from one of the upper bunks.*
This'll do for me an' Scotty to tie him.

SCOTTY
He's turnin' this way—he's comin'!
*He moves away from door.*

DAVIS
Stand by to lend a hand, Cocky.

COCKY
Righto.
*As* SMITTY *enters the forecastle he is seized roughly from both sides and his arms pinned behind him. At first he struggles fiercely, but seeing*

*the uselessness of this, he finally stands calmly and allows* DAVIS *and*
SCOTTY *to tie up his arms.*

SMITTY
*When they have finished—with cold contempt.*
If this is your idea of a joke I'll have to confess it's a bit too thick for
me to enjoy.

COCKY
*Angrily.*
Shut yer marf, 'ear!

DRISCOLL
*Roughly.*
Ye'll find ut's no joke, me bucko, b'fore we're done wid you.
*To* SCOTTY.
Kape your eye peeled, Scotty, and sing out if any one's comin'.
SCOTTY *resumes his post at the door.*

SMITTY
*With the same icy contempt.*
If you'd be good enough to explain—

DRISCOLL
*Furiously.*
Explain, is ut? 'Tis you'll do the explainin'—an' damn quick, or we'll
know the reason why.
*To* JACK *and* DAVIS.
Bring him here, now.
*They push* SMITTY *over to the bucket.*
Look here, ye murrdherin' swab. D'you see ut?
SMITTY *looks down with an expression of amazement which rapidly
changes to one of anguish.*

DAVIS
*With a sneer.*
Look at him! S'prised, ain't you? If you wants to try your dirty spyin'
tricks on us you've gotter git up earlier in the mornin'.

COCKY

Thorght yer weren't 'arf a fox, didn't yer?

SMITTY

*Trying to restrain his growing rage.*
What—what do you mean? That's only—How dare—What are you doing with my private belongings?

COCKY

*Sarcastically.*
Ho yus! Private b'longings!

DRISCOLL

*Shouting.*
What is ut, ye swine? Will you tell us to our faces? What's in ut?

SMITTY

*Biting his lips—holding himself in check with a great effort.*
Nothing but—That's my business. You'll please attend to your own.

DRISCOLL

Oho, ut is, is ut?
*Shaking his fist in* SMITTY's *face.*
Talk aisy now if ye know what's best for you. Your business, indade! Then we'll be makin' ut ours, I'm thinkin'.
*To* JACK *and* DAVIS.
Take his keys away from him an' we'll see if there's one'll open ut, maybe.
*They start in searching* SMITTY, *who tries to resist and kicks out at the bucket.* DRISCOLL *leaps forward and helps them push him away.*
Try to kick ut over, wud ye? Did ye see him then? Tryin' to murrdher us all, the scut! Take that pail out av his way, Cocky.
SMITTY *struggles with all of his strength and keeps them busy for a few seconds. As* COCKY *grabs the pail* SMITTY *makes a final effort and, lunging forward, kicks again at the bucket but only succeeds in hitting* COCKY *on the shin.* COCKY *immediately sets down the pail with a bang and, clutching his knee in both hands, starts hopping around the fore-castle, groaning and swearing.*

COCKY

Ooow! Gawd strike me pink! Kicked me, 'e did! Bloody, bleedin',
rotten Dutch 'og!

*Approaching* SMITTY, *who has given up the fight and is pushed back
against the wall near the doorway with* JACK *and* DAVIS *holding him
on either side—wrathfully, at the top of his lungs.*

Kick me, will yer? I'll show yer what for, yer bleedin' sneak!

*He draws back his fist.* DRISCOLL *pushes him to one side.*

DRISCOLL

Shut your mouth! D'you want to wake the whole ship?

COCKY *grumbles and retires to a bench, nursing his sore shin.*

JACK

*Taking a small bunch of keys from* SMITTY's *pocket.*

Here yuh are, Drisc.

DRISCOLL

*Taking them.*

We'll soon be knowin'.

*He takes the pail and sits down, placing it on the floor between his feet.*
SMITTY *again tries to break loose but he is too tired and is easily held
back against the wall.*

SMITTY

*Breathing heavily and very pale.*

Cowards!

JACK

*With a growl.*

Nix on the rough talk, see! That don't git yuh nothin'.

DRISCOLL

*Looking at the lock on the box in the water and then scrutinizing the
keys in his hand.*

This'll be ut, I'm thinkin'.

*He selects one and gingerly reaches his hand in the water.*

SMITTY

*His face grown livid—chokingly.*

Don't you open that box, Driscoll. If you do, so help me God, I'll kill you if I have to hang for it.

DRISCOLL
*Pausing—his hand in the water.*
Whin I open this box I'll not be the wan to be kilt, me sonny bye! I'm no dirty spy.

SMITTY
*His voice trembling with rage. His eyes are fixed on* DRISCOLL's *hand.*
Spy? What are you talking about? I only put that box there so I could get it quick in case we were torpedoed. Are you all mad? Do you think I'm—
*Chokingly.*
You stupid curs! You cowardly dolts!
DAVIS *claps his hand over* SMITTY's *mouth.*

DAVIS
That'll be enough from you!
DRISCOLL *takes the dripping box from the water and starts to fit in the key.* SMITTY *springs forward furiously, almost escaping from their grasp, and drags them after him half-way across the forecastle.*

DRISCOLL
Hold him, ye divils!
*He puts the box back in the water and jumps to their aid.* COCKY *hovers on the outskirts of the battle, mindful of the kick he received.*

SMITTY
*Raging.*
Cowards! Damn you! Rotten curs!
*He is thrown to the floor and held there.*
Cowards! Cowards!

DRISCOLL
I'll shut your dirty mouth for you.
*He goes to his bunk and pulls out a big wad of waste and comes back to* SMITTY.

SMITTY
Cowards! Cowards!

DRISCOLL
*With no gentle hand slaps the waste over* SMITTY's *mouth.*
That'll teach you to be misnamin' a man, ye sneak. Have ye a hand-
kerchief, Jack?
JACK *hands him one and he ties it tightly around* SMITTY's *head over
the waste.*
That'll fix your gab. Stand him up, now, and tie his feet, too, so he'll
not be movin'.
*They do so and leave him with his back against the wall near* SCOTTY.
*Then they all sit down beside* DRISCOLL, *who again lifts the box out
of the water and sets it carefully on his knees. He picks out the key, then
hesitates, looking from one to the other uncertainly.*
We'd best be takin' this to the skipper, d'you think, maybe?

JACK
*Irritably.*
To hell with the Old Man. This is our game and we c'n play it with-
out no help.

COCKY
Now bleedin' horficers, I says!

DAVIS
They'd only be takin' all the credit and makin' heroes of theyselves.

DRISCOLL
*Boldly.*
Here goes, thin!
*He slowly turns the key in the lock. The others instinctively turn away.
He carefully pushes the cover back on its hinges and looks at what he sees
inside with an expression of puzzled astonishment. The others crowd up
close. Even* SCOTTY *leaves his post to take a look.*
What is ut, Davis?

DAVIS
*Mystified.*

Looks funny, don't it? Somethin' square tied up in a rubber bag. Maybe it's dynamite—or somethin'—you can't never tell.

JACK

Aw, it ain't got no works so it ain't no bomb, I'll bet.

DAVIS

*Dubiously.*
They makes them all kinds, they do.

JACK

Open it up, Drisc.

DAVIS

Careful now!
DRISCOLL *takes a black rubber bag resembling a large tobacco pouch from the box and unties the string which is wound tightly around the top. He opens it and takes out a small packet of letters also tied up with string. He turns these over in his hands and looks at the others questioningly.*

JACK

*With a broad grin.*
On'y letters!
*Slapping* DAVIS *on the back.*
Yuh're a hell of a Sherlock Holmes, ain't yuh? Letters from his best girl too, I'll bet. Let's turn the Duke loose, what d'yuh say?
*He starts to get up.*

DAVIS

*Fixing him with a withering look.*
Don't be so damn smart, Jack. Letters, you says, 's if there never was no harm in 'em. How d'you s'pose spies gets their orders and sends back what they finds out if it ain't by letters and such things? There's many a letter is worser'n any bomb.

COCKY

Righto! They ain't as innercent as they looks, I'll take me oath, when you read 'em.
*Pointing at* SMITTY.
Not 'is Lordship's letters; not be no means!

JACK
*Sitting down again.*
Well, read 'em and find out.
DRISCOLL *commences untying the packet. There is a muffled groan of rage and protest from* SMITTY.

DAVIS
*Triumphantly.*
There! Listen to him! Look at him trying' to git loose! Ain't that proof enough? He knows well we're findin' him out. Listen to me! Love letters, you says, Jack, 's if they couldn't harm nothin'. Listen! I was readin' in some magazine in New York on'y two weeks back how some German spy in Paris was writin' love letters to some woman spy in Switzerland who sent 'em on to Berlin, Germany. To read 'em you wouldn't s'pect nothin'—just mush and all.
*Impressively.*
But they had a way o' doin' it—a damn sneakin' way. They had a piece o' plain paper with pieces cut out of it an' when they puts it on top o' the letter they sees on'y the words what tells them what they wants to know. An' the Frenchies gets beat in a fight all on account o' that letter.

COCKY
*Awed.*
Gawd blimey! They ain't 'arf smart bleeders!

DAVIS
*Seeing his audience is again all with him.*
An' even if these letters of his do sound all right they may have what they calls a code. You can't never tell.
*To* DRISCOLL, *who has finished untying the packet.*
Read one of 'em, Drisc. My eyes is weak.

DRISCOLL
*Takes the first one out of its envelope and bends down to the lantern with it. He turns up the wick to give him a better light.*
I'm no hand to be readin' but I'll try ut.
*Again there is a muffled groan from* SMITTY *as he strains at his bonds.*

DAVIS
*Gloatingly.*
Listen to him! He knows. Go ahead, Drisc!

DRISCOLL
*His brow furrowed with concentration.*
Ut begins: Dearest Man—
*His eyes travel down the page.*
An' thin there's a lot av blarney tellin' him how much she misses him
now she's gone away to singin' school—an' how she hopes he'll settle
down to rale worrk an' not be skylarkin' around now that she's away
loike he used to before she met up wid him—and ut ends: "I love you
betther than anythin' in the worrld. You know that, don't you, dear?
But b'fore I can agree to live out my life wid you, you must prove to
me that the black shadow—I won't menshun uts hateful name but
you know what I mean—which might wreck both our lives, does
not exist for you. You can do that, can't you, dear? Don't you see you
must for my sake?"
*He pauses for a moment—then adds gruffly.*
Uts signed: "Edith."
*At the sound of the name* SMITTY, *who has stood tensely with his eyes
shut as if he were undergoing torture during the reading, makes a muffled sound like a sob and half turns his face to the wall.*

JACK
*Sympathetically.*
Hell! What's the use of readin' that stuff even if—

DAVIS
*Interrupting him sharply.*
Wait! Where's that letter from, Drisc?

DRISCOLL
There's no address on the top av ut.

DAVIS
*Meaningly.*
What'd I tell you? Look at the postmark, Drisc,—on the envelope.

DRISCOLL

The name that's written is Sidney Davidson, wan hundred an'—

DAVIS

Never mind that. O' course it's a false name. Look at the postmark.

DRISCOLL

There's a furrin stamp on ut by the looks av ut. The mark's blurred
so it's hard to read.
*He spells it out laboriously.*
B-e-r—the nixt is an l, I think—i—an' an n.

DAVIS

*Excitedly.*
Berlin! What did I tell you? I knew them letters was from Germany.

COCKY

*Shaking his fist in* SMITTY's *direction.*
Rotten 'ound!
*The others look at* SMITTY *as if this last fact had utterly condemned him
in their eyes.*

DAVIS

Give me the letter, Drisc. Maybe I kin make somethin' out of it.
DRISCOLL *hands the letter to him.*
You go through the others, Drisc, and sing out if you sees anythin'
queer.
*He bends over the first letter as if he were determined to figure out its
secret meaning.* JACK, COCKY *and* SCOTTY *look over his shoulder with
eager curiosity.* DRISCOLL *takes out some of the other letters, running
his eyes quickly down the pages. He looks curiously over at* SMITTY *from
time to time, and sighs frequently with a puzzled frown.*

DAVIS

*Disappointedly.*
I gotter give it up. It's too deep for me, but we'll turn 'em over to
the perlice when we docks at Liverpool to look through. This one I
got was written a year before the war started, anyway. Find anythin'
in yours, Drisc?

DRISCOLL

They're all the same as the first—lovin' blarney, an' how her singin'
is doin', and the great things the Dutch teacher says about her voice,
an' how glad she is that her Sidney bye is worrkin' harrd an' makin'
a man av himself for her sake.

SMITTY *turns his face completely to the wall.*

DAVIS

*Disgustedly.*
If we on'y had the code!

DRISCOLL

*Taking up the bottom letter.*
Hullo! Here's wan addressed to this ship—S. S. Glencairn, ut says—
whin we was in Cape Town sivin months ago—
*Looking at the postmark.*
Ut's from London.

DAVIS

*Eagerly.*
Read it!
*There is another choking groan from* SMITTY.

DRISCOLL

*Reads slowly—his voice becomes lower and lower as he goes on.*
Ut begins wid simply the name Sidney Davidson—no dearest or
sweetheart to this wan. "Ut is only from your chance meetin' wid
Harry—whin you were drunk—that I happen to know where to
reach you. So you have run away to sea loike the coward you are
because you knew I had found out the truth—the truth you have
covered over with your mean little lies all the time I was away in Berlin and blindly trusted you. Very well, you have chosen. You have
shown that your drunkenness means more to you than any love or
faith av mine. I am sorry—for I loved you, Sidney Davidson—but
this is the end. I lave you—the mem'ries; an' if ut is any satisfaction
to you I lave you the real-i-zation that you have wrecked my loife as
you have wrecked your own. My one remainin' hope is that nivir in
God's worrld will I ivir see your face again. Good-by. Edith."
*As he finishes there is a deep silence, broken only by* SMITTY's *muffled*

*sobbing. The men cannot look at each other.* DRISCOLL *holds the rubber bag limply in his hand and some small white object falls out of it and drops noiselessly on the floor. Mechanically* DRISCOLL *leans over and picks it up, and looks at it wonderingly.*

DAVIS
*In a dull voice.*
What's that?

DRISCOLL
*Slowly.*
A bit av a dried-up flower,—a rose, maybe.
*He drops it into the bag and gathers up the letters and puts them back. He replaces the bag in the box, and locks it and puts it back under* SMITTY's *mattress. The others follow him with their eyes. He steps softly over to* SMITTY *and cuts the ropes about his arms and ankles with his sheath knife, and unties the handkerchief over the gag.* SMITTY *does not turn around but covers his face with his hands and leans his head against the wall. His shoulders continue to heave spasmodically but he makes no further sound.*

DRISCOLL
*Stalks back to the others—there is a moment of silence, in which each man is in agony with the hopelessness of finding a word he can say— then* DRISCOLL *explodes.*
God stiffen us, are we never goin' to turn in fur a wink av sleep?
*They all start as if awakening from a bad dream and gratefully crawl into their bunks, shoes and all, turning their faces to the wall, and pulling their blankets up over their shoulders.* SCOTTY *tiptoes past* SMITTY *out into the darkness . . .* DRISCOLL *turns down the light and crawls into his bunk as*

THE CURTAIN FALLS

*The Hairy Ape*
A Comedy of Ancient and
Modern Life in Eight Scenes

# Characters

ROBERT SMITH, "YANK"

PADDY

LONG

MILDRED DOUGLAS

HER AUNT

SECOND ENGINEER

A GUARD

A SECRETARY OF AN ORGANIZATION

STOKERS, LADIES, GENTLEMEN, ETC.

# Scenes

# Scene One

*The firemen's forecastle of a transatlantic liner an hour after sailing from
New York for the voyage across. Tiers of narrow, steel bunks, three deep,
on all sides. An entrance in rear. Benches on the floor before the bunks.
The room is crowded with men, shouting, cursing, laughing, singing—
a confused, inchoate uproar swelling into a sort of unity, a meaning—
the bewildered, furious, baffled defiance of a beast in a cage. Nearly all
the men are drunk. Many bottles are passed from hand to hand. All are
dressed in dungaree pants, heavy ugly shoes. Some wear singlets, but the
majority are stripped to the waist.*

*The treatment of this scene, or of any other scene in the play, should by
no means be naturalistic. The effect sought after is a cramped space in
the bowels of a ship, imprisoned by white steel. The lines of bunks, the
uprights supporting them, cross each other like the steel framework of a
cage. The ceiling crushes down upon the men's heads. They cannot stand
upright. This accentuates the natural stooping posture which shoveling
coal and the resultant over-development of back and shoulder muscles
have given them. The men themselves should resemble those pictures in
which the appearance of Neanderthal Man is guessed at. All are hairy-
chested, with long arms of tremendous power, and low, receding brows
above their small, fierce, resentful eyes. All the civilized white races are
represented, but except for the slight differentiation in color of hair, skin,
eyes, all these men are alike.*

*The curtain rises on a tumult of sound. Yank is seated in the foreground.
He seems broader, fiercer, more truculent, more powerful, more sure of
himself than the rest. They respect his superior strength—the grudging
respect of fear. Then, too, he represents to them a self-expression, the very
last word in what they are, their most highly developed individual.*

Gif me trink dere, you!

'Ave a wet!

Salute!

Gesundheit!

Skoal!

Drunk as a lord, God stiffen you!

Here's how!

Luck!

Pass back that bottle, damn you!

Pourin' it down his neck!

Ho, Froggy! Where the devil have you been?

*La Touraine.*

I hit him smash in yaw, py Gott!

Jenkins—the First—he's a rotten swine—

And the coppers nabbed him—and I run—

I like peer better. It don't pig head gif you.

A slut, I'm sayin'! She robbed me aslape—

To hell with 'em all!

You're a bloody liar!

Say dot again!

*Commotion. Two men about to fight are pulled apart.*

No scrappin' now!

Tonight—

See who's the best man!

Bloody Dutchman!

Tonight on the for'ard square.

I'll bet on Dutchy.

He packa da wallop, I tella you!

Shut up, Wop!

No fightin', maties. We're all chums, ain't we?

*A voice starts bawling a song.*

"Beer, beer, glorious beer!

Fill yourselves right up to here."

YANK

*For the first time seeming to take notice of the uproar about him, turns around threateningly—in a tone of contemptuous authority.*
Choke off dat noise! Where d'yuh get dat beer stuff? Beer, hell! Beer's for goils—and Dutchmen. Me for somep'n wit a kick to it! Gimme a drink, one of youse guys.
*Several bottles are eagerly offered. He takes a tremendous gulp at one of them; then, keeping the bottle in his hand, glares belligerently at the owner, who hastens to acquiesce in this robbery by saying* All righto, Yank. Keep it and have another. *Yank contemptuously turns his back on the crowd again. For a second there is an embarrassed silence. Then—*

VOICES
We must be passing the Hook.
She's beginning to roll to it.
Six days in hell—and then Southampton.
Py Yesus, I vish somepody take my first vatch for me!
Gittin' seasick, Square-head?
Drink up and forget it!
What's in your bottle?
Gin.
Dot's nigger trink.
Absinthe? It's doped. You'll go off your chump, Froggy!
Cochon!
Whisky, that's the ticket!
Where's Paddy?
Going asleep.
Sing us that whisky song, Paddy.
*They all turn to an old, wizened Irishman who is dozing, very drunk, on the benches forward. His face is extremely monkey-like with all the sad, patient pathos of that animal in his small eyes.*

Singa da song, Caruso Pat!
He's gettin' old. The drink is too much for him.
He's too drunk.

PADDY

*Blinking about him, starts to his feet resentfully, swaying, holding on to the edge of a bunk.*

I'm never too drunk to sing. 'Tis only when I'm dead to the world I'd be wishful to sing at all.

*With a sort of sad contempt.*

"Whisky Johnny," ye want? A chanty, ye want? Now that's a queer wish from the ugly like of you, God help you. But no matther.

*He starts to sing in a thin, nasal, doleful tone.*

Oh, whisky is the life of man!
    Whisky! O Johnny! (*They all join in on this.*)
Oh, whisky is the life of man!
    Whisky for my Johnny! (*Again chorus.*)
Oh, whisky drove my old man mad!
    Whisky! O Johnny!
Oh, whisky drove my old man mad!
    Whisky for my Johnny!

YANK

*Again turning around scornfully.*

Aw hell! Nix on dat old sailing ship stuff! All dat bull's dead, see? And you're dead, too, yuh damned old Harp, on'y yuh don't know it. Take it easy, see. Give us a rest. Nix on de loud noise.

*With a cynical grin.*

Can't youse see I'm tryin' to t'ink?

ALL

*Repeating the word after him as one with the same cynical amused mockery.*

Think!

*The chorused word has a brazen metallic quality as if their throats were phonograph horns. It is followed by a general uproar of hard, barking laughter.*

VOICES

Don't be cracking your head wit ut, Yank.

You gat headache, py yingo!

One thing about it—it rhymes with drink!

Ha, ha, ha!

Drink, don't think!

Drink, don't think!

Drink, don't think!

*A whole chorus of voices has taken up this refrain, stamping on the floor, pounding on the benches with fists.*

YANK

*Taking a gulp from his bottle—good-naturedly.*

Aw right. Can de noise. I got yuh de foist time.

*The uproar subsides. A very drunken sentimental tenor begins to sing.*

"Far away in Canada,
    Far across the sea,
There's a lass who fondly waits
    Making a home for me—"

YANK

*Fiercely contemptuous.*

Shut up, yuh lousy boob! Where d'yuh get dat tripe? Home? Home, hell! I'll make a home for yuh! I'll knock yuh dead. Home! T'hell wit home! Where d'yuh get dat tripe? Dis is home, see? What d'yuh want wit home?

*Proudly.*

I runned away from mine when I was a kid. On'y too glad to beat it, dat was me. Home was lickings for me, dat's all. But yuh can bet your shoit no one ain't never licked me since! Wanter try it, any of youse? Huh! I guess not.

*In a more placated but still contemptuous tone.*

Goils waitin' for yuh, huh? Aw, hell! Dat's all tripe. Dey don't wait for no one. Dey'd double-cross yuh for a nickel. Dey're all tarts, get me? Treat 'em rough, dat's me. To hell wit 'em. Tarts, dat's what, de whole bunch of 'em.

LONG

*Very drunk, jumps on a bench excitedly, gesticulating with a bottle in his hand.*

Listen 'ere, Comrades! Yank 'ere is right. 'E says this 'ere stinkin' ship is our 'ome. And 'e says as 'ome is 'ell. And 'e's right! This is 'ell. We lives in 'ell, Comrades—and right enough we'll die in it.

*Raging.*

And who's ter blame, I arsks yer? We ain't. We wasn't born this rotten way. All men is born free and ekal. That's in the bleedin' Bible, maties. But what d'they care for the Bible—them lazy, bloated swine what travels first cabin? Them's the ones. They dragged us down 'til we're on'y wage slaves in the bowels of a bloody ship, sweatin', burnin' up, eatin' coal dust! Hit's them's ter blame—the damned Capitalist clarss!

*There had been a gradual murmur of contemptuous resentment rising among the men until now he is interrupted by a storm of catcalls, hisses, boos, hard laughter.*

VOICES

Turn it off!

Shut up!

Sit down!

Closa da face!

Tamn fool!

*Etc.*

YANK

*Standing up and glaring at Long.*

Sit down before I knock yuh down!

*Long makes haste to efface himself. Yank goes on contemptuously.*

De Bible, huh? De Cap'tlist class, huh? Aw nix on dat Salvation Army–Socialist bull. Git a soapbox! Hire a hall! Come and be saved, huh? Jerk us to Jesus, huh? Aw g'wan! I've listened to lots of guys like you, see. Yuh're all wrong. Wanter know what I t'ink? Yuh ain't no good for no one. Yuh're de bunk. Yuh ain't got no noive, get me? Yuh're yellow, dat's what. Yellow, dat's you. Say! What's dem slobs in de foist cabin got to do wit us? We're better men dan dey are, ain't we? Sure! One of us guys could clean up de whole mob wit one mit. Put one of 'em down here for one watch in de stokehole, what'd happen? Dey'd carry him off on a stretcher. Dem boids don't amount to nothin'. Dey're just baggage. Who makes dis old tub run? Ain't it us guys? Well den, we belong, don't we? We belong and dey don't. Dat's all.

*A loud chorus of approval. Yank goes on.*

As for dis bein' hell — aw, nuts! Yuh lost your noive, dat's what. Dis is a man's job, get me? It belongs. It runs dis tub. No stiffs need apply. But yuh're a stiff, see? Yuh're yellow, dat's you.

VOICES

*With a great hard pride in them.*

Righto!

A man's job!

Talk is cheap, Long.

He never could hold up his end.

Divil take him!

Yank's right. We make it go.

Py Gott, Yank say right ting!

We don't need no one cryin' over us.

Makin' speeches.

Throw him out!

Yellow!

Chuck him overboard!

I'll break his jaw for him!

*They crowd around Long threateningly.*

YANK

*Half good-natured again — contemptuously.*

Aw, take it easy. Leave him alone. He ain't woith a punch. Drink up. Here's how, whoever owns dis.

*He takes a long swallow from his bottle. All drink with him. In a flash all is hilarious amiability again, back-slapping, loud talk, etc.*

PADDY

*Who has been sitting in a blinking, melancholy daze — suddenly cries out in a voice full of old sorrow.*

We belong to this, you're saying? We make the ship to go, you're saying? Yerra then, that Almighty God have pity on us!

*His voice runs into the wail of a keen, he rocks back and forth on his bench. The men stare at him, startled and impressed in spite of themselves.*

Oh, to be back in the fine days of my youth, ochone! Oh, there was fine beautiful ships them days—clippers wid tall masts touching the sky—fine strong men in them—men that was sons of the sea as if 'twas the mother that bore them. Oh, the clean skins of them, and the clear eyes, the straight backs and full chests of them! Brave men they was, and bold men surely! We'd be sailing out, bound down round the Horn maybe. We'd be making sail in the dawn, with a fair breeze, singing a chanty song wid no care to it. And astern the land would be sinking low and dying out, but we'd give it no heed but a laugh, and never a look behind. For the day that was, was enough, for we was free men—and I'm thinking 'tis only slaves do be giving heed to the day that's gone or the day to come—until they're old like me.

*With a sort of religious exaltation.*

Oh, to be scudding south again wid the power of the Trade Wind driving her on steady through the nights and the days! Full sail on her! Nights and days! Nights when the foam of the wake would be flaming wid fire, when the sky'd be blazing and winking wid stars. Or the full of the moon maybe. Then you'd see her driving through the gray night, her sails stretching aloft all silver and white, not a sound on the deck, the lot of us dreaming dreams, till you'd believe 'twas no real ship at all you was on but a ghost ship like the *Flying Dutchman* they say does be roaming the seas forevermore widout touching a port. And there was the days, too. A warm sun on the clean decks. Sun warming the blood of you, and wind over the miles of shiny green ocean like strong drink to your lungs. Work—aye, hard work—but who'd mind that at all? Sure, you worked under the sky and 'twas work wid skill and daring to it. And wid the day done, in the dog watch, smoking me pipe at ease, the lookout would be raising land maybe, and we'd see the mountains of South Americy wid the red fire of the setting sun painting their white tops and the clouds floating by them!

*His tone of exaltation ceases. He goes on mournfully.*

Yerra, what's the use of talking? 'Tis a dead man's whisper.

*To Yank resentfully.*

'Twas them days men belonged to ships, not now. 'Twas them days a ship was part of the sea, and a man was part of a ship, and the sea joined all together and made it one.

*Scornfully.*

Is it one wid this you'd be, Yank—black smoke from the funnels smudging the sea, smudging the decks—the bloody engines pounding and throbbing and shaking—wid divil a sight of sun or a breath of clean air—choking our lungs wid coal dust—breaking our backs and hearts in the hell of the stokehole—feeding the bloody furnace—feeding our lives along wid the coal, I'm thinking—caged in by steel from a sight of the sky like bloody apes in the Zoo!

*With a harsh laugh.*

Ho-ho, divil mend you! Is it to belong to that you're wishing? Is it a flesh and blood wheel of the engines you'd be?

YANK

*Who has been listening with a contemptuous sneer, barks out the answer.*
Sure ting! Dat's me. What about it?

PADDY

*As if to himself—with great sorrow.*
Me time is past due. That a great wave wid sun in the heart of it may sweep me over the side sometime I'd be dreaming of the days that's gone!

YANK

Aw, yuh crazy Mick!
*He springs to his feet and advances on Paddy threateningly—then stops, fighting some queer struggle within himself—lets his hands fall to his sides—contemptuously.*
Aw, take it easy. Yuh're aw right, at dat. Yuh're bugs, dat's all—nutty as a cuckoo. All dat tripe yuh been pullin'—Aw, dat's all right. On'y it's dead, get me? Yuh don't belong no more, see. Yuh don't get de stuff. Yuh're too old.

*Disgustedly.*

But aw say, come up for air onct in a while, can't yuh? See what's happened since yuh croaked.
*He suddenly bursts forth vehemently, growing more and more excited.*

Say! Sure! Sure I meant it! What de hell—Say, lemme talk! Hey! Hey, you old Harp! Hey, youse guys! Say, listen to me—wait a moment—I gotter talk, see. I belong and he don't. He's dead but I'm livin'. Listen to me! Sure I'm part of de engines! Why de hell not! Dey move, don't dey? Dey're speed, ain't dey! Dey smash trou, don't dey? Twenty-five knots a hour! Dat's goin' some! Dat's new stuff! Dat belongs! But him, he's too old. He gets dizzy. Say, listen. All dat crazy tripe about nights and days; all dat crazy tripe about stars and moons; all dat crazy tripe about suns and winds, fresh air and de rest of it—Aw hell, dat's all a dope dream! Hittin' de pipe of de past, dat's what he's doin'. He's old and don't belong no more. But me, I'm young! I'm in de pink! I move wit it! It, get me! I mean de ting dat's de guts of all dis. It ploughs trou all de tripe he's been sayin'. It blows dat up! It knocks dat dead! It slams dat offen de face of de oith! It, get me! De engines and de coal and de smoke and all de rest of it! He can't breathe and swallow coal dust, but I kin, see? Dat's fresh air for me! Dat's food for me! I'm new, get me? Hell in de stokehole? Sure! It takes a man to work in hell. Hell, sure, dat's my fav'rite climate. I eat it up! I git fat on it! It's me makes it hot! It's me makes it roar! It's me makes it move! Sure, on'y for me everyting stops. It all goes dead, get me? De noise and smoke and all de engines movin' de woild, dey stop. Dere ain't nothin' no more! Dat's what I'm sayin'. Everyting else dat makes de woild move, somep'n makes it move. It can't move witout somep'n else, see? Den yuh get down to me. I'm at de bottom, get me! Dere ain't nothin' foither. I'm de end! I'm de start! I start somep'n and de woild moves! It—dat's me!—de new dat's moiderin' de old! I'm de ting in coal dat makes it boin; I'm steam and oil for de engines; I'm de ting in noise dat makes yuh hear it; I'm smoke and express trains and steamers and factory whistles; I'm de ting in gold dat makes it money! And I'm what makes iron into steel! Steel, dat stands for de whole ting! And I'm steel—steel—steel! I'm de muscles in steel, de punch behind it!

*As he says this he pounds with his fist against the steel bunks. All the men, roused to a pitch of frenzied self-glorification by his speech, do likewise. There is a deafening metallic roar, through which Yank's voice can be heard bellowing.*

Slaves, hell! We run de whole woiks. All de rich guys dat tink dey're somep'n, dey ain't nothin'! Dey don't belong. But us guys, we're in de move, we're at de bottom, de whole ting is us!

*Paddy from the start of Yank's speech has been taking one gulp after another from his bottle, at first frightenedly, as if he were afraid to listen, then desperately, as if to drown his senses, but finally has achieved complete indifferent, even amused, drunkenness. Yank sees his lips moving. He quells the uproar with a shout.*

Hey, youse guys, take it easy! Wait a moment! De nutty Harp is sayin' somep'n.

PADDY

*Is heard now—throws his head back with a mocking burst of laughter.*
Ho-ho-ho-ho-ho—

YANK

*Drawing back his fist, with a snarl.*
Aw! Look out who yuh're givin' the bark!

PADDY

*Begins to sing the "Miller of Dee" with enormous good nature.*
　"I care for nobody, no, not I,
　　And nobody cares for me."

YANK

*Good-natured himself in a flash, interrupts Paddy with a slap on the bare back like a report.*
Dat's de stuff! Now yuh're gettin' wise to somep'n. Care for nobody, dat's de dope! To hell wit 'em all! And nix on nobody else carin'. I kin care for myself, get me!

*Eight bells sound, muffled, vibrating through the steel walls as if some enormous brazen gong were imbedded in the heart of the ship. All the men jump up mechanically, file through the door silently close upon each other's heels in what is very like a prisoners' lockstep. Yank slaps Paddy on the back.*

Our watch, yuh old Harp!

*Mockingly.*

Come on down in hell. Eat up de coal dust. Drink in de heat. It's it, see! Act like yuh liked it, yuh better—or croak yuhself.

PADDY

*With jovial defiance.*

To the divil wid it! I'll not report this watch. Let thim log me and be damned. I'm no slave the like of you. I'll be sittin' here at me ease, and drinking, and thinking, and dreaming dreams.

YANK

*Contemptuously.*

Tinkin' and dreamin', what'll that get yuh? What's tinkin' got to do wit it? We move, don't we? Speed, ain't it? Fog, dat's all you stand for. But we drive trou dat, don't we? We split dat up and smash trou— twenty-five knots a hour!

*Turns his back on Paddy scornfully.*

Aw, yuh make me sick! Yuh don't belong!

*He strides out the door in rear. Paddy hums to himself, blinking drowsily.*

CURTAIN

# Scene Two

*Two days out. A section of the promenade deck. Mildred Douglas and her aunt are discovered reclining in deck chairs. The former is a girl of twenty, slender, delicate, with a pale, pretty face marred by a self-conscious expression of disdainful superiority. She looks fretful, nervous and discontented, bored by her own anemia. Her aunt is a pompous and proud—and fat—old lady. She is a type even to the point of a double chin and lorgnettes. She is dressed pretentiously, as if afraid her face alone would never indicate her position in life. Mildred is dressed all in white.*

*The impression to be conveyed by this scene is one of the beautiful, vivid life of the sea all about—sunshine on the deck in a great flood, the fresh sea wind blowing across it. In the midst of this, these two incongruous, artificial figures, inert and disharmonious, the elder like a gray lump of dough touched up with rouge, the younger looking as if the vitality of her stock had been sapped before she was conceived, so that she is the expression not of its life energy but merely of the artificialities that energy had won for itself in the spending.*

MILDRED
*Looking up with affected dreaminess.*
How the black smoke swirls back against the sky! Is it not beautiful?

AUNT
*Without looking up.*
I dislike smoke of any kind.

MILDRED
My great-grandmother smoked a pipe—a clay pipe.

AUNT
*Ruffling.*

Vulgar!

MILDRED
She was too distant a relative to be vulgar. Time mellows pipes.

AUNT
*Pretending boredom but irritated.*
Did the sociology you took up at college teach you that—to play the
ghoul on every possible occasion, excavating old bones? Why not let
your great-grandmother rest in her grave?

MILDRED
*Dreamily.*
With her pipe beside her—puffing in Paradise.

AUNT
*With spite.*
Yes, you are a natural born ghoul. You are even getting to look like
one, my dear.

MILDRED
*In a passionless tone.*
I detest you, Aunt.
*Looking at her critically.*
Do you know what you remind me of? Of a cold pork pudding
against a background of linoleum tablecloth in the kitchen of a—
but the possibilities are wearisome.
*She closes her eyes.*

AUNT
*With a bitter laugh.*
Merci for your candor. But since I am and must be your chaperon—
in appearance, at least—let us patch up some sort of armed truce.
For my part you are quite free to indulge any pose of eccentricity
that beguiles you—as long as you observe the amenities—

MILDRED
*Drawling.*
The inanities?

AUNT

*Going on as if she hadn't heard.*

After exhausting the morbid thrills of social service work on New York's East Side—how they must have hated you, by the way, the poor that you made so much poorer in their own eyes!—you are now bent on making your slumming international. Well, I hope White-chapel will provide the needed nerve tonic. Do not ask me to chaperon you there, however. I told your father I would not. I loathe deformity. We will hire an army of detectives and you may investigate everything—they allow you to see.

MILDRED

*Protesting with a trace of genuine earnestness.*

Please do not mock at my attempts to discover how the other half lives. Give me credit for some sort of groping sincerity in that at least. I would like to help them. I would like to be some use in the world. Is it my fault I don't know how? I would like to be sincere, to touch life somewhere.

*With weary bitterness.*

But I'm afraid I have neither the vitality nor integrity. All that was burnt out in our stock before I was born. Grandfather's blast furnaces, flaming to the sky, melting steel, making millions—then father keeping those home fires burning, making more millions—and little me at the tail-end of it all. I'm a waste product in the Bessemer process—like the millions. Or rather, I inherit the acquired trait of the by-product, wealth, but none of the energy, none of the strength of the steel that made it. I am sired by gold and damned by it, as they say at the race track—damned in more ways than one.

*She laughs mirthlessly.*

AUNT

*Unimpressed—superciliously.*

You seem to be going in for sincerity today. It isn't becoming to you, really—except as an obvious pose. Be as artificial as you are, I advise. There's a sort of sincerity in that, you know. And, after all, you must confess you like that better.

MILDRED

*Again affected and bored.*

Yes, I suppose I do. Pardon me for my outburst. When a leopard complains of its spots, it must sound rather grotesque.

*In a mocking tone.*

Purr, little leopard. Purr, scratch, tear, kill, gorge yourself and be happy—only stay in the jungle where your spots are camouflage. In a cage they make you conspicuous.

AUNT

I don't know what you are talking about.

MILDRED

It would be rude to talk about anything to you. Let's just talk.

*She looks at her wrist watch.*

Well, thank goodness, it's about time for them to come for me. That ought to give me a new thrill, Aunt.

AUNT

*Affectedly troubled.*

You don't mean to say you're really going? The dirt—the heat must be frightful—

MILDRED

Grandfather started as a puddler. I should have inherited an immunity to heat that would make a salamander shiver. It will be fun to put it to the test.

AUNT

But don't you have to have the captain's—or someone's—permission to visit the stokehole?

MILDRED

*With a triumphant smile.*

I have it—both his and the chief engineer's. Oh, they didn't want to at first, in spite of my social service credentials. They didn't seem a bit anxious that I should investigate how the other half lives and works on a ship. So I had to tell them that my father, the president of Nazareth Steel, chairman of the board of directors of this line, had told me it would be all right.

AUNT
He didn't.

MILDRED
How naïve age makes one! But I said he did, Aunt. I even said he had
given me a letter to them—which I had lost. And they were afraid
to take the chance that I might be lying.
*Excitedly.*
So it's ho! for the stokehole. The second engineer is to escort me.
*Looking at her watch again.*
It's time. And here he comes, I think.
*The second engineer enters. He is a husky, fine-looking man of thirty-
five or so. He stops before the two and tips his cap, visibly embarrassed
and ill-at-ease.*

SECOND ENGINEER
Miss Douglas?

MILDRED
Yes.
*Throwing off her rugs and getting to her feet.*
Are we all ready to start?

SECOND ENGINEER
In just a second, ma'am. I'm waiting for the Fourth. He's coming
along.

MILDRED
*With a scornful smile.*
You don't care to shoulder this responsibility alone, is that it?

SECOND ENGINEER
*Forcing a smile.*
Two are better than one.
*Disturbed by her eyes, glances out to sea—blurts out.*
A fine day we're having.

MILDRED
Is it?

**SECOND ENGINEER**
A nice warm breeze—

**MILDRED**
It feels cold to me.

**SECOND ENGINEER**
But it's hot enough in the sun—

**MILDRED**
Not hot enough for me. I don't like Nature. I was never athletic.

**SECOND ENGINEER**
*Forcing a smile.*
Well, you'll find it hot enough where you're going.

**MILDRED**
Do you mean hell?

**SECOND ENGINEER**
*Flabbergasted, decides to laugh.*
Ho-ho! No, I mean the stokehole.

**MILDRED**
My grandfather was a puddler. He played with boiling steel.

**SECOND ENGINEER**
*All at sea—uneasily.*
Is that so? Hum, you'll excuse me, ma'am, but are you intending to wear that dress?

**MILDRED**
Why not?

**SECOND ENGINEER**
You'll likely rub against oil and dirt. It can't be helped.

**MILDRED**
It doesn't matter. I have lots of white dresses.

**SECOND ENGINEER**
I have an old coat you might throw over—

**MILDRED**

I have fifty dresses like this. I will throw this one into the sea when I come back. That ought to wash it clean, don't you think?

**SECOND ENGINEER**

*Doggedly.*

There's ladders to climb down that are none too clean—and dark alleyways—

**MILDRED**

I will wear this very dress and none other.

**SECOND ENGINEER**

No offense meant. It's none of my business. I was only warning you—

**MILDRED**

Warning? That sounds thrilling.

**SECOND ENGINEER**

*Looking down the deck—with a sigh of relief.*

There's the Fourth now. He's waiting for us. If you'll come—

**MILDRED**

Go on. I'll follow you.

*He goes. Mildred turns a mocking smile on her aunt.*

An oaf—but a handsome, virile oaf.

**AUNT**

*Scornfully.*

Poser!

**MILDRED**

Take care. He said there were dark alleyways—

**AUNT**

*In the same tone.*

Poser!

**MILDRED**

*Biting her lips angrily.*

You are right. But would that my millions were not so anemically chaste!

AUNT
Yes, for a fresh pose I have no doubt you would drag the name of Douglas in the gutter!

MILDRED
From which it sprang. Good-by, Aunt. Don't pray too hard that I may fall into the fiery furnace.

AUNT
Poser!

MILDRED
*Viciously.*
Old hag!
*She slaps her aunt insultingly across the face and walks off, laughing gaily.*

AUNT
*Screams after her.*
I said poser!

CURTAIN

# Scene Three

*The stokehole. In the rear, the dimly-outlined bulks of the furnaces and boilers. High overhead one hanging electric bulb sheds just enough light through the murky air laden with coal dust to pile up masses of shadows everywhere. A line of men, stripped to the waist, is before the furnace doors. They bend over, looking neither to right nor left, handling their shovels as if they were part of their bodies, with a strange, awkward, swinging rhythm. They use the shovels to throw open the furnace doors. Then from these fiery round holes in the black a flood of terrific light and heat pours full upon the men who are outlined in silhouette in the crouching, inhuman attitudes of chained gorillas. The men shovel with a rhythmic motion, swinging as on a pivot from the coal which lies in heaps on the floor behind to hurl it into the flaming mouths before them. There is a tumult of noise—the brazen clang of the furnace doors as they are flung open or slammed shut, the grating, teeth-gritting grind of steel against steel, of crunching coal. This clash of sounds stuns one's ears with its rending dissonance. But there is order in it, rhythm, a mechanical regulated recurrence, a tempo. And rising above all, making the air hum with the quiver of liberated energy, the roar of leaping flames in the furnaces, the monotonous throbbing beat of the engines.*

*As the curtain rises, the furnace doors are shut. The men are taking a breathing spell. One or two are arranging the coal behind them, pulling it into more accessible heaps. The others can be dimly made out leaning on their shovels in relaxed attitudes of exhaustion.*

PADDY
*From somewhere in the line—plaintively.*
Yerra, will this divil's own watch nivir end? Me back is broke. I'm destroyed entirely.

YANK

*From the center of the line—with exuberant scorn.*

Aw, yuh make me sick! Lie down and croak, why don't yuh? Always beefin', dat's you! Say, dis is a cinch! Dis was made for me! It's my meat, get me!

*A whistle is blown—a thin, shrill note from somewhere overhead in the darkness. Yank curses without resentment.*

Dere's de damn engineer crackin' de whip. He tinks we're loafin'.

PADDY

*Vindictively.*

God stiffen him!

YANK

*In an exultant tone of command.*

Come on, youse guys! Git into de game! She's gittin' hungry! Pile some grub in her. Trow it into her belly! Come on now, all of youse! Open her up!

*At this last all the men, who have followed his movements of getting into position, throw open their furnace doors with a deafening clang. The fiery light floods over their shoulders as they bend round for the coal. Rivulets of sooty sweat have traced maps on their backs. The enlarged muscles form bunches of high light and shadow.*

YANK

*Chanting a count as he shovels without seeming effort.*

One—two—tree—

*His voice rising exultantly in the joy of battle.*

Dat's de stuff! Let her have it! All togedder now! Sling it into her! Let her ride! Shoot de piece now! Call de toin on her! Drive her into it! Feel her move! Watch her smoke! Speed, dat's her middle name! Give her coal, youse guys! Coal, dat's her booze! Drink it up, baby! Let's see yuh sprint! Dig in and gain a lap! Dere she go-o-es.

*This last in the chanting formula of the gallery gods at the six-day bike race. He slams his furnace door shut. The others do likewise with as much unison as their wearied bodies will permit. The effect is of one fiery eye after another being blotted out with a series of accompanying bangs.*

PADDY

*Groaning.*

Me back is broke. I'm bate out—bate—

*There is a pause. Then the inexorable whistle sounds again from the dim regions above the electric light. There is a growl of cursing rage from all sides.*

YANK

*Shaking his fist upward—contemptuously.*

Take it easy dere, you! Who d'yuh tinks runnin' dis game, me or you? When I git ready, we move. Not before! When I git ready, get me!

VOICES

*Approvingly.*

That's the stuff!

Yank tal him, py golly!

Yank ain't affeerd.

Goot poy, Yank!

Give him hell!

Tell 'im 'e's a bloody swine!

Bloody slave-driver!

YANK

*Contemptuously.*

He ain't got no noive. He's yellow, get me? All de engineers is yellow. Dey got streaks a mile wide. Aw, to hell wit him! Let's move, youse guys. We had a rest. Come on, she needs it! Give her pep! It ain't for him. Him and his whistle, dey don't belong. But we belong, see! We gotter feed de baby! Come on!

*He turns and flings his furnace door open. They all follow his lead. At this instant the Second and Fourth Engineers enter from the darkness on the left with Mildred between them. She starts, turns paler, her pose is crumbling, she shivers with fright in spite of the blazing heat, but forces herself to leave the engineers and take a few steps nearer the men. She is right behind Yank. All this happens quickly while the men have their backs turned.*

YANK

Come on, youse guys!

*He is turning to get coal when the whistle sounds again in a peremptory, irritating note. This drives Yank into a sudden fury. While the other men have turned full around and stopped dumfounded by the spectacle of Mildred standing there in her white dress, Yank does not turn far enough to see her. Besides, his head is thrown back, he blinks upward through the murk trying to find the owner of the whistle, he brandishes his shovel murderously over his head in one hand, pounding on his chest, gorilla-like, with the other, shouting.*

Toin off dat whistle! Come down outa dere, yuh yellow, brass-buttoned, Belfast bum, yuh! Come down and I'll knock yer brains out! Yuh lousy, stinkin', yellow mut of a Catholic-moiderin' bastard! Come down and I'll moider yuh! Pullin' dat whistle on me, huh? I'll show yuh! I'll crash yer skull in! I'll drive yer teet' down yer troat! I'll slam yer nose trou de back of yer head! I'll cut yer guts out for a nickel, yuh lousy boob, yuh dirty, crummy, muck-eatin' son of a *Suddenly he becomes conscious of all the other men staring at something directly behind his back. He whirls defensively with a snarling, murderous growl, crouching to spring, his lips drawn back over his teeth, his small eyes gleaming ferociously. He sees Mildred, like a white apparition in the full light from the open furnace doors. He glares into her eyes, turned to stone. As for her, during his speech she has listened, paralyzed with horror, terror, her whole personality crushed, beaten in, collapsed, by the terrific impact of this unknown, abysmal brutality, naked and shameless. As she looks at his gorilla face, as his eyes bore into hers, she utters a low, choking cry and shrinks away from him, putting both hands up before her eyes to shut out the sight of his face, to protect her own. This startles Yank to a reaction. His mouth falls open, his eyes grow bewildered.*

MILDRED
*About to faint—to the engineers, who now have her one by each arm—whimperingly.*
Take me away! Oh, the filthy beast!
*She faints. They carry her quickly back, disappearing in the darkness at the left, rear. An iron door clangs shut. Rage and bewildered fury rush back on Yank. He feels himself insulted in some unknown fashion in the very heart of his pride. He roars* God damn yuh! *and hurls his shovel*

*after them at the door which has just closed. It hits the steel bulkhead with a clang and falls clattering on the steel floor. From overhead the whistle sounds again in a long, angry, insistent command.*

**CURTAIN**

# Scene Four

*The firemen's forecastle. Yank's watch has just come off duty and had dinner. Their faces and bodies shine from a soap and water scrubbing but around their eyes, where a hasty dousing does not touch, the coal dust sticks like black make-up, giving them a queer, sinister expression. Yank has not washed either face or body. He stands out in contrast to them, a blackened, brooding figure. He is seated forward on a bench in the exact attitude of Rodin's "The Thinker." The others, most of them smoking pipes, are staring at Yank half-apprehensively, as if fearing an outburst; half-amusedly, as if they saw a joke somewhere that tickled them.*

VOICES
He ain't ate nothin'.
Py golly, a fallar gat to gat grub in him.
Divil a lie.
Yank feeda da fire, no feeda da face.
Ha-ha.
He ain't even washed hisself.
He's forgot.
Hey, Yank, you forgot to wash.

YANK
*Sullenly.*
Forgot nothin'! To hell wit washin'.

VOICES
It'll stick to you.
It'll get under your skin.
Give yer the bleedin' itch, that's wot.
It makes spots on you—like a leopard.
Like a piebald nigger, you mean.

Better wash up, Yank.
You sleep better.
Wash up, Yank.
Wash up! Wash up!

YANK

*Resentfully.*
Aw say, youse guys. Lemme alone. Can't youse see I'm tryin' to tink?

ALL

*Repeating the word after him as one with cynical mockery.*
Think!
*The word has a brazen, metallic quality as if their throats were phono-
graph horns. It is followed by a chorus of hard, barking laughter.*

YANK

*Springing to his feet and glaring at them belligerently.*
Yes, tink! Tink, dat's what I said! What about it?
*They are silent, puzzled by his sudden resentment at what used to be one
of his jokes. Yank sits down again in the same attitude of "The Thinker."*

VOICES

Leave him alone.
He's got a grouch on.
Why wouldn't he?

PADDY

*With a wink at the others.*
Sure I know what's the matther. 'Tis aisy to see. He's fallen in love,
I'm telling you.

ALL

*Repeating the word after him as one with cynical mockery.*
Love!
*The word has a brazen, metallic quality as if their throats were phono-
graph horns. It is followed by a chorus of hard, barking laughter.*

YANK

*With a contemptuous snort.*
Love, hell! Hate, dat's what. I've fallen in hate, get me?

PADDY

*Philosophically.*

'Twould take a wise man to tell one from the other.

*With a bitter, ironical scorn, increasing as he goes on.*

But I'm telling you it's love that's in it. Sure what else but love for us poor bastes in the stokehole would be bringing a fine lady, dressed like a white quane, down a mile of ladders and steps to be havin' a look at us?

*A growl of anger goes up from all sides.*

LONG

*Jumping on a bench—hectically.*

Hinsultin' us! Hinsultin' us, the bloody cow! And them bloody engineers! What right 'as they got to be exhibitin' us 's if we was bleedin' monkeys in a menagerie? Did we sign for hinsults to our dignity as 'onest workers? Is that in the ship's articles? You kin bloody well bet it ain't! But I knows why they done it. I arsked a deck steward 'o she was and 'e told me. 'Er old man's a bleedin' millionaire, a bloody Capitalist! 'E's got enuf bloody gold to sink this bleedin' ship! 'E makes arf the bloody steel in the world! 'E owns this bloody boat! And you and me, Comrades, we're 'is slaves! And the skipper and mates and engineers, they're 'is slaves! And she's 'is bloody daughter and we're all 'er slaves, too! And she gives 'er orders as 'ow she wants to see the bloody animals below decks and down they takes 'er!

*There is a roar of rage from all sides.*

YANK

*Blinking at him bewilderedly.*

Say! Wait a moment! Is all dat straight goods?

LONG

Straight as string! The bleedin' steward as waits on 'em, 'e told me about 'er. And what're we goin' ter do, I arsks yer? 'Ave we got ter swaller 'er hinsults like dogs? It ain't in the ship's articles. I tell yer we got a case. We kin go to law—

YANK

*With abysmal contempt.*

Hell! Law!

ALL

*Repeating the word after him as one with cynical mockery.*
Law!
*The word has a brazen metallic quality as if their throats were phonograph horns. It is followed by a chorus of hard, barking laughter.*

LONG

*Feeling the ground slipping from under his feet—desperately.*
As voters and citizens we kin force the bloody governments—

YANK

*With abysmal contempt.*
Hell! Governments!

ALL

*Repeating the word after him as one with cynical mockery.*
Governments!
*The word has a brazen metallic quality as if their throats were phonograph horns. It is followed by a chorus of hard, barking laughter.*

LONG

*Hysterically.*
We're free and equal in the sight of God—

YANK

*With abysmal contempt.*
Hell! God!

ALL

*Repeating the word after him as one with cynical mockery.*
God!
*The word has a brazen metallic quality as if their throats were phonograph horns. It is followed by a chorus of hard, barking laughter.*

YANK

*Witheringly.*
Aw, join de Salvation Army!

ALL

Sit down! Shut up! Damn fool! Sea-lawyer!
*Long slinks back out of sight.*

PADDY

*Continuing the trend of his thoughts as if he had never been inter-rupted—bitterly.*

And there she was standing behind us, and the Second pointing at us like a man you'd hear in a circus would be saying: In this cage is a queerer kind of baboon than ever you'd find in darkest Africy. We roast them in their own sweat—and be damned if you won't hear some of thim saying they like it!

*He glances scornfully at Yank.*

YANK

*With a bewildered uncertain growl.*

Aw!

PADDY

And there was Yank roarin' curses and turning round wid his shovel to brain her—and she looked at him, and him at her—

YANK

*Slowly.*

She was all white. I tought she was a ghost. Sure.

PADDY

*With heavy, biting sarcasm.*

'Twas love at first sight, divil a doubt of it! If you'd seen the endearin' look on her pale mug when she shriveled away with her hands over her eyes to shut out the sight of him! Sure, 'twas as if she'd seen a great hairy ape escaped from the Zoo!

YANK

*Stung—with a growl of rage.*

Aw!

PADDY

And the loving way Yank heaved his shovel at the skull of her, only she was out the door!

*A grin breaking over his face.*

'Twas touching, I'm telling you! It put the touch of home, swate home in the stokehole.

There is a roar of laughter from all.

YANK

*Glaring at Paddy menacingly.*

Aw, choke dat off, see!

PADDY

*Not heeding him—to the others.*

And her grabbin' at the Second's arm for protection.

*With a grotesque imitation of a woman's voice.*

Kiss me, Engineer dear, for it's dark down here and me old man's in Wall Street making money! Hug me tight, darlin', for I'm afeerd in the dark and me mother's on deck makin' eyes at the skipper!

*Another roar of laughter.*

YANK

*Threateningly.*

Say! What yuh tryin' to do, kid me, yuh old Harp?

PADDY

Divil a bit! Ain't I wishin' myself you'd brained her?

YANK

*Fiercely.*

I'll brain her! I'll brain her yet, wait 'n' see!

*Coming over to Paddy—slowly.*

Say, is dat what she called me—a hairy ape?

PADDY

She looked it at you if she didn't say the word itself.

YANK

*Grinning horribly.*

Hairy ape, huh? Sure! Dat's de way she looked at me, aw right. Hairy ape! So dat's me, huh?

*Bursting into rage—as if she were still in front of him.*

Yuh skinny tart! Yuh white-faced bum, yuh! I'll show yuh who's a ape!

*Turning to the others, bewilderment seizing him again.*

Say, youse guys. I was bawlin' him out for pullin' de whistle on us. You heard me. And den I seen youse lookin' at somep'n and I tought he'd sneaked down to come up in back of me, and I hopped round to knock him dead wit de shovel. And dere she was wit de light on her! Christ, yuh coulda pushed me over with a finger! I was scared, get me? Sure! I tought she was a ghost, see? She was all in white like dey wrap around stiffs. You seen her. Kin yuh blame me? She didn't belong, dat's what. And den when I come to and seen it was a real skoit and seen de way she was lookin' at me—like Paddy said—Christ, I was sore, get me? I don't stand for dat stuff from nobody. And I flung de shovel—on'y she'd beat it.

*Furiously.*

I wished it'd banged her! I wished it'd knocked her block off!

LONG

And be 'anged for murder or 'lectrocuted? She ain't bleedin' well worth it.

YANK

I don't give a damn what! I'd be square wit her, wouldn't I? Tink I wanter let her put somep'n over on me? Tink I'm goin' to let her git away wit dat stuff? Yuh don't know me! No one ain't never put nothin' over on me and got away wit it, see!—not dat kind of stuff— no guy and no skoit neither! I'll fix her! Maybe she'll come down again—

VOICE

No chance, Yank. You scared her out of a year's growth.

YANK

I scared her? Why de hell should I scare her? Who de hell is she? Ain't she de same as me? Hairy ape, huh?

*With his old confident bravado.*

I'll show her I'm better'n her, if she on'y knew it. I belong and she don't, see! I move and she's dead! Twenty-five knots a hour, dat's me! Dat carries her but I make dat. She's on'y baggage. Sure!

*Again bewilderedly.*

But, Christ, she was funny lookin'! Did yuh pipe her hands? White and skinny. Yuh could see de bones through 'em. And her mush, dat was dead white, too. And her eyes, dey was like dey'd seen a ghost. Me, dat was! Sure! Hairy ape! Ghost, huh? Look at dat arm!

*He extends his right arm, swelling out the great muscles.*

I coulda took her wit dat, wit' just my little finger even, and broke her in two.

*Again bewilderedly.*

Say, who is dat skoit, huh? What is she? What's she come from? Who made her? Who give her de noive to look at me like dat? Dis ting's got my goat right. I don't get her. She's new to me. What does a skoit like her mean, huh? She don't belong, get me! I can't see her.

*With growing anger.*

But one ting I'm wise to, aw right, aw right! Youse all kin bet your shoits I'll git even wit her. I'll show her if she tinks she— She grinds de organ and I'm on de string, huh? I'll fix her! Let her come down again and I'll fling her in de furnace! She'll move den! She won't shiver at nothin', den! Speed, dat'll be her! She'll belong den!

*He grins horribly.*

PADDY

She'll never come. She's had her belly-full, I'm telling you. She'll be in bed now, I'm thinking, wid ten doctors and nurses feedin' her salts to clean the fear out of her.

YANK

*Enraged.*

Yuh tink I made her sick, too, do yuh? Just lookin' at me, huh? Hairy ape, huh?

*In a frenzy of rage.*

I'll fix her! I'll tell her where to git off! She'll git down on her knees and take it back or I'll bust de face offen her!

*Shaking one fist upward and beating on his chest with the other.*

I'll find yuh! I'm comin', d'yuh hear? I'll fix yuh, God damn yuh!

*He makes a rush for the door.*

VOICES

Stop him!

He'll get shot!

He'll murder her!

Trip him up!

Hold him!

He's gone crazy!

Gott, he's strong!
Hold him down!
Look out for a kick!
Pin his arms!
*They have all piled on him and, after a fierce struggle, by sheer weight of numbers have borne him to the floor just inside the door.*

PADDY
*Who has remained detached.*
Kape him down till he's cooled off.
*Scornfully.*
Yerra, Yank, you're a great fool. Is it payin' attention at all you are to the like of that skinny sow widout one drop of rale blood in her?

YANK
*Frenziedly, from the bottom of the heap.*
She done me doit! She done me doit, didn't she? I'll git square wit her! I'll get her some way! Git offen me, youse guys! Lemme up! I'll show her who's a ape!

CURTAIN

# FRESH CHOICE #055
# (650)949-4901
# 15% Off Next Meal!
# Take Short Survey

At Freshcomments.com
or at 1-800-785-6629
Redemption Code: _____

YOUR ORDER # 147

|               | NO PERSN 1 |   | S/R # 44 |
|---------------|------------|---|----------|
| Lunch         |            |   | 8.19     |
| Sr Lunch 15%  |            |   | -1.23    |
| Bev/Lem/IceT  |            |   | 2.29     |
| TAX           |            |   | 0.86     |

| TOTAL   | **$10.11** |
|---------|------------|
| VISA/MC | 10.11      |

| C-ID 001 |                    | CASH1       |
|----------|--------------------|-------------|
| 0047     | 2:28PM  7/27/09    | 0000-000    |

FRESH CHOICE #055
(650)949-4901
15% Off Next Meal!
Take Short Survey

or at 1-800-785-6629
Redemption Code: _____

YOUR ORDER # 147
NO PRSN 1                    S/R # 44
                                  8.19
                                 -1.23
                                  2.29
                                  0.96

# Scene Five

*Three weeks later. A corner of Fifth Avenue in the Fifties on a fine Sunday morning. A general atmosphere of clean, well-tidied, wide street; a flood of mellow, tempered sunshine; gentle, genteel breezes. In the rear, the show windows of two shops, a jewelry establishment on the corner, a furrier's next to it. Here the adornments of extreme wealth are tantalizingly displayed. The jeweler's window is gaudy with glittering diamonds, emeralds, rubies, pearls, etc., fashioned in ornate tiaras, crowns, necklaces, collars, etc. From each piece hangs an enormous tag from which a dollar sign and numerals in intermittent electric lights wink out the incredible prices. The same in the furrier's. Rich furs of all varieties hang there bathed in a downpour of artificial light. The general effect is of a background of magnificence cheapened and made grotesque by commercialism, a background in tawdry disharmony with the clear light and sunshine on the street itself.*

*Up the side street Yank and Long come swaggering. Long is dressed in shore clothes, wears a black Windsor tie, cloth cap. Yank is in his dirty dungarees. A fireman's cap with black peak is cocked defiantly on the side of his head. He has not shaved for days and around his fierce, resentful eyes—as around those of Long to a lesser degree—the black smudge of coal dust still sticks like make-up. They hesitate and stand together at the corner, swaggering, looking about them with a forced, defiant contempt.*

LONG
*Indicating it all with an oratorical gesture.*
Well, 'ere we are. Fif' Avenoo. This 'ere's their bleedin' private lane, as yer might say.
*Bitterly.*
We're trespassers 'ere. Proletarians keep orf the grass!

YANK

*Dully.*

I don't see no grass, yuh boob.

*Staring at the sidewalk.*

Clean, ain't it? Yuh could eat a fried egg offen it. The white wings
got some job sweepin' dis up.

*Looking up and down the avenue—surlily.*

Where's all de white-collar stiffs yuh said was here—and de skoits—
*her* kind?

LONG

In church, blarst 'em! Arskin' Jesus to give 'em more money.

YANK

Choich, huh? I useter go to choich onct—sure—when I was a kid.
Me old man and woman, dey made me. Dey never went demselves,
dough. Always got too big a head on Sunday mornin', dat was dem.

*With a grin.*

Dey was scrappers for fair, bot' of dem. On Satiday nights when dey
bot' got a skinful dey could put up a bout oughter been staged at
de Garden. When dey got trou dere wasn't a chair or table wit a leg
under it. Or else dey bot' jumped on me for somep'n. Dat was where
I loined to take punishment.

*With a grin and a swagger.*

I'm a chip offen de old block, get me?

LONG

Did yer old man follow the sea?

YANK

Naw. Worked along shore. I runned away when me old lady croaked
wit de tremens. I helped at truckin' and in de market. Den I shipped
in de stokehole. Sure. Dat belongs. De rest was nothin'.

*Looking around him.*

I ain't never seen dis before. De Brooklyn waterfront, dat was where
I was dragged up.

*Taking a deep breath.*

Dis ain't so bad at dat, huh?

LONG

Not bad? Well, we pays for it wiv our bloody sweat, if yer wants to know!

YANK

*With sudden angry disgust.*

Aw, hell! I don't see no one, see—like her. All dis gives me a pain. It don't belong. Say, ain't dere a back room around dis dump? Let's go shoot a ball. All dis is too clean and quiet and dolled-up, get me! It gives me a pain.

LONG

Wait and yer'll bloody well see—

YANK

I don't wait for no one. I keep on de move. Say, what yuh drag me up here for, anyway? Tryin' to kid me, yuh simp, yuh?

LONG

Yer wants to get back at 'er, don't yer? That's what yer been sayin' every bloomin' hour since she hinsulted yer.

YANK

*Vehemently.*

Sure ting I do! Didn't I try to get even wit her in Southhampton? Didn't I sneak on de dock and wait for her by de gangplank? I was goin' to spit in her pale mug, see! Sure, right in her pop-eyes! Dat woulda made me even, see? But no chanct. Dere was a whole army of plainclothes bulls around. Dey spotted me and gimme de bum's rush. I never seen her. But I'll git square wit her yet, you watch!

*Furiously.*

De lousy tart! She tinks she kin get away wit moider—but not wit me! I'll fix her! I'll tink of a way!

LONG

*As disgusted as he dares to be.*

Ain't that why I brought yer up 'ere—to show yer? Yer been lookin' at this 'ere 'ole affair wrong. Yer been actin' an' talkin' 's if it was all a bleedin' personal matter between yer and that bloody cow. I wants to convince yer she was on'y a representative of 'er clarss. I wants to awaken yer bloody clarss consciousness. Then yer'll see it's 'er clarss yer've got to fight, not 'er alone. There's a 'ole mob of 'em like 'er, Gawd blind 'em!

YANK

*Spitting on his hands—belligerently.*
De more de merrier when I gits started. Bring on de gang!

LONG

Yer'll see 'em in arf a mo', when that church lets out.
*He turns and sees the window display in the two stores for the first time.*
Blimey! Look at that, will yer?
*They both walk back and stand looking in the jeweler's. Long flies into a fury.*
Just look at this 'ere bloomin' mess! Just look at it! Look at the bleedin' prices on 'em—more'n our 'ole bloody stokehole makes in ten voyages sweatin' in 'ell! And they—'er and 'er bloody clarss—buys 'em for toys to dangle on 'em! One of these 'ere would buy scoff for a starvin' family for a year!

YANK

Aw, cut de sob stuff! T' hell wit de starvin' family! Yuh'll be passin' de hat to me next.
*With naïve admiration.*
Say, dem tings is pretty, huh? Bet yuh dey'd hock for a piece of change aw right.
*Then turning away, bored.*
But, aw hell, what good are dey? Let her have 'em. Dey don't belong no more'n she does.
*With a gesture of sweeping the jewelers into oblivion.*
All dat don't count, get me?

LONG

*Who has moved to the furrier's—indignantly.*
And I s'pose this 'ere don't count neither—skins of poor, 'armless animals slaughtered so as 'er and 'ers can keep their bleedin' noses warm!

YANK

*Who has been staring at something inside—with queer excitement.*

Take a slant at dat! Give it de once-over! Monkey fur—two t'ousand bucks!

*Bewilderedly.*

Is dat straight goods—monkey fur? What de hell—?

LONG

*Bitterly.*

It's straight enuf.

*With grim humor.*

They wouldn't bloody well pay that for a 'airy ape's skin—no, nor for the 'ole livin' ape with all 'is 'ead, and body, and soul thrown in!

YANK

*Clenching his fists, his face growing pale with rage as if the skin in the window were a personal insult.*

Trowin' it up in my face! Christ! I'll fix her!

LONG

*Excitedly.*

Church is out. 'Ere they come, the bleedin' swine.

*After a glance at Yank's lowering face—uneasily.*

Easy goes, Comrade. Keep yer bloomin' temper. Remember force defeats itself. It ain't our weapon. We must impress our demands through peaceful means—the votes of the on-marching proletarians of the bloody world!

YANK

*With abysmal contempt.*

Votes, hell! Votes is a joke, see. Votes for women! Let dem do it!

LONG

*Still more uneasily.*

Calm, now. Treat 'em wiv the proper contempt. Observe the bleedin' parasites but 'old yer 'orses.

YANK

*Angrily.*

Git away from me! Yuh're yellow, dat's what. Force, dat's me! De punch, dat's me every time, see!

*The crowd from church enter from the right, sauntering slowly and affectedly, their heads held stiffly up, looking neither to right nor left, talking in toneless, simpering voices. The women are rouged, calcimined, dyed, overdressed to the nth degree. The men are in Prince Alberts, high hats, spats, canes, etc. A procession of gaudy marionettes, yet with something of the relentless horror of Frankensteins in their detached, mechanical unawareness.*

VOICES

Dear Doctor Caiaphas! He is so sincere!

What was the sermon? I dozed off.

About the radicals, my dear—and the false doctrines that are being preached.

We must organize a hundred per cent American bazaar.

And let everyone contribute one one-hundredth per cent of their income tax.

What an original idea!

We can devote the proceeds to rehabilitating the veil of the temple.

But that has been done so many times.

YANK

*Glaring from one to the other of them—with an insulting snort of scorn.*

Huh! Huh!

*Without seeming to see him, they make wide detours to avoid the spot where he stands in the middle of the sidewalk.*

LONG

*Frightenedly.*

Keep yer bloomin' mouth shut, I tells yer.

YANK

*Viciously.*

G'wan! Tell it to Sweeney!

*He swaggers away and deliberately lurches into a top-hatted gentleman, then glares at him pugnaciously.*

Say, who d'yuh tink yuh're bumpin'? Tink yuh own de oith?

GENTLEMAN

*Coldly and affectedly.*

I beg your pardon.

*He has not looked at Yank and passes on without a glance, leaving him bewildered.*

LONG

*Rushing up and grabbing Yank's arm.*

'Ere! Come away! This wasn't what I meant. Yer'll 'ave the bloody coppers down on us.

YANK

*Savagely—giving him a push that sends him sprawling.*

G'wan!

LONG

*Picks himself up—hysterically.*

I'll pop orf then. This ain't what I meant. And whatever 'appens, yer can't blame me.

*He slinks off left.*

YANK

T' hell wit youse!

*He approaches a lady—with a vicious grin and a smirking wink.*

Hello, Kiddo. How's every little ting? Got anyting on for tonight? I know an old boiler down to de docks we kin crawl into.

*The lady stalks by without a look, without a change of pace. Yank turns to others—insultingly.*

Holy smokes, what a mug! Go hide yuhself before de horses shy at yuh. Gee, pipe de heine on dat one! Say, youse, yuh look like de stoin of a ferryboat. Paint and powder! All dolled up to kill! Yuh look like stiffs laid out for de boneyard! Aw, g'wan, de lot of youse! Yuh give me de eyeache. Yuh don't belong, get me! Look at me, why don't youse dare? I belong, dat's me!

*Pointing to a skyscraper across the street which is in process of construction—with bravado.*

See dat building goin' up dere? See de steel work? Steel, dat's me! Youse guys live on it and tink yuh're somep'n. But I'm *in* it, see! I'm de hoistin' engine dat makes it go up! I'm it—de inside and bottom of it! Sure! I'm steel and steam and smoke and de rest of it! It moves—speed—twenty-five stories up—and me at de top and bottom—movin'! Youse simps don't move. Yuh're on'y dolls I winds up to see 'em spin. Yuh're de garbage, get me—de leavins—de ashes we dump over de side! Now, what 'a' yuh gotta say?

*But as they seem neither to see nor hear him, he flies into a fury.*

Bums! Pigs! Tarts! Bitches!

*He turns in a rage on the men, bumping viciously into them but not jarring them the least bit. Rather it is he who recoils after each collision. He keeps growling.*

Git off de oith! G'wan, yuh bum! Look where yuh're goin', can't yuh? Git outa here! Fight, why don't yuh? Put up yer mits! Don't be a dog! Fight or I'll knock yuh dead!

*But, without seeming to see him, they all answer with mechanical affected politeness:* I beg your pardon. *Then at a cry from one of the women, they all scurry to the furrier's window.*

THE WOMAN

*Ecstatically, with a gasp of delight.*

Monkey fur!

*The whole crowd of men and women chorus after her in the same tone of affected delight:* Monkey fur!

YANK

*With a jerk of his head back on his shoulders, as if he had received a punch full in the face—raging.*

I see yuh, all in white! I see yuh, yuh white-faced tart, yuh! Hairy ape, huh? I'll hairy ape yuh!

*He bends down and grips at the street curbing as if to pluck it out and hurl it. Foiled in this, snarling with passion, he leaps to the lamp-post on the corner and tries to pull it up for a club. Just at that moment a bus is heard rumbling up. A fat, high-hatted, spatted gentleman runs out from the side street. He calls out plaintively:* Bus! Bus! Stop there! *and runs full tilt into the bending, straining Yank, who is bowled off his balance.*

YANK

*Seeing a fight—with a roar of joy as he springs to his feet.*

At last! Bus, huh? I'll bust yuh!

*He lets drive a terrific swing, his fist landing full on the fat gentleman's face. But the gentleman stands unmoved as if nothing had happened.*

GENTLEMAN
I beg your pardon.
*Then irritably.*
You have made me lose my bus.
*He claps his hands and begins to scream.*
Officer! Officer!
*Many police whistles shrill out on the instant and a whole platoon of policemen rush in on Yank from all sides. He tries to fight but is clubbed to the pavement and fallen upon. The crowd at the window have not moved or noticed this disturbance. The clanging gong of the patrol wagon approaches with a clamoring din.*

CURTAIN

# Scene Six

*Night of the following day. A row of cells in the prison on Blackwells Island. The cells extend back diagonally from right front to left rear. They do not stop, but disappear in the dark background as if they ran on, numberless, into infinity. One electric bulb from the low ceiling of the narrow corridor sheds its light through the heavy steel bars of the cell at the extreme front and reveals part of the interior. Yank can be seen within, crouched on the edge of his cot in the attitude of Rodin's "The Thinker." His face is spotted with black and blue bruises. A blood-stained bandage is wrapped around his head.*

YANK
*Suddenly starting as if awakening from a dream, reaches out and shakes the bars—aloud to himself, wonderingly.*
Steel. Dis is de Zoo, huh?
*A burst of hard, barking laughter comes from the unseen occupants of the cells, runs back down the tier, and abruptly ceases.*

VOICES
*Mockingly.*
The Zoo? That's a new name for this coop—a damn good name!
Steel, eh? You said a mouthful. This is the old iron house.
Who is that boob talkin'?
He's the bloke they brung in out of his head. The bulls had beat him up fierce.

YANK
*Dully.*
I musta been dreamin'. I tought I was in a cage at de Zoo—but de apes don't talk, do dey?

VOICES

*With mocking laughter.*

You're in a cage aw right.

A coop!

A pen!

A sty!

A kennel!

*Hard laughter—a pause.*

Say, guy! Who are you? No, never mind lying. What are you?

Yes, tell us your sad story. What's your game?

What did they jug yuh for?

YANK

*Dully.*

I was a fireman—stokin' on de liners.

*Then with sudden rage, rattling his cell bars.*

I'm a hairy ape, get me? And I'll bust youse all in de jaw if yuh don't
lay off kiddin' me.

VOICES

Huh! You're a hard boiled duck, ain't you!

When you spit, it bounces!

*Laughter.*

Aw, can it. He's a regular guy. Ain't you?

What did he say he was—a ape?

YANK

*Defiantly.*

Sure ting! Ain't dat what youse all are—apes?

*A silence. Then a furious rattling of bars from down the corridor.*

A VOICE

*Thick with rage.*

I'll show yuh who's a ape, yuh bum!

VOICES

Ssshh! Nix!

Can de noise!

Piano!
You'll have the guard down on us!

YANK
*Scornfully.*
De guard? Yuh mean de keeper, don't yuh?
*Angry exclamations from all the cells.*

VOICE
*Placatingly.*
Aw, don't pay no attention to him. He's off his nut from the beatin'-
up he got. Say, you guy! We're waitin' to hear what they landed you
for — or ain't yuh tellin'?

YANK
Sure, I'll tell youse. Sure! Why de hell not? On'y — youse won't get
me. Nobody gets me but me, see? I started to tell de Judge and all
he says was: "Toity days to tink it over." Tink it over! Christ, dat's
all I been doin' for weeks!
*After a pause.*
I was tryin' to git even wit someone, see? — someone dat done me
doit.

VOICES
*Cynically.*
De old stuff, I bet. Your goil, huh?
Give yuh the double-cross, huh?
That's them every time!
Did yuh beat up de odder guy?

YANK
*Disgustedly.*
Aw, yuh're all wrong! Sure dere was a skoit in it — but not what youse
mean, not dat old tripe. Dis was a new kind of skoit. She was dolled
up all in white — in de stokehole. I tought she was a ghost. Sure.
*A pause.*

VOICES
*Whispering.*

Gee, he's still nutty.

Let him rave. It's fun listenin'.

YANK

*Unheeding—groping in his thoughts.*

Her hands—dey was skinny and white like dey wasn't real but painted on somep'n. Dere was a million miles from me to her—twenty-five knots a hour. She was like some dead ting de cat brung in. Sure, dat's what. She didn't belong. She belonged in de window of a toy store, or on de top of a garbage can, see! Sure!

*He breaks out angrily.*

But would yuh believe it, she had de noive to do me doit. She lamped me like she was seein' somep'n broke loose from de menagerie. Christ, yuh'd oughter seen her eyes!

*He rattles the bars of his cell furiously.*

But I'll get back at her yet, you watch! And if I can't find her I'll take it out on de gang she runs wit. I'm wise to where dey hangs out now. I'll show her who belongs! I'll show her who's in de move and who ain't. You watch my smoke!

VOICES

*Serious and joking.*

Dat's de talkin'!

Take her for all she's got!

What was this dame, anyway? Who was she, eh?

YANK

I dunno. First cabin stiff. Her old man's a millionaire, dey says—name of Douglas.

VOICES

Douglas? That's the president of the Steel Trust, I bet.

Sure. I seen his mug in de papers.

He's filthy with dough.

VOICE

Hey, feller, take a tip from me. If you want to get back at that dame, you better join the Wobblies. You'll get some action then.

YANK

Wobblies? What de hell's dat?

VOICE

Ain't you ever heard of the I. W. W.?

YANK

Naw. What is it?

VOICE

A gang of blokes—a tough gang. I been readin' about 'em today in
the paper. The guard give me the *Sunday Times*. There's a long spiel
about 'em. It's from a speech made in the Senate by a guy named
Senator Queen.
*He is in the cell next to Yank's. There is a rustling of paper.*
Wait'll I see if I got light enough and I'll read you. Listen.
*He reads.*
"There is a menace existing in this country today which threatens
the vitals of our fair Republic—as foul a menace against the very life-
blood of the American Eagle as was the foul conspiracy of Cataline
against the eagles of ancient Rome!"

VOICE

*Disgustedly.*
Aw, hell! Tell him to salt de tail of dat eagle!

VOICE

*Reading.*
"I refer to that devil's brew of rascals, jailbirds, murderers and cut-
throats who libel all honest working men by calling themselves the
Industrial Workers of the World; but in the light of their nefarious
plots, I call them the Industrious *Wreckers* of the World!"

YANK

*With vengeful satisfaction.*
Wreckers, dat's de right dope! Dat belongs! Me for dem!

VOICE

Ssshh!
*Reading.*

"This fiendish organization is a foul ulcer on the fair body of our
Democracy—"

VOICE
Democracy, hell! Give him the boid, fellers—the raspberry!
*They do.*

VOICE
*Ssshh!*
*Reading.*
"Like Cato I say to this Senate, the I. W. W. must be destroyed! For
they represent an ever-present dagger pointed at the heart of the
greatest nation the world has ever known, where all men are born
free and equal, with equal opportunities to all, where the Founding
Fathers have guaranteed to each one happiness, where Truth, Honor,
Liberty, Justice, and the Brotherhood of Man are a religion absorbed
with one's mother milk, taught at our father's knee, sealed, signed,
and stamped upon in the glorious Constitution of these United
States!"
*A perfect storm of hisses, catcalls, boos, and hard laughter.*

VOICES
*Scornfully.*
Hurrah for de Fort' of July!
Pass de hat!
Liberty!
Justice!
Honor!
Opportunity!
Brotherhood!

ALL
*With abysmal scorn.*
Aw, hell!

VOICE
Give that Queen Senator guy the bark! All togedder now—one—
two—tree—
*A terrific chorus of barking and yapping.*

GUARD
*From a distance.*
Quiet there, youse—or I'll git the hose.
*The noise subsides.*

YANK
*With growling rage.*
I'd like to catch dat senator guy alone for a second. I'd loin him some
trute!

VOICE
Ssshh! Here's where he gits down to cases on the Wobblies.
*Reads.*
"They plot with fire in one hand and dynamite in the other. They
stop not before murder to gain their ends, nor at the outraging of defenseless womanhood. They would tear down society, put the lowest
scum in the seats of the mighty, turn Almighty God's revealed plan
for the world topsy-turvy, and make of our sweet and lovely civiliza-
tion a shambles, a desolation where man, God's masterpiece, would
soon degenerate back to the ape!"

VOICE
*To Yank.*
Hey, you guy. There's your ape stuff again.

YANK
*With a growl of fury.*
I got him. So dey blow up tings, do dey? Dey turn tings round, do
dey? Hey, lend me dat paper, will yuh?

VOICE
Sure. Give it to him. On'y keep it to yourself, see. We don't wanter
listen to no more of that slop.

VOICE
Here you are. Hide it under your mattress.

YANK
*Reaching out.*

262    The Hairy Ape

Tanks. I can't read much but I kin manage.

*He sits, the paper in the hand at his side, in the attitude of Rodin's "The Thinker." A pause. Several snores from down the corridor. Suddenly Yank jumps to his feet with a furious groan as if some appalling thought had crashed on him—bewilderedly.*

Sure—her old man—president of de Steel Trust—makes half de steel in de world—steel—where I tought I belonged—drivin' trou—movin'—in dat—to make *her*—and cage me in for her to spit on! Christ!

*He shakes the bars of his cell door till the whole tier trembles. Irritated, protesting exclamations from those awakened or trying to get to sleep.*

He made dis—dis cage! Steel! *It* don't belong, dat's what! Cages, cells, locks, bolts, bars—dat's what it means!—holdin' me down wit him at de top! But I'll drive trou! Fire, dat melts it! I'll be fire—under de heap—fire dat never goes out—hot as hell—breakin' out in de night—

*While he has been saying this last he has shaken his cell door to a clanging accompaniment. As he comes to the "breakin' out" he seizes one bar with both hands and, putting his two feet up against the others so that his position is parallel to the floor like a monkey's, he gives a great wrench backwards. The bar bends like a licorice stick under his tremendous strength. Just at this moment the prison guard rushes in, dragging a hose behind him.*

GUARD

*Angrily.*

I'll loin youse bums to wake me up!

*Sees Yank.*

Hello, it's you, huh? Got the D. Ts., hey? Well, I'll cure 'em. I'll drown your snakes for yuh!

*Noticing the bar.*

Hell, look at dat bar bended! On'y a bug is strong enough for dat!

YANK

*Glaring at him.*

Or a hairy ape, yuh big yellow bum! Look out! Here I come!

*He grabs another bar.*

GUARD

*Scared now — yelling off left.*

Toin de hose on, Ben! — full pressure! And call de others — and a straitjacket!

*The curtain is falling. As it hides Yank from view, there is a splattering smash as the stream of water hits the steel of Yank's cell.*

CURTAIN

# Scene Seven

*Nearly a month later. An I. W. W. local near the waterfront, showing
the interior of a front room on the ground floor, and the street outside.
Moonlight on the narrow street, buildings massed in black shadow. The
interior of the room, which is general assembly room, office, and reading room, resembles some dingy settlement boys' club. A desk and high
stool are in one corner. A table with papers, stacks of pamphlets, chairs
about it, is at center. The whole is decidedly cheap, banal, commonplace
and unmysterious as a room could well be. The secretary is perched on
the stool making entries in a large ledger. An eye shade casts his face into
shadows. Eight or ten men, longshoremen, iron workers, and the like,
are grouped about the table. Two are playing checkers. One is writing a
letter. Most of them are smoking pipes. A big signboard is on the wall at
the rear, "Industrial Workers of the World—Local No. 57."*

YANK

*Comes down the street outside. He is dressed as in Scene Five. He moves
cautiously, mysteriously. He comes to a point opposite the door; tiptoes
softly up to it, listens, is impressed by the silence within, knocks carefully, as if he were guessing at the password to some secret rite. Listens.
No answer. Knocks again a bit louder. No answer. Knocks impatiently,
much louder.*

SECRETARY

*Turning around on his stool.*

What the hell is that—someone knocking?

*Shouts.*

Come in, why don't you?

*All the men in the room look up. Yank opens the door slowly, gingerly, as
if afraid of an ambush. He looks around for secret doors, mystery, is taken
aback by the commonplaceness of the room and the men in it, thinks he*

265

*may have gotten in the wrong place, then sees the signboard on the wall and is reassured.*

YANK
*Blurts out.*
Hello.

MEN
*Reservedly.*
Hello.

YANK
*More easily.*
I tought I'd bumped into de wrong dump.

SECRETARY
*Scrutinizing him carefully.*
Maybe you have. Are you a member?

YANK
Naw, not yet. Dat's what I come for—to join.

SECRETARY
That's easy. What's your job—longshore?

YANK
Naw. Fireman—stoker on de liners.

SECRETARY
*With satisfaction.*
Welcome to our city. Glad to know you people are waking up at last. We haven't got many members in your line.

YANK
Naw. Dey're all dead to de woild.

SECRETARY
Well, you can help to wake 'em. What's your name? I'll make out your card.

YANK
*Confused.*

Name? Lemme tink.

SECRETARY
*Sharply.*
Don't you know your own name?

YANK
Sure; but I been just Yank for so long—Bob, dat's it—Bob Smith.

SECRETARY
*Writing.*
Robert Smith.
*Fills out the rest of card.*
Here you are. Cost you half a dollar.

YANK
Is dat all—four bits? Dat's easy.
*Gives the Secretary the money.*

SECRETARY
*Throwing it in drawer.*
Thanks. Well, make yourself at home. No introductions needed.
There's literature on the table. Take some of those pamphlets with
you to distribute aboard ship. They may bring results. Sow the seed,
only go about it right. Don't get caught and fired. We got plenty out
of work. What we need is men who can hold their jobs—and work
for us at the same time.

YANK
Sure.
*But he still stands, embarrassed and uneasy.*

SECRETARY
*Looking at him—curiously.*
What did you knock for? Think we had a coon in uniform to open
doors?

YANK
Naw. I tought it was locked—and dat yuh'd wanter give me the
once-over trou a peep-hole or somep'n to see if I was right.

SECRETARY

*Alert and suspicious but with an easy laugh.*

Think we were running a crap game? That door is never locked. What put that in your nut?

YANK

*With a knowing grin, convinced that this is all camouflage, a part of the secrecy.*

Dis burg is full of bulls, ain't it?

SECRETARY

*Sharply.*

What have the cops got to do with us? We're breaking no laws.

YANK

*With a knowing wink.*

Sure. Youse wouldn't for woilds. Sure. I'm wise to dat.

SECRETARY

You seem to be wise to a lot of stuff none of us knows about.

YANK

*With another wink.*

Aw, dat's aw right, see.

*Then made a bit resentful by the suspicious glances from all sides.*

Aw, can it! Youse needn't put me trou de toid degree. Can't youse see I belong? Sure! I'm reg'lar. I'll stick, get me? I'll shoot de woiks for youse. Dat's why I wanted to join in.

SECRETARY

*Breezily, feeling him out.*

That's the right spirit. Only are you sure you understand what you've joined? It's all plain and above board; still, some guys get a wrong slant on us.

*Sharply.*

What's your notion of the purpose of the I. W. W.?

YANK

Aw, I know all about it.

SECRETARY
*Sarcastically.*
Well, give us some of your valuable information.

YANK
*Cunningly.*
I know enough not to speak outa my toin.
*Then resentfully again.*
Aw, say! I'm reg'lar. I'm wise to de game. I know yuh got to watch
your step wit a stranger. For all youse know, I might be a plain-
clothes dick, or somep'n, dat's what yuh're tinkin', huh? Aw, forget
it! I belong, see? Ask any guy down to de docks if I don't.

SECRETARY
Who said you didn't?

YANK
After I'm 'nitiated, I'll show yuh.

SECRETARY
*Astounded.*
Initiated? There's no initiation.

YANK
*Disappointed.*
Ain't there no password—no grip nor nothin'?

SECRETARY
What'd you think this is—the Elks—or the Black Hand?

YANK
De Elks, hell! De Black Hand, dey're a lot of yellow backstickin'
Ginees. Naw. Dis is a man's gang, ain't it?

SECRETARY
You said it! That's why we stand on our two feet in the open. We got
no secrets.

YANK
*Surprised but admiringly.*
Yuh mean to say yuh always run wide open—like dis?

SECRETARY

Exactly.

YANK

Den yuh sure got your noive wit youse!

SECRETARY

*Sharply.*

Just what was it made you want to join us? Come out with that straight.

YANK

Yuh call me? Well, I got noive, too! Here's my hand. Yuh wanter blow tings up, don't yuh? Well, dat's me! I belong!

SECRETARY

*With pretended carelessness.*

You mean change the unequal conditions of society by legitimate direct action—or with dynamite?

YANK

Dynamite! Blow it offen de oith—steel—all de cages—all de factories, steamers, buildings, jails—de Steel Trust and all dat makes it go.

SECRETARY

So—that's your idea, eh? And did you have any special job in that line you wanted to propose to us?

*He makes a sign to the men, who get up cautiously one by one and group behind Yank.*

YANK

*Boldly.*

Sure, I'll come out wit it. I'll show youse I'm one of de gang. Dere's dat millionaire guy, Douglas—

SECRETARY

President of the Steel Trust, you mean? Do you want to assassinate him?

YANK

Naw, dat don't get yuh nothin'. I mean blow up de factory, de woiks, where he makes de steel. Dat's what I'm after—to blow up de steel, knock all de steel in de woild up to de moon. Dat'll fix tings!

*Eagerly, with a touch of bravado.*

I'll do it by me lonesome! I'll show yuh! Tell me where his woiks is, how to git there, all de dope. Gimme de stuff, de old butter—and watch me do de rest! Watch de smoke and see it move! I don't give a damn if dey nab me—long as it's done! I'll soive life for it—and give 'em de laugh!

*Half to himself.*

And I'll write her a letter and tell her de hairy ape done it. Dat'll square tings.

SECRETARY

*Stepping away from Yank.*

Very interesting.

*He gives a signal. The men, huskies all, throw themselves on Yank and before he knows it they have his legs and arms pinioned. But he is too flabbergasted to make a struggle, anyway. They feel him over for weapons.*

MAN

No gat, no knife. Shall we give him what's what and put the boots to him?

SECRETARY

No. He isn't worth the trouble we'd get into. He's too stupid.

*He comes closer and laughs mockingly in Yank's face.*

Ho-ho! By God, this is the biggest joke they've put up on us yet. Hey, you Joke! Who sent you—Burns or Pinkerton? No, by God, you're such a bonehead I'll bet you're in the Secret Service! Well, you dirty spy, you rotten agent provocator, you can go back and tell whatever skunk is paying you blood-money for betraying your brothers that he's wasting his coin. You couldn't catch a cold. And tell him that all he'll ever get on us, or ever has got, is just his own sneaking plots that he's framed up to put us in jail. We are what our manifesto says we are, neither more nor less—and we'll give him a copy of that any time he calls. And as for you—

*He glares scornfully at Yank, who is sunk in an oblivious stupor.*

Oh, hell, what's the use of talking? You're a brainless ape.

YANK

*Aroused by the word to fierce but futile struggles.*

What's dat, yuh Sheeny bum, yuh!

SECRETARY

Throw him out, boys.

*In spite of his struggles, this is done with gusto and éclat. Propelled by several parting kicks, Yank lands sprawling in the middle of the narrow cobbled street. With a growl he starts to get up and storm the closed door, but stops bewildered by the confusion in his brain, pathetically impotent. He sits there, brooding, in as near to the attitude of Rodin's "Thinker" as he can get in his position.*

YANK

*Bitterly.*

So dem boids don't tink I belong, neider. Aw, to hell wit 'em! Dey're in de wrong pew—de same old bull—soapboxes and Salvation Army —no guts! Cut out an hour offen de job a day and make me happy! Gimme a dollar more a day and make me happy! Tree square a day, and cauliflowers in de front yard—ekal rights—a woman and kids— a lousy vote—and I'm all fixed for Jesus, huh? Aw, hell! What does dat get yuh? Dis ting's in your inside, but it ain't your belly. Feedin' your face—sinkers and coffee—dat don't touch it. It's way down— at de bottom. Yuh can't grab it, and yuh can't stop it. It moves, and everything moves. It stops and de whole woild stops. Dat's me now—I don't tick, see?—I'm a busted Ingersoll, dat's what. Steel was me, and I owned de woild. Now I ain't steel, and de woild owns me. Aw, hell! I can't see—it's all dark, get me? It's all wrong!

*He turns a bitter mocking face up like an ape gibbering at the moon.*

Say, youse up dere, Man in de Moon, yuh look so wise, gimme de answer, huh? Slip me de inside dope, de information right from de stable—where do I get off at, huh?

A POLICEMAN

*Who has come up the street in time to hear this last—with grim humor.*
You'll get off at the station, you boob, if you don't get up out of that
and keep movin'.

YANK

*Looking up at him—with a hard, bitter laugh.*
Sure! Lock me up! Put me in a cage! Dat's de on'y answer yuh know.
G'wan, lock me up!

POLICEMAN

What you been doin'?

YANK

Enuf to gimme life for! I was born, see? Sure, dat's de charge. Write
it in de blotter. I was born, get me!

POLICEMAN

*Jocosely.*
God pity your old woman!
*Then matter-of-fact.*
But I've no time for kidding. You're soused. I'd run you in but it's
too long a walk to the station. Come on now, get up, or I'll fan your
ears with this club. Beat it now!
*He hauls Yank to his feet.*

YANK

*In a vague mocking tone.*
Say, where do I go from here?

POLICEMAN

*Giving him a push—with a grin, indifferently.*
Go to hell.

CURTAIN

# Scene Eight

*Twilight of the next day. The monkey house at the Zoo. One spot of clear gray light falls on the front of one cage so that the interior can be seen. The other cages are vague, shrouded in shadow from which chatterings pitched in a conversational tone can be heard. On the one cage a sign from which the word "gorilla" stands out. The gigantic animal himself is seen squatting on his haunches on a bench in much the same attitude as Rodin's "Thinker." Yank enters from the left. Immediately a chorus of angry chattering and screeching breaks out. The gorilla turns his eyes but makes no sound or move.*

YANK
*With a hard, bitter laugh.*
Welcome to your city, huh? Hail, hail, de gang's all here!
*At the sound of his voice the chattering dies away into an attentive silence. Yank walks up to the gorilla's cage and, leaning over the railing, stares in at its occupant, who stares back at him, silent and motionless. There is a pause of dead stillness. Then Yank begins to talk in a friendly confidential tone, half-mockingly, but with a deep undercurrent of sympathy.*
Say, yuh're some hard-lookin' guy, ain't yuh? I seen lots of tough nuts dat de gang called gorillas, but yuh're de foist real one I ever seen. Some chest yuh got, and shoulders, and dem arms and mits! I bet yuh got a punch in eider fist dat'd knock 'em all silly!
*This with genuine admiration. The gorilla, as if he understood, stands upright, swelling out his chest and pounding on it with his fist. Yank grins sympathetically.*
Sure, I get yuh. Yuh challenge de whole woild, huh? Yuh got what I was sayin' even if yuh muffed de woids.
*Then bitterness creeping in.*

And why wouldn't yuh get me? Ain't we both members of de same club—de Hairy Apes?

*They stare at each other—a pause—then Yank goes on slowly and bitterly.*

So yuh're what she seen when she looked at me, de white-faced tart! I was you to her, get me? On'y outa de cage—broke out—free to moider her, see? Sure! Dat's what she tought. She wasn't wise dat I was in a cage, too—worser'n yours—sure—a damn sight—'cause you got some chanct to bust loose—but me—

*He grows confused.*

Aw, hell! It's all wrong, ain't it?

*A pause.*

I s'pose yuh wanter know what I'm doin' here, huh? I been warmin' a bench down to de Battery—ever since last night. Sure. I seen de sun come up. Dat was pretty, too—all red and pink and green. I was lookin' at de skyscrapers—steel—and all de ships comin' in, sailin' out, all over de oith—and dey was steel, too. De sun was warm, dey wasn't no clouds, and dere was a breeze blowin'. Sure, it was great stuff. I got it aw right—what Paddy said about dat bein' de right dope—on'y I couldn't get *in* it, see? I couldn't belong in dat. It was over my head. And I kept tinkin'—and den I beat it up here to see what youse was like. And I waited till dey was all gone to git yuh alone. Say, how d'yuh feel sittin' in dat pen all de time, havin' to stand for 'em comin' and starin' at yuh—de white-faced, skinny tarts and de boobs what marry 'em—makin' fun of yuh, laughin' at yuh, gittin' scared of yuh—damn 'em!

*He pounds on the rail with his fist. The gorilla rattles the bars of his cage and snarls. All the other monkeys set up an angry chattering in the darkness. Yank goes on excitedly.*

Sure! Dat's de way it hits me, too. On'y yuh're lucky, see? Yuh don't belong wit 'em and yuh know it. But me, I belong wit 'em—but I don't, see? Dey don't belong wit me, dat's what. Get me? Tinkin' is hard—

*He passes one hand across his forehead with a painful gesture. The gorilla growls impatiently. Yank goes on gropingly.*

It's dis way, what I'm drivin' at. Youse can sit and dope dream in de past, green woods, de jungle and de rest of it. Den yuh belong and dey don't. Den yuh kin laugh at 'em, see? Yuh're de champ of de woild. But me—I ain't got no past to tink in, nor nothin' dat's comin', on'y what's now—and dat don't belong. Sure, you're de best off! Yuh can't tink, can yuh? Yuh can't talk neider. But I kin make a bluff at talkin' and tinkin'—a'most git away wit it—a'most!—and dat's where de joker comes in.

*He laughs.*

I ain't on oith and I ain't in heaven, get me? I'm in de middle tryin' to separate 'em, takin' all de woist punches from bot' of 'em. Maybe dat's what dey call hell, huh? But you, yuh're at de bottom. You belong! Sure! Yuh're de on'y one in de woild dat does, yuh lucky stiff!

*The gorilla growls proudly.*

And dat's why dey gotter put yuh in a cage, see?

*The gorilla roars angrily.*

Sure! Yuh get me. It beats it when you try to tink it or talk it—it's way down—deep—behind—you 'n' me we feel it. Sure! Bot' members of dis club!

*He laughs—then in a savage tone.*

What de hell! T' hell wit it! A little action, dat's our meat! Dat belongs! Knock 'em down and keep bustin' 'em till dey croaks yuh wit a gat—wit steel! Sure! Are yuh game? Dey've looked at youse, ain't dey—in a cage? Wanter git even? Wanter wind up like a sport 'stead of croakin' slow in dere?

*The gorilla roars an emphatic affirmative. Yank goes on with a sort of furious exaltation.*

Sure! Yuh're reg'lar! Yuh'll stick to de finish! Me 'n' you, huh?—bot' members of this club! We'll put up one last star bout dat'll knock 'em offen deir seats! Dey'll have to make de cages stronger after we're trou!

*The gorilla is straining at his bars, growling, hopping from one foot to the other. Yank takes a jimmy from under his coat and forces the lock on the cage door. He throws this open.*

Pardon from de governor! Step out and shake hands! I'll take yuh for a walk down Fif' Avenoo. We'll knock 'em offen de oith and croak wit de band playin'. Come on, Brother.

*The gorilla scrambles gingerly out of his cage. Goes to Yank and stands looking at him. Yank keeps his mocking tone—holds out his hand.*

Shake—de secret grip of our order.

*Something, the tone of mockery, perhaps, suddenly enrages the animal. With a spring he wraps his huge arms around Yank in a murderous hug. There is a crackling snap of crushed ribs—a gasping cry, still mocking, from Yank.*

Hey, I didn't say kiss me!

*The gorilla lets the crushed body slip to the floor; stands over it uncertainly, considering; then picks it up, throws it in the cage, shuts the door, and shuffles off menacingly into the darkness at left. A great uproar of frightened chattering and whimpering comes from the other cages. Then Yank moves, groaning, opening his eyes, and there is silence. He mutters painfully.*

Say—dey oughter match him—wit Zybszko. He got me, aw right. I'm trou. Even him didn't tink I belonged.

*Then, with sudden passionate despair.*

Christ, where do I get off at? Where do I fit in?

*Checking himself as suddenly.*

Aw, what de hell! No squawkin', see! No quittin', get me! Croak wit your boots on!

*He grabs hold of the bars of the cage and hauls himself painfully to his feet—looks around him bewilderedly—forces a mocking laugh.*

In de cage, huh?

*In the strident tones of a circus barker.*

Ladies and gents, step forward and take a slant at de one and only—

*His voice weakening.*

—one and original—Hairy Ape from de wilds of—

*He slips in a heap on the floor and dies. The monkeys set up a chattering, whimpering wail. And, perhaps, the Hairy Ape at last belongs.*

CURTAIN

*Hughie*
A Play in One Act

# Characters

NIGHT CLERK

ERIE SMITH

# Hughie

*The desk and a section of lobby of a small hotel on a West Side street in midtown New York. It is between 3 and 4 A.M. of a day in the summer of 1928.*

*It is one of those hotels, built in the decade 1900–10 on the side streets of the Great White Way sector, which began as respectable second class but soon were forced to deteriorate in order to survive. Following the First World War and Prohibition, it had given up all pretense of respectability, and now is anything a paying guest wants it to be, a third class dump, catering to the catch-as-catch-can trade. But still it does not prosper. It has not shared in the Great Hollow Boom of the twenties. The Everlasting Opulence of the New Economic Law has overlooked it. It manages to keep running by cutting the overhead for service, repairs, and cleanliness to a minimum.*

*The desk faces left along a section of seedy lobby with shabby chairs. The street entrance is off-stage, left. Behind the desk are a telephone switchboard and the operator's stool. At right, the usual numbered tiers of mailboxes, and above them a clock.*

*The* NIGHT CLERK *sits on the stool, facing front, his back to the switchboard. There is nothing to do. He is not thinking. He is not sleepy. He simply droops and stares acquiescently at nothing. It would be discouraging to glance at the clock. He knows there are several hours to go before his shift is over. Anyway, he does not need to look at clocks. He has been a night clerk in New York hotels so long he can tell time by sounds in the street.*

He is in his early forties. Tall, thin, with a scrawny neck and jutting Adam's apple. His face is long and narrow, greasy with perspiration, sallow, studded with pimples from ingrowing hairs. His nose is large and without character. So is his mouth. So are his ears. So is his thinning brown hair, powdered with dandruff. Behind horn-rimmed spectacles, his blank brown eyes contain no discernible expression. One would say they had even forgotten how it feels to be bored. He wears an ill-fitting blue serge suit, white shirt and collar, a blue tie. The suit is old and shines at the elbows as if it had been waxed and polished.

Footsteps echo in the deserted lobby as someone comes in from the street. The Night Clerk rises wearily. His eyes remain empty but his gummy lips part automatically in a welcoming The-Patron-Is-Always-Right grimace, intended as a smile. His big uneven teeth are in bad condition.

ERIE SMITH enters and approaches the desk. He is about the same age as the Clerk and has the same pasty, perspiry, night-life complexion. There the resemblance ends. Erie is around medium height but appears shorter because he is stout and his fat legs are too short for his body. So are his fat arms. His big head squats on a neck which seems part of his beefy shoulders. His face is round, his snub nose flattened at the tip. His blue eyes have drooping lids and puffy pouches under them. His sandy hair is falling out and the top of his head is bald. He walks to the desk with a breezy, familiar air, his gait a bit waddling because of his short legs. He carries a Panama hat and mops his face with a red and blue silk handkerchief. He wears a light grey suit cut in the extreme, tightwaisted, Broadway mode, the coat open to reveal an old and faded but expensive silk shirt in a shade of blue that sets teeth on edge, and a gay red and blue foulard tie, its knot stained by perspiration. His trousers are held up by a braided brown leather belt with a brass buckle. His shoes are tan and white, his socks white silk.

In manner, he is consciously a Broadway sport and a Wise Guy—the type of small fry gambler and horse player, living hand to mouth on the fringe of the rackets. Infesting corners, doorways, cheap restaurants, the bars of minor speakeasies, he and his kind imagine they are in the Real Know, cynical oracles of the One True Grapevine.

*Erie usually speaks in a low, guarded tone, his drooplidded eyes suspiciously wary of nonexistent eavesdroppers. His face is set in the prescribed pattern of gambler's dead pan. His small, pursy mouth is always crooked in the cynical leer of one who possesses superior, inside information, and his shifty once-over glances never miss the price tags he detects on everything and everybody. Yet there is something phoney about his characterization of himself, some sentimental softness behind it which doesn't belong in the hard-boiled picture.*

*Erie avoids looking at the Night Clerk, as if he resented him.*

ERIE
*Peremptorily.*
Key.
*Then as the Night Clerk gropes with his memory—grudgingly.*
Forgot you ain't seen me before. Erie Smith's the name. I'm an old timer in this fleabag. 492.

NIGHT CLERK
*In a tone of one who is wearily relieved when he does not have to remember anything—he plucks out the key.*
492. Yes, sir.

ERIE
*Taking the key, gives the Clerk the once-over. He appears not unfavorably impressed but his tone still holds resentment.*
How long you been on the job? Four, five days, huh? I been off on a drunk. Come to now, though. Tapering off. Well, I'm glad they fired that young squirt they took on when Hughie got sick. One of them fresh wise punks. Couldn't tell him nothing. Pleased to meet you, Pal. Hope you stick around.
*He shoves out his hand. The Night Clerk takes it obediently.*

NIGHT CLERK
*With a compliant, uninterested smile.*
Glad to know you, Mr. Smith.

ERIE
What's your name?

NIGHT CLERK
*As if he had half forgotten because what did it matter, anyway?*
Hughes. Charlie Hughes.

ERIE
*Starts.*
Huh? Hughes? Say, is that on the level?

NIGHT CLERK
Charlie Hughes.

ERIE
Well, I be damned! What the hell d'you know about that!
*Warming toward the Clerk.*
Say, now I notice, you don't look like Hughie, but you remind me
of him somehow. You ain't by any chance related?

NIGHT CLERK
You mean to the Hughes who had this job so long and died recently?
No, sir. No relation.

ERIE
*Gloomily.*
No, that's right. Hughie told me he didn't have no relations left—
except his wife and kids, of course.
*He pauses—more gloomily.*
Yeah. The poor guy croaked last week. His funeral was what started
me off on a bat.
*Then boastfully, as if defending himself against gloom.*
Some drunk! I don't go on one often. It's bum dope in my book. A
guy gets careless and gabs about things he knows and when he comes
to he's liable to find there's guys who'd feel easier if he wasn't around
no more. That's the trouble with knowing things. Take my tip, Pal.
Don't never know nothin'. Be a sap and stay healthy.
*His manner has become secretive, with sinister undertones. But the Night
Clerk doesn't notice this. Long experience with guests who stop at his desk
in the small hours to talk about themselves has given him a foolproof
technique of self-defense. He appears to listen with agreeable submissive-
ness and be impressed, but his mind is blank and he doesn't hear unless a*

*direct question is put to him, and sometimes not even then. Erie thinks
he is impressed.*
But hell, I always keep my noggin working, booze or no booze. I'm
no sucker. What was I sayin'? Oh, some drunk. I sure hit the high
spots. You shoulda seen the doll I made night before last. And did
she take me to the cleaners! I'm a sucker for blondes.
*He pauses—giving the Night Clerk a cynical, contemptuous glance.*
You're married, ain't you?

NIGHT CLERK
*Long ago he gave up caring whether questions were personal or not.*
Yes, sir.

ERIE
Yeah, I'd'a laid ten to one on it. You got that old look. Like Hughie
had. Maybe that's the resemblance.
*He chuckles contemptuously.*
Kids, too, I bet?

NIGHT CLERK
Yes, sir. Three.

ERIE
You're worse off than Hughie was. He only had two. Three, huh?
Well, that's what comes of being careless!
*He laughs. The Night Clerk smiles at a guest. He had been a little of-
fended when a guest first made that crack—must have been ten years
ago—yes, Eddie, the oldest, is eleven now—or is it twelve? Erie goes on
with good-natured tolerance.*
Well, I suppose marriage ain't such a bum racket, if you're made for
it. Hughie didn't seem to mind it much, although if you want my
low-down, his wife is a bum—in spades! Oh, I don't mean cheatin'.
With her puss and figure, she'd never make no one except she raided
a blind asylum.
*The Night Clerk feels that he has been standing a long time and his feet
are beginning to ache and he wishes 492 would stop talking and go to
bed so he can sit down again and listen to the noises in the street and
think about nothing. Erie gives him an amused, condescending glance.*

How old are you? Wait! Let me guess. You look fifty or over but I'll lay ten to one you're forty-three or maybe forty-four.

NIGHT CLERK
I'm forty-three.
*He adds vaguely.*
Or maybe it is forty-four.

ERIE
*Elated.*
I win, huh? I sure can call the turn on ages, Buddy. You ought to see the dolls get sored up when I work it on them! You're like Hughie. He looked like he'd never see fifty again and he was only forty-three. Me, I'm forty-five. Never think it, would you? Most of the dames don't think I've hit forty yet.
*The Night Clerk shifts his position so he can lean more on the desk. Maybe those shoes he sees advertised for fallen arches—But they cost eight dollars, so that's out—Get a pair when he goes to heaven. Erie is sizing him up with another cynical, friendly glance.*
I make another bet about you. Born and raised in the sticks, wasn't you?

NIGHT CLERK
*Faintly aroused and defensive.*
I come originally from Saginaw, Michigan, but I've lived here in the Big Town so long I consider myself a New Yorker now.
*This is a long speech for him and he wonders sadly why he took the trouble to make it.*

ERIE
I don't deserve no medal for picking that one. Nearly every guy I know on the Big Stem—and I know most of 'em—hails from the sticks. Take me. You'd never guess it but I was dragged up in Erie, P-a. Ain't that a knockout! Erie, P-a! That's how I got my moniker. No one calls me nothing but Erie. You better call me Erie, too, Pal, or I won't know when you're talkin' to me.

NIGHT CLERK
All right, Erie.

Atta Boy.

*He chuckles.*

Here's another knockout. Smith is my real name. A Broadway guy like me named Smith and it's my real name! Ain't that a knockout! *He explains carefully so there will be no misunderstanding.*

I don't remember nothing much about Erie, P-a, you understand—or want to. Some punk burg! After grammar school, my Old Man put me to work in his store, dealing out groceries. Some punk job! I stuck it till I was eighteen before I took a run-out powder.

*The Night Clerk seems turned into a drooping waxwork, draped along the desk. This is what he used to dread before he perfected his technique of not listening: The Guest's Story of His Life. He fixes his mind on his aching feet. Erie chuckles.*

Speaking of marriage, that was the big reason I ducked. A doll nearly had me hooked for the old shotgun ceremony. Closest I ever come to being played for a sucker. This doll in Erie—Daisy's her name—was one of them dumb wide-open dolls. All the guys give her a play. Then one day she wakes up and finds she's going to have a kid. I never figured she meant to frame me in particular. Way I always figured, she didn't have no idea who, so she holds a lottery all by herself. Put about a thousand guys' names in a hat—all she could remember—and drew one out and I was it. Then she told her Ma, and her Ma told her Pa, and her Pa come round looking for me. But I was no fall guy even in them days. I took it on the lam. For Saratoga, to look the bangtails over. I'd started to be a horse player in Erie, though I'd never seen a track. I been one ever since.

*With a touch of bravado.*

And I ain't done so bad, Pal. I've made some killings in my time the gang still gab about. I've been in the big bucks. More'n once, and I will be again. I've had tough breaks too, but what the hell, I always get by. When the horses won't run for me, there's draw or stud. When they're bad, there's a crap game. And when they're all bad, there's always bucks to pick up for little errands I ain't talkin' about, which they give a guy who can keep his clam shut. Oh, I get along, Buddy. I get along fine.

*He waits for approving assent from the Night Clerk, but the latter is not hearing so intently he misses his cue until the expectant silence crashes his ears.*

NIGHT CLERK
*Hastily, gambling on "yes."*
Yes, Sir.

ERIE
*Bitingly.*
Sorry if I'm keeping you up, Sport.
*With an aggrieved air.*
Hughie was a wide-awake guy. He was always waiting for me to roll in. He'd say, "Hello, Erie, how'd the bangtails treat you?" Or, "How's luck?" Or, "Did you make the old bones behave?" Then I'd tell him how I'd done. He'd ask, "What's new along the Big Stem?" and I'd tell him the latest off the grapevine.
*He grins with affectionate condescension.*
It used to hand me a laugh to hear old Hughie crackin' like a sport. In all the years I knew him, he never bet a buck on nothin'.
*Excusingly.*
But it ain't his fault. He'd have took a chance, but how could he with his wife keepin' cases on every nickel of his salary? I showed him lots of ways he could cross her up, but he was too scared.
*He chuckles.*
The biggest knockout was when he'd kid me about dames. He'd crack, "What? No blonde to-night, Erie? You must be slippin'." Jeez, you never see a guy more bashful with a doll around than Hughie was. I used to introduce him to the tramps I'd drag home with me. I'd wise them up to kid him along and pretend they'd fell for him. In two minutes, they'd have him hanging on the ropes. His face'd be red and he'd look like he wanted to crawl under the desk and hide. Some of them dolls was raw babies. They'd make him pretty raw propositions. He'd stutter like he was paralyzed. But he ate it up, just the same. He was tickled pink. I used to hope maybe I could nerve him up to do a little cheatin'. I'd offer to fix it for him with one of my dolls. Hell, I got plenty, I wouldn't have minded. I'd tell him, "Just let that wife of yours know you're cheatin', and she'll have some respect for you." But he was too scared.

*He pauses—boastfully.*

Some queens I've brought here in my time, Brother—frails from the Follies, or the Scandals, or the Frolics, that'd knock your eye out! And I still can make 'em. You watch. I ain't slippin'.

*He looks at the Night Clerk expecting reassurance, but the Clerk's mind has slipped away to the clanging bounce of garbage cans in the outer night. He is thinking: "A job I'd like. I'd bang those cans louder than they do! I'd wake up the whole damned city!" Erie mutters disgustedly to himself.*

Jesus, what a dummy!

*He makes a move in the direction of the elevator, off right front—gloomily.*

Might as well hit the hay, I guess.

NIGHT CLERK

*Comes to—with the nearest approach to feeling he has shown in many a long night—approvingly.*

Good night, Mr. Smith. I hope you have a good rest.

*But Erie stops, glancing around the deserted lobby with forlorn distaste, jiggling the room key in his hand.*

ERIE

What a crummy dump! What did I come back for? I shoulda stayed on a drunk. You'd never guess it, Buddy, but when I first come here this was a classy hotel—and clean, can you believe it?

*He scowls.*

I've been campin' here, off and on, fifteen years, but I've got a good notion to move out. It ain't the same place since Hughie was took to the hospital.

*Gloomily.*

Hell with going to bed! I'll just lie there worrying—

*He turns back to the desk. The Clerk's face would express despair, but the last time he was able to feel despair was back around World War days when the cost of living got so high and he was out of a job for three months. Erie leans on the desk—in a dejected, confidential tone.*

Believe me, Brother, I never been a guy to worry, but this time I'm on a spot where I got to, if I ain't a sap.

*In the vague tone of a corpse which admits it once overheard a favorable rumor about life.*

That's too bad, Mr. Smith. But they say most of the things we worry about never happen.

*His mind escapes to the street again to play bouncing cans with the garbage men.*

ERIE

*Grimly.*

This thing happens, Pal. I ain't won a bet at nothin' since Hughie was took to the hospital. I'm jinxed. And that ain't all—But to hell with it! You're right, at that. Something always turns up for me. I was born lucky. I ain't worried. Just moaning low. Hell, who don't when they're getting over a drunk? You know how it is. The Brooklyn Boys march over the bridge with bloodhounds to hunt you down. And I'm still carrying the torch for Hughie. His checking out was a real K.O. for me. Damn if I know why. Lots of guys I've been pals with, in a way, croaked from booze or something, or got rubbed out, but I always took it as part of the game. Hell, we all gotta croak. Here today, gone tomorrow, so what's the good of beefin'? When a guy's dead, he's dead. He don't give a damn, so why should anybody else?

*But this fatalistic philosophy is no comfort and Erie sighs.*

I miss Hughie, I guess. I guess I'd got to like him a lot.

*Again he explains carefully so there will be no misunderstanding.*

Not that I was ever real pals with him, you understand. He didn't run in my class. He didn't know none of the answers. He was just a sucker.

*He sighs again.*

But I sure am sorry he's gone. You missed a lot not knowing Hughie, Pal. He sure was one grand little guy.

*He stares at the lobby floor. The Night Clerk regards him with vacant, bulging eyes full of a vague envy for the blind. The garbage men have gone their predestined way. Time is that much older. The Clerk's mind remains in the street to greet the noise of a far-off El train. Its approach is pleasantly like a memory of hope; then it roars and rocks and rattles past the nearby corner, and the noise pleasantly deafens memory; then it re-*

cedes and dies, and there is something melancholy about that. But there is hope. Only so many El trains pass in one night, and each one passing leaves one less to pass, so the night recedes, too, until at last it must die and join all the other long nights in Nirvana, the Big Night of Nights. And that's life. "What I always tell Jess when she nags me to worry about something: 'That's life, isn't it? What can you do about it?'" Erie sighs again—then turns to the Clerk, his foolishly wary, wise-guy eyes defenseless, his poker face as self-betraying as a hurt dog's—appealingly.

Say, you do remind me of Hughie somehow, Pal. You got the same look on your map.

But the Clerk's mind is far away attending the obsequies of night, and it takes it some time to get back. Erie is hurt—contemptuously.

But I guess it's only that old night clerk look! There's one of 'em born every minute!

NIGHT CLERK

His mind arrives just in time to catch this last—with a bright grimace.

Yes, Mr. Smith. That's what Barnum said, and it's certainly true, isn't it?

ERIE

Grateful even for this sign of companionship, growls.

Nix on the Mr. Smith stuff, Charlie. There's ten of *them* born every minute. Call me Erie, like I told you.

NIGHT CLERK

Automatically, as his mind tiptoes into the night again.

All right, Erie.

ERIE

Encouraged, leans on the desk, clacking his room key like a castanet.

Yeah. Hughie was one grand little guy. All the same, like I said, he wasn't the kind of guy you'd ever figger a guy like me would take to. Because he was a sucker, see—the kind of sap you'd take to the cleaners a million times and he'd never wise up he was took. Why, night after night, just for a gag, I'd get him to shoot crap with me here on the desk. With *my* dice. And he'd never ask to give 'em the once-over. Can you beat that!

He chuckles—then earnestly.

Not that I'd ever ring in no phoneys on a pal. I'm no heel.

*He chuckles again.*

And anyway, I didn't need none to take Hughie because he never even made me knock 'em against nothing. Just a roll on the desk here. Boy, if they'd ever let me throw 'em that way in a real game, I'd be worth ten million dollars.

*He laughs.*

You'da thought Hughie woulda got wise something was out of order when, no matter how much he'd win on a run of luck like suckers have sometimes, I'd always take him to the cleaners in the end. But he never suspicioned nothing. All he'd say was "Gosh, Erie, no wonder you took up gambling. You sure were born lucky."

*He chuckles.*

Can you beat that?

*He hastens to explain earnestly.*

Of course, like I said, it was only a gag. We'd play with real jack, just to make it look real, but it was all my jack. He never had no jack. His wife dealt him four bits a day for spending money. So I'd stake him at the start to half of what I got—in chicken feed, I mean. We'd pretend a cent was a buck, and a nickel was a fin and so on. Some big game! He got a big kick out of it. He'd get all het up. It give me a kick, too—especially when he'd say, "Gosh, Erie, I don't wonder you never worry about money, with your luck."

*He laughs.*

That guy would believe anything! Of course, I'd stall him off when he'd want to shoot nights when I didn't have a goddamned nickel.

*He chuckles.*

What laughs he used to hand me! He'd always call horses "the bangtails," like he'd known 'em all his life—and he'd never seen a race horse, not till I kidnaped him one day and took him down to Belmont. What a kick he got out of that! I got scared he'd pass out with excitement. And he wasn't doing no betting either. All he had was four bits. It was just the track, and the crowd, and the horses got him. Mostly the horses.

*With a surprised, reflective air.*

Y'know, it's funny how a dumb, simple guy like Hughie will all of a sudden get something right. He says, "They're the most beautiful things in the world, I think." And he wins! I tell you, Pal, I'd rather sleep in the same stall with old Man o' War than make the whole damn Follies. What do you think?

NIGHT CLERK

*His mind darts back from a cruising taxi and blinks bewilderedly in the light: "Say yes."*

Yes, I agree with you, Mr.—I mean, Erie.

ERIE

*With good-natured contempt.*

Yeah? I bet you never seen one, except back at the old Fair Grounds in the sticks. I don't mean them kind of turtles. I mean a real horse. *The Clerk wonders what horses have to do with anything—or for that matter, what anything has to do with anything—then gives it up. Erie takes up his tale.*

And what d'you think happened the next night? Damned if Hughie didn't dig two bucks out of his pants and try to slip 'em to me. "Let this ride on the nose of whatever horse you're betting on tomorrow," he told me. I got sore. "Nix," I told him, "if you're going to start playin' sucker and bettin' on horse races, you don't get no assist from me."

*He grins wryly.*

Was that a laugh! Me advising a sucker not to bet when I've spent a lot of my life tellin' saps a story to make 'em bet! I said, "Where'd you grab this dough? Outa the Little Woman's purse, huh? What tale you going to give her when you lose it? She'll start breaking up the furniture with you!" "No," he says, "she'll just cry." "That's worse," I said, "no guy can beat that racket. I had a doll cry on me once in a restaurant full of people till I had to promise her a diamond engagement ring to sober her up." Well, anyway, Hughie sneaked the two bucks back in the Little Woman's purse when he went home that morning, and that was the end of that.

*Cynically.*

Boy Scouts got nothin' on me, Pal, when it comes to good deeds. That was one I done. It's too bad I can't remember no others.

*He is well wound up now and goes on without noticing that the Night Clerk's mind has left the premises in his sole custody.*

Y'know I had Hughie sized up for a sap the first time I see him. I'd just rolled in from Tia Juana. I'd made a big killing down there and I was lousy with jack. Came all the way in a drawing room, and I wasn't lonely in it neither. There was a blonde movie doll on the train—and I was lucky in them days. Used to follow the horses South every winter. I don't no more. Sick of traveling. And I ain't as lucky as I was—

*Hastily.*

Anyway, this time I'm talkin' about, soon as I hit this lobby I see there's a new night clerk, and while I'm signing up for the bridal suite I make a bet with myself he's never been nothin' but a night clerk. And I win. At first, he wouldn't open up. Not that he was cagey about gabbin' too much. But like he couldn't think of nothin' about himself worth saying. But after he'd seen me roll in here the last one every night, and I'd stop to kid him along and tell him the tale of what I'd win that day, he got friendly and talked. He'd come from a hick burg upstate. Graduated from high school, and had a shot at different jobs in the old home town but couldn't make the grade until he was took on as night clerk in the hotel there. Then he made good. But he wasn't satisfied. Didn't like being only a night clerk where everybody knew him. He'd read somewhere—in the Suckers' Almanac, I guess—that all a guy had to do was come to the Big Town and Old Man Success would be waitin' at the Grand Central to give him the key to the city. What a gag that is! Even I believed that once, and no one could ever call me a sap. Well, anyway, he made the break and come here and the only job he could get was night clerk. Then he fell in love—or kidded himself he was—and got married. Met her on a subway train. It stopped sudden and she was jerked into him, and he put his arms around her, and they started talking, and the poor boob never stood a chance. She was a sales girl in some punk department store, and she was sick of standing on her dogs all day, and all the way home to Brooklyn, too. So, the way I figger it, knowing Hughie and dames, she proposed and said "yes" for him, and married him, and after that, of course, he never dared stop being a night clerk, even if he could.

*He pauses.*

Maybe you think I ain't giving her a square shake. Well, maybe I ain't. She never give me one. She put me down as a bad influence, and let her chips ride. And maybe Hughie couldn't have done no better. Dolls didn't call him no riot. Hughie and her seemed happy enough the time he had me out to dinner in their flat. Well, not happy. Maybe contented. No, that's boosting it, too. Resigned comes nearer, as if each was givin' the other a break by thinking, "Well, what more could I expect?"

*Abruptly he addresses the Night Clerk with contemptuous good nature.*
How d'you and your Little Woman hit it off, Brother?

NIGHT CLERK
*His mind has been counting the footfalls of the cop on the beat as they recede, sauntering longingly toward the dawn's release. "If he'd only shoot it out with a gunman some night! Nothing exciting has happened in any night I've ever lived through!" He stammers gropingly among the echoes of Erie's last words.*
Oh—you mean *my* wife? Why, we get along all right, I guess.

ERIE
*Disgustedly.*
Better lay off them headache pills, Pal. First thing you know, some guy is going to call you a dope.
*But the Night Clerk cannot take this seriously. It is years since he cared what anyone called him. So many guests have called him so many things. The Little Woman has, too. And, of course, he has, himself. But that's all past. Is daybreak coming now? No, too early yet. He can tell by the sound of that surface car. It is still lost in the night. Flat wheeled and tired. Distant the carbarn, and far way the sleep. Erie, having soothed resentment with his wisecrack, goes on with a friendly grin.*
Well, keep hoping, Pal. Hughie was as big a dope as you until I give him some interest in life.
*Slipping back into narrative.*
That time he took me home to dinner. Was that a knockout! It took him a hell of a while to get up nerve to ask me. "Sure, Hughie," I told him, "I'll be tickled to death." I was thinking, I'd rather be shot. For one thing, he lived in Brooklyn, and I'd sooner take a trip to China. Another thing, I'm a guy that likes to eat what I order and not what somebody deals me. And he had kids and a wife, and

the family racket is out of my line. But Hughie looked so tickled I couldn't welsh on him. And it didn't work out so bad. Of course, what he called home was only a dump of a cheap flat. Still, it wasn't so bad for a change. His wife had done a lot of stuff to doll it up. Nothin' with no class, you understand. Just cheap stuff to make it comfortable. And his kids wasn't the gorillas I'd expected, neither. No throwin' spitballs in my soup or them kind of gags. They was quiet like Hughie. I kinda liked 'em. After dinner I started tellin' 'em a story about a race horse a guy I know owned once. I thought it was up to me to put out something, and kids like animal stories, and this one was true, at that. This old turtle never wins a race, but he was as foxy as ten guys, a natural born crook, the goddamnedest thief, he'd steal anything in reach that wasn't nailed down — Well, I didn't get far. Hughie's wife butt in and stopped me cold. Told the kids it was bedtime and hustled 'em off like I was giving 'em measles. It got my goat, kinda. I coulda liked her — a little — if she'd give me a chance. Not that she was nothin' Ziegfeld would want to glorify. When you call her plain, you give her all the breaks.

*Resentfully.*

Well, to hell with it. She had me tagged for a bum, and seein' me made her sure she was right. You can bet she told Hughie never invite me again, and he never did. He tried to apologize, but I shut him up quick. He says, "Irma was brought up strict. She can't help being narrow-minded about gamblers." I said, "What's it to me? I don't want to hear your dame troubles. I got plenty of my own. Remember that doll I brung home night before last? She gives me an argument I promised her ten bucks. I told her, 'Listen, Baby, I got an impediment in my speech. Maybe it sounded like ten, but it was two, and that's all you get. Hell, I don't want to buy your soul! What would I do with it?' Now she's peddling the news along Broadway I'm a rat and a chiseler, and of course all the rats and chiselers believe her. Before she's through, I won't have a friend left."

*He pauses — confidentially.*

I switched the subject on Hughie, see, on purpose. He never did beef to me about his wife again.

*He gives a forced chuckle.*

Believe me, Pal, I can stop guys that start telling me their family troubles!

NIGHT CLERK

*His mind has hopped an ambulance clanging down Sixth, and is asking without curiosity: "Will he die, Doctor, or isn't he lucky?" "I'm afraid not, but he'll have to be absolutely quiet for months and months." "With a pretty nurse taking care of him?" "Probably not pretty." "Well, anyway, I claim he's lucky. And now I must get back to the hotel. 492 won't go to bed and insists on telling me jokes. It must have been a joke because he's chuckling." He laughs with a heartiness which has forgotten that heart is more than a word used in "Have a heart," an old slang expression.*

Ha—Ha! That's a good one, Erie. That's the best I've heard in a long time!

ERIE

*For a moment is so hurt and depressed he hasn't the spirit to make a sarcastic crack. He stares at the floor, twirling his room key—to himself.*

Jesus, this sure is a dead dump. About as homey as the Morgue.

*He glances up at the clock.*

Gettin' late. Better beat it up to my cell and grab some shut eye.

*He makes a move to detach himself from the desk but fails and remains wearily glued to it. His eyes prowl the lobby and finally come to rest on the Clerk's glistening, sallow face. He summons up strength for a withering crack.*

Why didn't you tell me you was deef, Buddy? I know guys is sensitive about them little afflictions, but I'll keep it confidential.

*But the Clerk's mind has rushed out to follow the siren wail of a fire engine. "A fireman's life must be exciting." His mind rides the engine, and asks a fireman with disinterested eagerness: "Where's the fire? Is it a real good one this time? Has it a good start? Will it be big enough, do you think?" Erie examines his face—bitingly.*

Take my tip, Pal, and don't never try to buy from a dope peddler. He'll tell you you had enough already.

*The Clerk's mind continues its dialogue with the fireman: "I mean, big enough to burn down the whole damn city?" "Sorry, Brother, but there's no chance. There's too much stone and steel. There'd always be something left." "Yes, I guess you're right. There's too much stone and steel. I wasn't really hoping, anyway. It really doesn't matter to me." Erie gives him up and again attempts to pry himself from the desk, twirling his key frantically as if it were a fetish which might set him free.*

Well, me for the hay.

*But he can't dislodge himself—dully.*

Christ, it's lonely. I wish Hughie was here. By God, if he was, I'd tell him a tale that'd make his eyes pop! The bigger the story the harder he'd fall. He was that kind of sap. He thought gambling was romantic. I guess he saw me like a sort of dream guy, the sort of guy he'd like to be if he could take a chance. I guess he lived a sort of double life listening to me gabbin' about hittin' the high spots. Come to figger it, I'll bet he even cheated on his wife that way, using me and my dolls.

*He chuckles.*

No wonder he liked me, huh? And the bigger I made myself the more he lapped it up. I went easy on him at first. I didn't lie—not any more'n a guy naturally does when he gabs about the bets he wins and the dolls he's made. But I soon see he was cryin' for more, and when a sucker cries for more, you're a dope if you don't let him have it. Every tramp I made got to be a Follies' doll. Hughie liked 'em to be Follies' dolls. Or in the Scandals or Frolics. He wanted me to be the Sheik of Araby, or something that any blonde'd go round-heeled about. Well, I give him plenty of that. And I give him plenty of gambling tales. I explained my campin' in this dump was because I don't want to waste jack on nothin' but gambling. It was like dope to me, I told him. I couldn't quit. He lapped that up. He liked to kid himself I'm mixed up in the racket. He thought gangsters was romantic. So I fed him some baloney about highjacking I'd done once. I told him I knew all the Big Shots. Well, so I do, most of 'em, to say hello, and sometimes they hello back. Who wouldn't know 'em that hangs around Broadway and the joints? I run errands for 'em sometimes, because there's dough in it, but I'm cagey about gettin' in where it ain't healthy. Hughie wanted to think me and Legs Diamond was old pals. So I give him that too. I give him anything he cried for.

*Earnestly.*

Don't get the wrong idea, Pal. What I fed Hughie wasn't all lies. The tales about gambling wasn't. They was stories of big games and killings that really happened since I've been hangin' round. Only I wasn't in on 'em like I made out—except one or two from way back when I had a run of big luck and was in the bucks for a while until I was took to the cleaners.

*He stops to pay tribute of a sigh to the memory of brave days that were and that never were—then meditatively.*

Yeah, Hughie lapped up my stories like they was duck soup, or a beakful of heroin. I sure took him around with me in tales and showed him one hell of a time.

*He chuckles—then seriously.*

And, d'you know, it done me good, too, in a way. Sure. I'd get to seein' myself like he seen me. Some nights I'd come back here without a buck, feeling lower than a snake's belly, and first thing you know I'd be lousy with jack, bettin' a grand a race. Oh, I was wise I was kiddin' myself. I ain't a sap. But what the hell, Hughie loved it, and it didn't cost nobody nothin', and if every guy along Broadway who kids himself was to drop dead there wouldn't be nobody left. Ain't it the truth, Charlie?

*He again stares at the Night Clerk appealingly, forgetting past rebuffs. The Clerk's face is taut with vacancy. His mind has been trying to fasten itself to some noise in the night, but a rare and threatening pause of silence has fallen on the city, and here he is, chained behind a hotel desk forever, awake when everyone else in the world is asleep, except Room 492, and he won't go to bed, he's still talking, and there is no escape.*

NIGHT CLERK

*His glassy eyes stare through Erie's face. He stammers deferentially.*

Truth? I'm afraid I didn't get—What's the truth?

ERIE

*Hopelessly.*

Nothing, Pal. Not a thing.

*His eyes fall to the floor. For a while he is too defeated even to twirl his room key. The Clerk's mind still cannot make a getaway because the city remains silent, and the night vaguely reminds him of death, and he is vaguely frightened, and now that he remembers, his feet are giving him hell, but that's no excuse not to act as if the Guest is always right: "I should have paid 492 more attention. After all, he is company. He is awake and alive. I should use him to help me live through the night. What's he been talking about? I must have caught some of it without meaning to."* The Night Clerk's forehead puckers perspiringly as he tries to remember. Erie begins talking again but this time it is obviously aloud to himself, without hope of a listener.

I could tell by Hughie's face before he went to the hospital, he was through. I've seen the same look on guys' faces when they knew they was on the spot, just before guys caught up with them. I went to see him twice in the hospital. The first time, his wife was there and give me a dirty look, but he cooked up a smile and said, "Hello, Erie, how're the bangtails treating you?" I see he wants a big story to cheer him, but his wife butts in and says he's weak and he mustn't get excited. I felt like crackin', "Well, the Docs in this dump got the right dope. Just leave you with him and he'll never get excited." The second time I went, they wouldn't let me see him. That was near the end. I went to his funeral, too. There wasn't nobody but a coupla his wife's relations. I had to feel sorry for her. She looked like she ought to be parked in a coffin, too. The kids was bawlin'. There wasn't no flowers but a coupla lousy wreaths. It woulda been a punk showing for poor old Hughie, if it hadn't been for my flower piece.

*He swells with pride.*

That was some display, Pal. It'd knock your eye out! Set me back a hundred bucks, and no kiddin'! A big horseshoe of red roses! I knew Hughie'd want a horseshoe because that made it look like he'd been a horse player. And around the top printed in forget-me-nots was "Good-by, Old Pal." Hughie liked to kid himself he was my pal.

*He adds sadly.*

And so he was, at that—even if he was a sucker.

*He pauses, his false poker face as nakedly forlorn as an organ grinder's monkey's. Outside, the spell of abnormal quiet presses suffocatingly upon the street, enters the deserted, dirty lobby. The Night Clerk's mind cowers away from it. He cringes behind the desk, his feet aching like hell. There is only one possible escape. If his mind could only fasten onto something 492 has said. "What's he been talking about? A clerk should always be attentive. You even are duty bound to laugh at a guest's smutty jokes, no matter how often you've heard them. That's the policy of the hotel. 492 has been gassing for hours. What's he been telling me? I must be slip-*

*ping. Always before this I've been able to hear without bothering to listen, but now when I need company—Ah! I've got it! Gambling! He said a lot about gambling. That's something I've always wanted to know more about, too. Maybe he's a professional gambler. Like Arnold Rothstein."*

NIGHT CLERK
*Blurts out with an uncanny, almost lifelike eagerness.*
I beg your pardon, Mr.—Erie—but did I understand you to say you are a gambler by profession? Do you, by any chance, know the Big Shot, Arnold Rothstein?
*But this time it is Erie who doesn't hear him. And the Clerk's mind is now suddenly impervious to the threat of Night and Silence as it pursues an ideal of fame and glory within itself called Arnold Rothstein.*

ERIE
*With mournful longing.*
Christ, I wish Hughie was alive and kickin'. I'd tell him I win ten grand from the bookies, and ten grand at stud, and ten grand in a crap game! I'd tell him I bought one of those Mercedes sport road-sters with nickel pipes sticking out of the hood! I'd tell him I lay three babes from the Follies—two blondes and one brunette!
*The Night Clerk dreams, a rapt hero worship transfiguring his pimply face: "Arnold Rothstein! He must be some guy! I read a story about him. He'll gamble for any limit on anything, and always wins. The story said he wouldn't bother playing in a poker game unless the smallest bet you could make—one white chip!—was a hundred dollars. Christ, that's going some! I'd like to have the dough to get in a game with him once! The last pot everyone would drop out but him and me. I'd say, 'Okay, Arnold, the sky's the limit,' and I'd raise him five grand, and he'd call, and I'd have a royal flush to his four aces. Then I'd say, 'Okay, Arnold, I'm a good sport, I'll give you a break. I'll cut you double or nothing. Just one cut. I want quick action for my dough.' And I'd cut the ace of spades and win again." Beatific vision swoons on the empty pools of the Night Clerk's eyes. He resembles a holy saint, recently elected to Paradise. Erie breaks the silence—bitterly resigned.*
But Hughie's better off, at that, being dead. He's got all the luck. He needn't do no worryin' now. He's out of the racket. I mean, the whole goddamned racket. I mean life.

NIGHT CLERK

*Kicked out of his dream—with detached, pleasant acquiescence.*

Yes, it is a goddamned racket when you stop to think, isn't it, 492?
But we might as well make the best of it, because—Well, you can't
burn it all down, can you? There's too much steel and stone. There'd
always be something left to start it going again.

ERIE

*Scowls bewilderedly.*

Say, what is this? What the hell you talkin' about?

NIGHT CLERK

*At a loss—in much confusion.*

Why, to be frank, I really don't—Just something that came into my
head.

ERIE

*Bitingly, but showing he is comforted at having made some sort of con-
tact.*

Get it out of your head quick, Charlie, or some guys in uniform will
walk in here with a butterfly net and catch you.

*He changes the subject—earnestly.*

Listen, Pal, maybe you guess I was kiddin' about that flower piece for
Hughie costing a hundred bucks? Well, I ain't! I didn't give a damn
what it cost. It was up to me to give Hughie a big-time send-off,
because I knew nobody else would.

NIGHT CLERK

Oh, I'm not doubting your word, Erie. You won the money gambling, I suppose—I mean, I beg your pardon if I'm mistaken, but
you are a gambler, aren't you?

ERIE

*Preoccupied.*

Yeah, sure, when I got scratch to put up. What of it? But I don't win
that hundred bucks. I don't win a bet since Hughie was took to the
hospital. I had to get down on my knees and beg every guy I know
for a sawbuck here and a sawbuck there until I raised it.

NIGHT CLERK
*His mind concentrated on the Big Ideal — insistently.*
Do you by any chance know — Arnold Rothstein?

ERIE
*His train of thought interrupted — irritably.*
Arnold? What's he got to do with it? He wouldn't loan a guy like me
a nickel to save my grandmother from streetwalking.

NIGHT CLERK
*With humble awe.*
Then you do know him!

ERIE
Sure I know the bastard. Who don't on Broadway? And he knows
me — when he wants to. He uses me to run errands when there ain't
no one else handy. But he ain't my trouble, Pal. My trouble is, some
of these guys I put the bit on is dead wrong G's, and they expect to
be paid back next Tuesday, or else I'm outa luck and have to take it
on the lam, or I'll get beat up and maybe sent to a hospital.
*He suddenly rouses himself and there is something pathetically but genu-
inely gallant about him.*
But what the hell. I was wise I was takin' a chance. I've always took
a chance, and if I lose I pay, and no welshing! It sure was worth it to
give Hughie the big send-off.
*He pauses. The Night Clerk hasn't paid any attention except to his own
dream. A question is trembling on his parted lips, but before he can get
it out Erie goes on gloomily.*
But even that ain't my big worry, Charlie. My big worry is the run
of bad luck I've had since Hughie got took to the hospital. Not a
win. That ain't natural. I've always been a lucky guy — lucky enough
to get by and pay up, I mean. I wouldn't never worry about owing
guys, like I owe them guys. I'd always know I'd make a win that'd fix
it. But now I got a lousy hunch when I lost Hughie I lost my luck —
I mean, I've lost the old confidence. He used to give me confidence.
*He turns away from the desk.*
No use gabbin' here all night. You can't do me no good.
*He starts toward the elevator.*

NIGHT CLERK
*Pleadingly.*
Just a minute, Erie, if you don't mind.
*With awe.*
So you're an old friend of Arnold Rothstein! Would you mind telling me if it's really true when Arnold Rothstein plays poker, one white chip is—a hundred dollars?

ERIE
*Dully exasperated.*
Say, for Christ's sake, what's it to you—?
*He stops abruptly, staring probingly at the Clerk. There is a pause. Suddenly his face lights up with a saving revelation. He grins warmly and saunters confidently back to the desk.*
Say, Charlie, why didn't you put me wise before, you was interested in gambling? Hell, I got you all wrong, Pal. I been tellin' myself, this guy ain't like old Hughie. He ain't got no sportin' blood. He's just a dope.
*Generously.*
Now I see you're a right guy. Shake.
*He shoves out his hand which the Clerk clasps with a limp pleasure. Erie goes on with gathering warmth and self-assurance.*
That's the stuff. You and me'll get along. I'll give you all the breaks, like I give Hughie.

NIGHT CLERK
*Gratefully.*
Thank you, Erie.
*Then insistently.*
Is it true when Arnold Rothstein plays poker, one white chip—

ERIE
*With magnificent carelessness.*
Sets you back a hundred bucks? Sure. Why not? Arnold's in the bucks, ain't he? And when you're in the bucks, a C note is chicken feed. I ought to know, Pal. I was in the bucks when Arnold was a piker. Why, one time down in New Orleans I lit a cigar with a C note, just for a gag, y'understand. I was with a bunch of high class dolls

and I wanted to see their eyes pop out—and believe me, they sure popped! After that, I coulda made 'em one at a time or all together! Hell, I once win twenty grand on a single race. That's action! A good crap game is action, too. Hell, I've been in games where there was a hundred grand in real folding money lying around the floor. That's travelin'!

*He darts a quick glance at the Clerk's face and begins to hedge warily. But he needn't. The Clerk sees him now as the Gambler in 492, the Friend of Arnold Rothstein—and nothing is incredible. Erie goes on.*

Of course, I wouldn't kid you. I'm not in the bucks now—not right this moment. You know how it is, Charlie. Down today and up tomorrow. I got some dough ridin' on the nose of a turtle in the 4th at Saratoga. I hear a story he'll be so full of hop, if the joc can keep him from jumpin' over the grandstand, he'll win by a mile. So if I roll in here with a blonde that'll knock your eyes out, don't be surprised. *He winks and chuckles.*

NIGHT CLERK

*Ingratiatingly pally, smiling.*

Oh, you can't surprise me that way. I've been a night clerk in New York all my life, almost.

*He tries out a wink himself.*

I'll forget the house rules, Erie.

ERIE

*Dryly.*

Yeah. The manager wouldn't like you to remember something he ain't heard of yet.

*Then slyly feeling his way.*

How about shootin' a little crap, Charlie? I mean just in fun, like I used to with Hughie. I know you can't afford takin' no chances. I'll stake you, see? I got a coupla bucks. We gotta use real jack or it don't look real. It's all my jack, get it? You can't lose. I just want to show you how I'll take you to the cleaners. It'll give me confidence.

*He has taken two one-dollar bills and some change from his pocket. He pushes most of it across to the Clerk.*

Here y'are.

*He produces a pair of dice—carelessly.*

Want to give these dice the once-over before we start?

NIGHT CLERK
*Earnestly.*

What do you think I am? I know I can trust you.

ERIE
*Smiles.*

You remind me a lot of Hughie, Pal. He always trusted me. Well, don't blame me if I'm lucky.

*He clicks the dice in his hand—thoughtfully.*

Y'know, it's time I quit carryin' the torch for Hughie. Hell, what's the use? It don't do him no good. He's gone. Like we all gotta go. Him yesterday, me or you tomorrow, and who cares, and what's the difference? It's all in the racket, huh?

*His soul is purged of grief, his confidence restored.*

I shoot two bits.

NIGHT CLERK
*Manfully, with an excited dead-pan expression he hopes resembles Arnold Rothstein's.*

I fade you.

ERIE
*Throws the dice.*

Four's my point.

*Gathers them up swiftly and throws them again.*

Four it is.

*He takes the money.*

Easy when you got my luck—and know how. Huh, Charlie?

*He chuckles, giving the Night Clerk the slyly amused, contemptuous, affectionate wink with which a Wise Guy regales a Sucker.*

CURTAIN

Eugene O'Neill (1888–1953) was born in New York City, the son of James O'Neill, a popular actor, and Mary Ellen Quinlan. During his childhood years he lived mainly in hotels with his family, following the tours of his father's company; the only permanent home the young O'Neill knew was a summer cottage in New London, Connecticut, which later became the setting for *Long Day's Journey into Night*.

As an adolescent, O'Neill attended eastern preparatory schools and then Princeton University for one year until he was expelled. During the next five years he worked as a gold prospector, a sailor, an actor, and a reporter.

O'Neill began writing plays in 1913, and by 1916 his one-act play *Bound East for Cardiff* was produced in New York by the Provincetown Players, a group he had helped found. In 1920 his full-length play *Beyond the Horizon* was produced in New York and won O'Neill the first of his four Pulitzer Prizes. During decades of extraordinary productivity, O'Neill published 24 other full-length plays. After receiving the Nobel Prize for literature in 1936, he published two of his most highly acclaimed plays, *The Iceman Cometh* and *A Moon for the Misbegotten*. O'Neill died in Boston in 1953. *Long Day's Journey into Night,* often regarded as his finest work, was published three years after his death.

($) LSI Cancel Dunne
  800722 0300

(2)

---

(1) Palo Alto Housing $350,700 CURVAL

(2) Lewis re: Rickey's
    8669705330 x25014

(3) → Ron Fellows $1,300 – 500 up front
    Can start right away

(4)